Wellington's Doctors

*The British Army Medical Services
in the Napoleonic Wars*

WELLINGTON'S DOCTORS

THE BRITISH ARMY MEDICAL SERVICES IN THE NAPOLEONIC WARS

by

Dr Martin Howard

MBChB MD FRCP FRCPath

SPELLMOUNT
Staplehurst

British Library Cataloguing in Publication Data:
A catalogue record for this book is available
from the British Library

Copyright © Martin Howard 2002
Map © Spellmount 2002

ISBN 1-86227-143-7

First published in the UK in 2002 by
Spellmount Limited
The Old Rectory
Staplehurst
Kent TN12 0AZ

Tel: 01580 893730
Fax: 01580 893731
E-mail: enquiries@spellmount.com
Website: www.spellmount.com

1 3 5 7 9 8 6 4 2

Typeset in Palatino by MATS, Southend-on-Sea, Essex
Printed in Great Britain by
TJ International Ltd, Padstow, Cornwall

Contents

Acknowledgements

I am much indebted to the following for their help in locating books, journals and manuscripts: The Wellcome Library for the History and Understanding of Medicine, London; Aberdeen University Library; York District Library; Bristol University Medical School Library; Leeds University Medical School Library; The Royal College of Physicians Library; Jeffrey Stern Antiquarian Books. For their help with illustrations many thanks to: The Army Medical Services Museum (particularly Captain Pete Starling); The National Army Museum, London; The National Museums of Scotland; The British Museum; The Hulton Getty Picture Library.

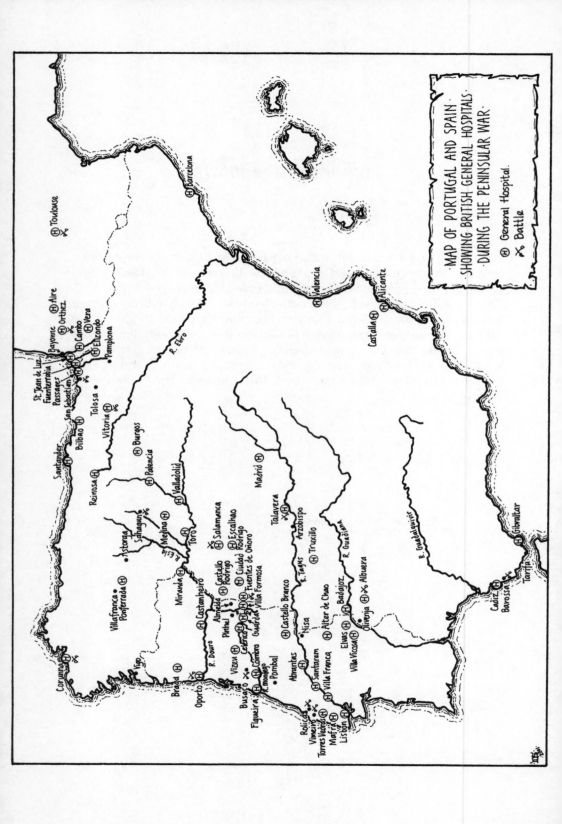

MAP OF PORTUGAL AND SPAIN.
SHOWING BRITISH GENERAL HOSPITALS.
DURING THE PENINSULAR WAR.
Ⓗ General Hospital.
✕ Battle

CHAPTER I
The Army Doctor

The soldier should not be consigned to the ignorant and un-educated of the profession. He is clearly entitled to the same quality of medical advice as when he was a civilian, and is not to be put off with a cheap article of a doctor, and with one who could not afford the expense of a regular medical education.

James McGrigor[1]

As night fell over the Spanish city of Badajoz, Wellington started to write his dispatch. The events of the previous days had been painful for the army's commander. Although the British had emerged victorious, it was at a terrible cost. Five thousand men and officers had been lost, 3,000 of them perishing in the final desperate assault. At the breaches the dead, the dying, and the wounded had lain in their hundreds. Even the usually stern-faced and self-controlled Duke had shed tears when James McGrigor, his Surgeon General, had told him of the full scale of the casualties. McGrigor, near to his chief during the crucial hours, entered the army's headquarters building as Wellington carefully composed his report to the Prime Minister. The army's senior doctor had also had a torrid time during the siege but, allowing for the inevitable deficiencies, he was happy with his hospital arrangements and with the work of his staff. After he had updated Wellington on the state of the wounded, he sensed an opportunity to rectify what he felt to be a longstanding omission.

> I trust, my Lord, you are satisfied that the medical officers during last night did their duty, as well as the military officers, and that you will receive my testimony that they discharged their arduous and laborious duties most zealously, and often under circumstances of personal danger.

Wellington agreed, saying that he had witnessed the doctors' efforts. McGrigor persevered.

> Nothing could more gratify those officers, nothing could be a greater incentive to their exertions on further occasions than noting them in the public dispatches.

1

The Duke hesitated; 'Is that usual?'
It would be of the most essential service; really their extraordinary exertions give them justice and a claim to this.'
'I have finished my dispatch – but very well, I will add something about the doctors.'

Camp at Badajoz, April 8th 1812.

My Lord
It gives me great pleasure to inform your Lordship that our numerous wounded officers and soldiers are doing well. I have great reason to be satisfied with the attention paid to these by Mr McGrigor the Inspector general of Hospitals and the Medical Gentlemen under his direction, and I trust that the loss to the Service upon this occasion will not eventually be great.
I have the honour to be
My Lord
Your Lordship's obedient servant, Wellington

It was hardly effusive, but then that was also a feature of Wellington's character. It was the first time that British army doctors had been commended for their role in action. When the dispatch was published in the London newspapers, doctors at home were delighted that their colleagues had been acknowledged in the same manner as military officers. For the doctors of the Peninsular Army it was a small and possibly overdue recognition of their contribution to the war.[2]

Even nearly two hundred years later Wellington's doctors are easily overlooked. They feature little in conventional histories of the Napoleonic Wars. In soldiers' memoirs they are shadowy figures, making cameo appearances to treat wounds or disease. Sometimes they are portrayed as heroes and life-savers. At other times they are ignorant 'butcher's boys' or comic 'saw-bones', out of their depth in the heat of battle. To understand who these doctors were, what they did, and what they believed in, it is necessary to strip away the superficial glamour of the wars. Of course there was heroism, glory, and triumph on the road to Waterloo. The story has been told many times. But there was also wounding, disease, despair, and death. It was often only Wellington's doctors who stood between the Napoleonic soldier and an early grave.

To talk simply of the 'army doctor' is an overgeneralisation. Many medical officers did not accompany the troops into battle, instead occupying administrative and hospital posts. At the beginning of the Napoleonic Wars, the British Army Medical Department was broadly divided into three parts: the administrative officers, the hospital and medical 'staff', and the regimental surgeons. For much of the duration of the wars, the department's administrative affairs were overseen by the much maligned Army Medical Board.[3] The first attempt to form a medical board of control had been made as early as 1756, but this was short-lived, the board breaking up on the commencement of war. It was only reconstituted in 1794, when three senior doctors assumed what ought to have been an onerous responsibility.[4]

Sir Lucas Pepys was appointed Physician-General as a reward for his services to George III during the King's illness in 1789. He was an eminent and highly qualified civilian physician, but he had no particular knowledge of army affairs or of the diseases that affected troops in the field. John Gunning, also a civilian, was nominated Surgeon-General and Thomas Keate, the only one of the three who had previously served as an army medical officer, was made Inspector of Regimental Infirmaries, a title later changed to Inspector of Army Hospitals. In the early years of the board, the members had some collective responsibility, but in 1798 the commander-in-chief issued orders which effectively made each of the three members supreme in his own department. In fact, this royal warrant ordered discontinuation of the board but, rather confusingly, official documents continued to use this term in references to the work of the three men. By this stage John Rush had replaced Thomas Keate as Inspector of Regimental Infirmaries, and on his death in 1801 he was in turn replaced by Francis Knight. A weighty book could easily be written on the subsequent painful demise of the board. Distracted by their own private medical practice, starved of administrative support, antagonistic to each other, and in large part distanced from the reality of an army on campaign, ultimate failure was ensured from the outset. Although there is not space here to relate the events in full, some appreciation of the board's problems is helpful as their decisions impinged considerably on the working life and prospects of the ordinary army doctor.

Even after careful study of relevant documents, it is difficult to comprehend the responsibilities of the board's individual members – it is very likely that they were also perplexed. It would be hard to improve on the summary penned by Arnold Chaplin in his masterly resume of the Army Medical Department.

> Surely it is impossible to imagine a more clumsy and impossible arrangement ... The position, so far as can be ascertained, was as follows: Collectively the Board was supposed to meet if questions were submitted to it. It was to obey orders, but it was no part of its business to make representations, and when it did meet the Physician-General took the chair. In their individual capacities the members were assigned special duties, but the conduct of these duties could not be brought under the criticism of the Board as a whole.

The Physician-General, with a salary of 40s. (i.e. £2) per diem, was responsible for the choice of physicians, for the supervision of medical drugs, and for the examination of candidates for the posts of physician in the Army. The Surgeon-General, with a salary of 40s. per diem, and also an extra £800 per annum as the holder of the sinecure post of surgeon to Chelsea Hospital, appointed the Surgeons for the Army and provided surgical drugs and appliances. He occupied a seat on the Court of Examiners at the College of Surgeons for granting a certificate to hospital mates [junior hospital doctors]. He consulted with the authorities on medical matters while the troops were on foreign service, and he received the returns of sick and wounded. The Inspector-General was entrusted with the duties of providing Inspectors of hospitals and hospital mates. He had charge of regimental hospitals, and had the position of surgeon to the staff of the Commander-in-Chief. In addition to his salary of 40s. a day, he received an equivalent amount on account of his position of Controller of Army Hospital Accounts. Finally, he was responsible for the provision of drugs for the Guards regiments, and superintended the education of cadets for hospital mates.

To complete this description of this edifice of inconsistencies, it remains to be said that the Guards chose their own surgeons, that the medical department of the Ordnance was a separate concern under the control of an Inspector-General, and that the medical comforts were under the control of the Commissary-General.[5]

Chaplin might also have mentioned the Apothecary-General who controlled the supply of medicines, dressings and surgical instruments from civil firms, and the Purveyor-in-Chief who directed the provision of hospital equipment.

Unsurprisingly, the muddled lines of demarcation detailed above led to many anomalies. For instance, although the Surgeon-General was responsible for sending physicians, surgeons, apothecaries and purveyors to their various posts at home and abroad, he was not allowed to promote them. Conversely, the Inspector-General of Hospitals could both appoint and promote apothecaries and purveyors, but he could only select medical officers for his hospitals from those who had been nominated and promoted on the recommendation of others. It would, however, be overly generous to ascribe the poor performance of the board's members entirely to a lack of clarity regarding their roles. The evidence suggests that they were less than fully committed to their military duties. Despite the extensive campaigning of the army in Europe and the West Indies, their official office hours extended only from 12 o'clock to 2 o'clock daily. Even during this time they were not invariably to be found at their desks. General Orders stated that the three were to meet monthly or more frequently to sign the returns of the sick of the army. Keate later admitted that the board met on 'very few occasions'. He was quick to point out that it was not the role of the medical board to take the initiative in managing the health concerns of the army: 'The medical board have only to obey orders and it was not their province, as I conceive, to form arrangements ... they conceived they would have exceeded their duty if they had voluntarily stepped forward.' The members' reluctance to be proactive and their greater commitment to private practice were accompanied by a totally inadequate infrastructure for the board's activities. The medical department headquarters in Upper Brook Street, and later in Berkeley Street, was a hopelessly small facility with only a niggardly allowance from the government for essential clerical help and other office expenses.

When the three doctors did meet it was mainly to argue with each other. The quarrels gradually intensified in their bitterness, petty jealousies grew, and the situation became increasingly chaotic. Particular points of contention were the methods of appointing medical officers to the army and the relative roles of regimental and general hospitals. The medical catastrophe of the Walcheren expedition in 1809 took place during the board's continuing power struggles. The Secretary of War was forced to write to the Treasury: 'The divisions which exist among the principal members of the Army Medical Board is productive of very serious inconvenience to the public service.' It is often assumed that it was the medical incompetence of the Walcheren expedition which led to the dissolution of the medical board. In truth the board was already doomed. The Walcheren debacle was at most a final nail in its coffin.[6]

In 1807 the Commission of Military Enquiry had conducted a painstaking investigation into the workings of the medical service. This was not prompted by the deficiencies of the department, similar enquiries initiated by the Treasury were underway for the barrack-master's department, the board of works, the pay-master's department, the stamp officers and the customs and excise. The report, which relied heavily on the testimony of critics of the medical board, appeared in January 1808.[7] It recommended changes in the way army medical officers were appointed, better defined the various grades of army doctor, supported the increased use of regimental hospitals, and encouraged better supervision of the supply of drugs. Most significantly it recommended the creation of a new medical board with a supreme head and two assistants. It was specified that 'the chairman should be well acquainted with the details of military service, both at home and abroad, and that the two minor members should be medical officers who have served in the capacity of regimental and staff surgeon in different climates and on active service'. This effectively removed the old members of the board from consideration as neither Pepys nor Keate had significant military experience and even Knight's regimental service had been limited to the Helder in 1799.

There followed some prevarication for political reasons. Keate used the time to indulge in a war of words with the authors of the report and several of his colleagues. He was fighting a lost cause, and in late 1809 the commander-in-chief summoned a committee of general officers to carry out the necessary reforms to the medical department. At the top they supported the appointment of a Director General with an income of £2,000 a year with a number of supporting principal inspectors. This 'new medical board' was constituted in February 1810 with John Weir the first Director-General and Theodore Gordon and Charles Ker as the first Principal Inspectors. In accordance with the report's strictures, all these men had considerably more military and medical experience than their predecessors. However, Weir's experience was rather dated. He had been commissioned as early as 1775 and had been on half-pay for the previous twelve years. The Duke of York, who had no personal influence in his appointment, ungenerously referred to the 55-year-old Weir as 'an old driveller'.

Perhaps in part due to Weir's deficiencies the new board, although an improvement on the old, did not bring about the transformation in the medical department's affairs that might have been hoped for. It remained unpopular with staff and regimental surgeons who slightingly referred to the three men as the 'wigs in Berkeley Street'. The major reasons for the resentment were the board's propensity to promote medical officers at home rather than those already serving in the Peninsula, and their obsession with economy. No doubt because of the commission's criticism of the earlier board as being profligate, the new board apparently subjected all of the department's interests to a series of cost-cutting measures. This contributed substantially to the serious shortage of medical officers in 1812 and 1813. Even after the siege of Badajoz, a demand for bandages, splints and linen was likely to be queried. However, it would be jaundiced to portray the new board as a further failure. The new structure worked better than the old and many sensible decisions were taken, not least of which was the appointment of James McGrigor as head of the medical department in the Peninsula.

Whatever the machinations of the administrative machine in London, medical officers in the field were largely autonomous from home. This was inevitable in view of the distances involved and the crude communications which made it virtually impossible for the medical board to directly influence policy or treatment. Senior doctors with the army on campaign were accountable to the commander of the forces rather than to their medical superiors elsewhere. Thus, in the Peninsula, McGrigor reported to Wellington and could to some extent outmanoeuvre the board with which he frequently disagreed. Wellington was sympathetic to his senior doctor as he was fighting a similar battle with the Horseguards.

The second major division of the medical department was that of the medical staff. Wellington referred to them as the 'medical gentlemen', which was strictly correct as they were members of a civil organisation and only held relative military rank. They included inspectors, physicians, staff surgeons, hospital mates, apothecaries and purveyors. The inspectors were the senior medical officers in the field. The nomenclature of inspectatorial posts is confusing as it changed during the wars with some posts becoming obsolete. The commanding medical officer of an army in the field usually assumed the title 'Inspector-General of Hospitals'. Answerable to him were the Deputy Inspectors of Hospitals. Their exact role varied. Some were the Principal Medical Officer of a whole force or division; others had responsibility for a large general hospital. The title 'Senior Medical Officer' was usually applied to a staff surgeon who had been given additional responsibility such as overseeing the medical arrangements for a brigade, organising the regimental hospitals, or directing a brigade dressing station in battle. Their adminis-trative tasks might include making recommendations for disease prevention, arranging transport for the wounded, and ensuring the supply of medical equipment.[8]

In the early years of the wars the physicians were commissioned on the recommendation of the Physician-General, Lucas Pepys. They were the undoubted elite of the army medical profession, a status that was jealously guarded. Men of high academic qualifications, they drew a handsome salary of £1 a day. In war, physicians were either the personal medical attendant of the commander-in-chief or were appointed to large hospitals or garrisons in a supervisory role. They were never numerous. In 1807, for instance, there were only seventeen on the establishment.[9] The average soldier in the Peninsula was extremely unlikely to meet a physician.

Despite its scarcity and relatively small contribution to the army's medical care, the post of physician was a constant source of debate and acrimony throughout the period. Prior to the Napoleonic Wars, John Hunter, the Surgeon General, had sensibly decreed that no person should be appointed to the rank of physician without first having served as a staff surgeon, regimental surgeon or apothecary. However, Pepys discounted previous experience of military medicine and limited physician posts to those who were graduates of Oxford or Cambridge and who were licentiates, members or fellows of the College of Physicians of London.[10] This rule was both arbitrary and in disagreement with the royal warrant of 1798 which stated that 'for physicians, a medical degree in an English university, or a license from the College of Physicians, although desirable, must not be considered indispensable'. The restriction to Oxford and Cambridge was ironic as neither university had a proper school of medicine, and thus the relevant knowledge would have to be gained elsewhere. The decision to exclude other universities was justified by damning them. 'It is well known,' stated the medical board, 'that from many of the Scottish universities a degree may be sent for by the stage coach on paying eleven pounds.'

The most damaging effect of Pepys's directive was that able staff and regimental surgeons were entirely excluded from promotion to the senior position of physician. Scarcely any army medical men held the necessary qualifications. All fourteen physicians appointed during Pepys's tenure as Physician-General came from civilian life without previous army experience. The discontent of experienced army doctors when these newly qualified civilian physicians were appointed above them was understandable. Pepys justified his regulations by saying that the education of the army surgeons was not adequate. 'It does not lead them to a knowledge of principles.' He was not without support. Nathaniel Bancroft, himself a physician nominated by Pepys, wrote that the physicians' education, 'inevitably made them superior to the surgeons who were often of obscure origin, sons of millers or bakers who trust in curing diseases without license. They have neither the knowledge, habits, nor manners of members of a learned profession, and many assume the title of doctor without any justification.'[11] It is clear that there was not only intellectual prejudice but also snobbery. For men such as Pepys it was unthinkable that an ordinary regimental surgeon, a man of 'obscure origin', would be able to rise to the socially privileged rank of physician.

Apart from demoralising army surgeons, the appointment of physicians directly from civilian life had other obvious deficiencies. James McGrigor was quick to concede that most army surgeons were not adequately equipped to become physicians, but he decried the appointment of educated men with no previous experience to responsible posts.

> Physicians found that they practised with great disadvantage in a military hospital, in total ignorance of usage of the service, and of the diseases peculiar to soldiers. Of them, not a few malingered as it is called, played all manner of tricks in feigning diseases which they had not, and exposed the physician to the ridicule of the C.O. of a regiment, as well as of its surgeon.[12]

This view of the helpless, aristocratic physician was even more forcefully expressed by William Fergusson who campaigned widely in the Low Countries, West Indies and the Peninsula, rising from a regimental surgeon to Inspector of Hospitals. The following scathing attack was written after the disastrous Flanders campaign of 1793–4.

> The position of the young physicians was both pitiable and ridiculous. Divested of the pride they had imbibed at the universities,

they might have made excellent hospital-assistants: and, from their high general education, would have been deserving of every promotion the rules of military service – which in due time they would have come to grace and elevate – could permit. Their station in society, too, proclaimed them to be a class far superior to what the army had commonly received: but as physicians, setting aside their utter ignorance of diseases at so early an age, more especially military ones, they were far too fine for common use.

To one of them I was attached in the first campaign. He could read Hippocrates in the original Greek, but he did not know the grain scales and weights when he saw them; and to have touched a bleeding wound, even while the sound of cannon was booming in our ears, would have been to lose caste. He was my superior by at least four degrees of military rank, but I had to teach him what I myself was taught in the early days of my apprenticeship. With an apothecary, an assistant, a nurse, and a clerk in his train, he might have made a routine book prescription in classical Latin out of the military medicine chest; but had the ingredients of his own prescription been put into his hands, he would have known as much about them as if they had been sent from Timbuctoo. He had worn a cap and gown at Cambridge, but it is not to be supposed that he had ever entered an apothecary's shop, or contaminated his hands with drugs.[13]

Pepys's restrictive practices led to what might be regarded as test cases, where very experienced and eminent army surgeons were ludicrously excluded from advancement to physician. For instance, John Wright, a Fellow of the College of Physicians of Edinburgh, had served for seventeen years in the army and had extensive experience of diseases in the West Indies. His scientific attainments were of a high order, and when the expedition to the tropics under Sir Ralph Abercromby was being prepared, the general was anxious to secure his services as a physician to the force. Pepys predictably refused to appoint him unless he held the licence of the College of Physicians of London. Wright agreed to sit the examination but the expedition sailed before this was possible.[14] An even more notorious case was that of Robert Jackson, one of the great army doctors of the period. Jackson, a classical scholar, wrote extensively on the health of soldiers and was a particular authority on fevers and other diseases of the West Indies. He had served in the American War of Independence, and on the outbreak of the Napoleonic Wars in 1793 he re-entered the service as a regimental surgeon to the Buffs with a promise from John Hunter that he would shortly be elevated to physician. However, on Hunter's death Pepys's new rule effectively excluded Jackson from the promised promotion. Jackson went to London to argue his case with Pepys, drawing attention to his previous practical experience as an army physician as well as the fact that he had written a book on the fevers of Jamaica. Sir Lucas apparently lost his temper, replying, 'Had you the knowledge of Sydenham or of Radcliffe, you are the surgeon of a regiment, and the surgeon of a regiment can never be allowed to be a physician to His Majesty's Army.' Jackson's arguments with the medical board persisted throughout the war, culminating in an incident where he struck the surgeon-general with a cane and was sentenced to six months' imprisonment in the King's Bench Prison.[15]

Significantly, Wright and Jackson eventually achieved their promotion to physician, both on the recommendation of the commander in the field over the head of the Physician-General. Jackson, like Wright, proceeded to obtain the licence of the College of Physicians of London on his return to England. Undoubtedly, these promotions against his wishes undermined Pepys's position. He also had opposition within the medical board, as Francis Knight, the Inspector of Hospitals, held different views, prioritising previous army experience in selecting his staff.[16] Even the favoured army physicians began to suffer. As it was not possible to promote staff-surgeons to physician posts, they were instead promoted to assistant or deputy-inspectors of hospitals. The latter rank was senior to the physicians who were generally excluded from this promotion. The effect was that the army did not attract the best physicians from civil life. Hence, even Pepys's stated aim of raising the academic standard of army medicine was defeated. The writing was on the wall for the Physician-General. With the collapse of the old medical board it was instructed in 1811 that in future the opportunity of appointment to physician should be extended to those regimental and staff surgeons who held a British university degree.

The designation 'staff surgeon' was applied to all surgeons who did not belong to a particular regiment. Thus, it included surgeons employed on the staff of a general in the field, in a general hospital, or in a garrison. Staff surgeons were chosen predominantly for their surgical skills and were often promoted from hospital mates, apothecaries and regimental surgeons, although significant numbers came straight from civilian life. During the Napoleonic period it was a war-time post only, and in peace-time staff surgeons were removed from the active list and went on half-pay. As has been alluded to, the post could include administrative duties in the field, for instance acting as senior medical officer to a brigade or division. The hospital attachments were usually entirely surgical in nature. Staff surgeons were more often on foreign service than based at home. In 1807 of sixty staff surgeons all but seven were abroad.[17]

If the physicians were the cream of the army medical staff, there is no doubt that the poor hospital mates were at the bottom of the pile. Hospital mates provided the basic medical care in the army's general hospitals.

Few viewed them as 'medical gentlemen'. When a captain of a transport at Lisbon was asked what he had on board he apparently replied 'horses and hospital mates for the army'. The mates were treated as hospital drudges, in the words of one doctor, 'scarcely ranking with wardmasters and sergeants . . . and despised by every new ensign'. This execrable reputation was a result of the demand for ordinary hospital doctors exceeding the supply of suitable applicants. As expeditions sailed with only a fraction of the hospital mates required, the medical board was forced to lower already lenient standards. Many of the so-called doctors appointed as hospital mates had no proper qualifications, their previous exposure to medicine perhaps limited to a brief visit to hospital wards or an attachment to a country apothecary. The Inspector of Hospitals questioned the case of a 17-year-old hospital mate serving with the army whose apprenticeship was limited to four months.[18] Even this minimal experience was often not properly authenticated.

The mates themselves were demoralised by the reputation of the post. When Walter Henry joined the army as a doctor, he had few illusions about the status of his new job.

> The wise men on the medical bench having examined me and reported that I could physic as well as bleed, I was in due course gazetted 'Hospital Mate' for general service to His Majesty's Force. The title grated on my ear at first, as cacophonous to the last degree: but one gets accustomed to disagreeable sounds.[19]

Changes were made to the post of hospital mate during the wars. By a royal warrant of 1804 hospital mates serving in general hospitals were divided into a warrant class and a commissioned class. The first commission did not actually appear in the London Gazette until 1809 when twenty-three 'gentlemen' were gazetted hospital mates for general service. This continued until 1813 when commissioned hospital mates were re-named 'hospital assistants'. Those appointed by warrant continued as hospital mates but were encouraged by the medical board to 'improve themselves towards a due qualification for admission as commissioned officers'.[20]

To complete this review of the army's medical staff, we need briefly to consider apothecaries and purveyors. Apothecaries managed the medicines and medical stores. They were medical men and were usually selected from assistant surgeons and hospital mates. Some were highly qualified and were subsequently promoted to physician.[21] Purveyors were originally medically qualified, but by the time of the Peninsular War doctor shortages meant that they were raised from purveyors' clerks. Their role was as commissariat officers to a hospital with responsibility for the purchase and distribution of food and medical comforts. They were generally distrusted by other parts of the service who believed, possibly with some justification, that many yielded to temptation and feathered their own nests.[22]

This brings us to the third and largest part of the medical department, the regimental medical organisation. These were the surgeons who provided the routine medical care to the men of Wellington's army and who accompanied them into battle. That they were the most numerous group of doctors in the army is confirmed by the following breakdown of medical officers in 1814 at the height of the Peninsular War: medical staff officers 354, regimental surgeons 313, and regimental assistant surgeons 573.[23] In previous wars each cavalry regiment and infantry battalion had a surgeon and a surgeon's mate. The former was a commissioned officer, but the latter only a warrant officer. Thus the mate, who might be an educated man, was of low status in the regiment and just as exposed to flogging and other indignities as the rank and file. At the outbreak of the war with France, many mates either transferred to hospital mate posts or were promoted. In 1796 the title was changed to assistant surgeon. An extra assistant surgeon was added to larger regiments in 1803, and by Waterloo most regiments of cavalry and battalions of infantry had a surgeon and two assistants. In the infantry the surgeon ranked as a captain and the assistant surgeon as a subaltern. However, this was a relative rank and the doctors had no real military authority over either hospital attendants or patients.[24]

The professional attainments of most of the regimental surgeons were modest. After an apprenticeship in a country practice, attendance at a course of private lectures, and a period in a hospital, they might have entered for examination at the Corporation of Surgeons (later the Royal College of Surgeons) or the Society of Apothecaries. In the early years of the wars there was strictly no need for any diploma. From 1803 an attempt was made to exercise greater control of appointments, and regimental surgeons had to be approved by the medical board rather than just being selected by the colonel of the regiment. Three years later it was directed that assistant surgeons of regiments were to be chosen from the hospital mates and the regimental surgeons from the assistant surgeons, promotion depending on ability and length of service. Before receiving advancement the mates had to pass an examination at Surgeons Hall and be examined by senior army doctors. However, from 1812 onwards, as the scope of the war widened and casualties mounted, the authorities were again forced to relax these standards with some regimental surgeons with limited experience and qualifications enrolled directly from civilian life.

It is important not to overgeneralise regarding the regimental surgeons. At best they were well educated and conscientious men capable of great things. All the eminent British army doctors of the period, men such as James McGrigor, William Fergusson, Robert Jackson, John Hennen and

George Guthrie, started their careers as surgeons attached to regiments. James McGrigor was quick to defend his fellow regimental officers. He acknowledged that they were not universally highly qualified, but regarded them as 'a respectable body of men'.[25] At worst there were regimental surgeons who had received hardly any relevant training. This was particularly true of the regimental mates at the outset of the wars. Some had only the briefest attachment to a country apothecary with no attendance at lectures or visits to a hospital. On occasion, even private soldiers who had applied a few dressings in the role of hospital orderlies were summarily elevated to mate. Changing the title of hospital mate to assistant surgeon was not in itself a solution. In 1799 a surgeon in the West Middlesex militia wrote a damning account of the appointment of assistant surgeons. He compared their training unfavourably with occupations such as tailoring and carpentry, pointing out that these craftsmen had to undergo a proper apprenticeship. Family connections and patronage were still important in obtaining regimental medical posts.

> Mere apprentice boys were appointed as surgeons and many without exhibiting their proper testimonials of their knowledge or ability . . . such a man, [he wrote would] deal out his poisons to the aggravation of disease; and . . . too frequently, deprive us of our dearest friends.[26]

George Guthrie, the greatest British surgeon of the Peninsular War, joined in the condemnation. Medical personnel, he stated, 'were appointed without having served a single day in a regiment. They were taken to learn their profession at the expense and great inconvenience of the unfortunate soldiers committed to their care.'[27] Such men, implied Guthrie, could damage the army more effectively than the enemy. The competence of the doctors of Wellington's army attracted much comment from both medical and military commentators and it is a subject to which we will return.

It is easy to become immersed in, and at times perplexed by, the numerous changes in the regulations pertaining to regimental surgeons, mates and assistant surgeons that occurred between 1793 and 1815. The best insights into the formative years of regimental doctors are gained by reading their correspondence and diaries written as they pursued their education, passed the required examinations, and finally took the fateful decision to join the army. There is not a profusion of such writings, but there are a few valuable accounts. Notable amongst these are the letters of James Dickson who, in early 1794, was appointed as surgeon's mate to a regiment of Dragoons accompanying the army to Flanders. Dickson's little known correspondence, gathered together in a small publication by A A Cormack, gives explicit details of his gradual progress from his early schooldays to his ultimate regimental and hospital appointments. Born in

Aberdeen, he won a bursary to study arts at the local Marischal College and soon decided on a medical career. There was no formal medical course available in Aberdeen, so he became apprenticed to two respectable local doctors whilst continuing with his arts degree. His apprenticeship was a three-year commitment for both parties and was formalised in a contract drawn up in 1785 when Dickson was 16 years old. Dickson undertook to, 'abstain from gaming, debauchery, and bad company, and in general shall behave properly and decently in every respect as becoming an apprentice'. His father had to continue to keep him and also made a payment of '300 Merks Scots money' (£16 17/6d) as an apprentice fee. On their part the two doctors promised to 'teach and instruct the said James Dickson in all and everything relating to their Business and employment'.[28]

When Robert Jackson was similarly attached to a local doctor he simply says that he 'learned to compound drugs and let blood, & c'.[29] Apprenticeships varied greatly in quality, but Dickson appears to have been fortunate in his choice of teachers. Initially, his level of responsibility was equivalent to that of a modern day medical student, but he quickly moved on to tasks which we would associate with a junior doctor. After only a week or so of his apprenticeship, he was visiting the local infirmary on a daily basis to make up the medicines, apply dressings, and witness treatments and operations. In the following month he updated his father and sister on his progress.

> I have now a good opportunity of acquiring medical knowledge. A man who was lately hanged here we have had upon the dissecting table since Friday was [sic] eight days – and although he begins to putrefy, we will go through the whole anatomy of the parts.

He continued to dress simple wounds and was given the additional responsibility of visiting patients at home.

In the spring of 1787 he graduated MA at Aberdeen and proceeded to the great medical school at Edinburgh to complete his medical training. Here the esteemed professors gave lectures on subjects such as botany, materia medica, chemistry and natural history. In a further illuminating letter to his father, Dickson discusses his future career plans and especially the role of qualifications.

> The obtaining of a degree of MD [doctor of medicine] from this university is attached with much expense and difficulty, as it requires the graduate to have attended every medical class in the college and to pass a very strict examination. The expense which depends upon you, I make no doubt but you may be ready to defray; but the abilities requisite to obtain it which must belong to me, I am afraid I am not

possessed of. When I began the Study of Medicine, I was much biased in favour of Surgery from a conviction of its greater use and a natural desire to excel in the art. As I advanced in my studies, I retained this predilection and consequently have paid more attention to it than to the practice of medicine. As my inclination is for this branch of Medicine, and my genius is some degree mechanical, I should wish that my education may correspond with it, and this, when you consider it rightly, I dare say you will comply with. A Degree from this university would in this case be of no service to me – and I imagine this may answer your question with respect to what I principally intend to pursue – the place where I shall exercise my profession is for you to determine.[30]

By deciding to pursue surgery rather than medicine as a career, Dickson was effectively reducing his requirement for a higher qualification. Surgery was at this time regarded as a mechanical speciality, requiring the skill of an able craftsman, but relatively little formal education or theoretical knowledge. Surgeons were compromised by their long association with the barbers and the public linked them with the ghoulish body-snatchers. In contrast, the university degree of doctor of medicine was a prerequisite for a career as a respected physician. As we have seen, the Physician-General was discriminatory in his appointment of army physicians preferring degrees from Oxford and Cambridge. An alternative professional qualification open to Dickson, aspiring surgeon, was membership of the Edinburgh College of Surgeons. However, his name does not appear in the records of the Royal College, suggesting that he did not take this examination. The lack of college membership was at this time not a major omission considering Dickson's final choice of an army career and his entry into the forces as a humble surgeon's mate.

James Dickson's education and early career decisions are remarkably similar to those of his illustrious countryman, James McGrigor. Although McGrigor was eventually to rise to be Director General of the Army Medical Department and was a fervent campaigner for better qualified medical officers, he also entered the army with no paper qualifications in medicine. He graduated in arts at Marischal College before being apprenticed to a physician at the local Aberdeen Infirmary. Later he attended Edinburgh University but failed to gain the MD degree and he did not take the examination of the College of Surgeons. He joined the army by purchasing a commission in the 88th Foot, the famed Connaught Rangers, in 1793. Dickson was 25 years old and McGrigor 22 when they received their regimental appointments. At this time young age was no bar to the ambitious army surgeon. George Guthrie commenced his apprenticeship at 13, was appointed a hospital assistant at 15, passed the membership of the college of surgeons at the same age, and joined the 29th Regiment as assistant surgeon when just 16 years old. A year later, in 1802, some restrictions were introduced.

Those wishing to pursue formal qualifications, notably a university degree, needed financial support. For many, for instance in James Dickson's case, this was provided by their family. Not all were so fortunate. Robert Jackson attributed his inability to gain proper qualifications early in his career to the failure of his finances:

> I had not the means of paying teachers. I was therefore under the necessity of teaching myself, or remaining untaught. I never attended a hospital in the United Kingdom; I could not afford to pay the fees.[31]

William Dent came from a wealthy Yorkshire farming family and was able to attend St Thomas' and other famous London teaching hospitals. He also aspired to a career in surgery and joined the Peninsular army in 1810, first as a hospital mate and then as an assistant surgeon to the 9th (East Norfolk) Regiment. His letters home describe his life as a London medical student in 1808 and 1809. The following excerpt is typical.

> I told you that I had got very good lodgings, along with two young men who belonged [sic] the hospitals, they are both of them very steady and studious, one of them attended last season, and we derive a good deal of information from him, as he is very clever indeed, we are kept close at work both day and night, writing out the lectures. We have a great deal of practice in the Hospitals, and accidents are continually brought in, we have an opportunity of seeing them all, as our lodgings are only a few doors from Guy's hospital.[32]

If we assume his letters to be truthful and not written simply for parental consumption, Dent was a very conscientious student. He achieved a professional qualification by passing the examination to become a member of the Royal College of Surgeons. He informed his mother that this was, 'more than most medical Practitioners in the North can boast of'. The college diploma cost the not inconsiderable sum of £ 22 7s. 6d. Before being commissioned as an assistant surgeon, he was also expected to pass an examination at the medical board office. Unlike most of his contemporaries, Dent had an opportunity to treat sick and wounded soldiers prior to his joining the army. Following the battle of Corunna in January 1809, the British Army embarked for the south coast of England. Approximately 6,000 sick were landed, and such was the necessity for medical assistance in the hospitals, that London medical students were asked to help. Dent was sent to Colchester, where he was placed under the supervision of a surgeon of the 4th Regiment. There were 197 men from this regiment in the hospital and Dent had to look after half of them himself. In a letter to his mother he enthuses:

> I am glad that I came here for besides attending the sick and wounded, we have the privilege of dissecting those who die; and in London we could not get a dead body under three guineas.[33]

William Dent's experiences at Colchester must have been invaluable to him when he became a fully fledged army doctor. In the latter years of the war there was some attempt to give instruction in the treatment of the diseases of soldiers to new army doctors by attaching them to the York Hospital in Chelsea. William Gibney, later a regimental assistant surgeon at Waterloo, attended the hospital for a few months in 1813. From Gibney's account it seems that the hospital at least provided an introduction to the privations of army life and an initiation into the tricks of malingerers.

> I first commenced my military career and found myself something like a fish out of water among the comical set of fellows I met with at the York Hospital. Physicians, staff surgeons, hospital assistants, apothecaries, and the queer lot generally, comprising the staff of a general hospital ... There were two or three staff surgeons, under whose orders the assistants acted. They did their duties efficiently and systematically, one being always officer of the day, and consequently never quitted the hospital on the day of duty, so as to be prepared to receive any sent in wounded or seriously ill. This duty came around disagreeably often: of course the confinement to the hospital walls was monotonous enough but it was the bad commons and disgusting bedding which tried one most. 'The Ordinary', or, as it would now be termed, 'Hospital Mess', was very bad. One pound of beef was anything in the shape of meat, and as tough as shoe leather; the potatoes bad and badly boiled; one pound of bread of the brickbat nature; and a pint of porter sufficiently sour to necessitate our practising on ourselves the cure of diarrhoea; as for the bedding it was damp and dirty: with sheets so coarse as to act like nutmeg graters.
>
> It might have been disagreeable, this duty, but it gave us a good insight into practice, and brought us into contact with all manner of characters among the soldiers who from time to time became the inmates of the hospital. Some of them were really good, brave, and heroic fellows, who submitted to every kind of treatment and operation with undaunted courage; but others were most obstinate and discontented, using every kind of dodge to impose upon us young doctors, and to avoid being sent back to duty. To this end,

some even of the younger soldiers, benefiting by the instruction given to them by old malingerers, caused sores and slight wounds, which under ordinary circumstances, would have healed quickly, to become inflamed and daily worse. Tongues rubbed against the white washed walls certainly puzzled us doctors. Fits were common and constantly acted in the barrack yard, lameness was a general complaint, and not a few declared themselves to be hopelessly paralysed.[34]

The education provided at the York Hospital led to the proposal of the formation of a proper school of military medicine. However this was summarily rejected. The medical board did take the more modest initiative of paying for the education of potential medical officers, the so-called 'medical cadetships'. With the gradual increase in the scale of the wars, it became increasingly difficult to attract adequate numbers of recruits for both hospital mate and regimental surgeon posts. In desperation, advertisements were placed on the college gates of Dublin, Edinburgh and Glasgow offering favourable pay, good quarters and full travelling expenses. In retrospect, James McGrigor was critical of this practice:

> . . . it was the occasion of many uneducated and unqualified persons being introduced to the service, not a few of whom, in quarters where the promotion was rapid, found means to pass through different grades to the rank of regimental and staff surgeons. Not a few apothecaries and even druggists apparently found their way into the service in this manner.[35]

It is understandable that ill-educated and poorly qualified men saw some gain in becoming army surgeons; the alternatives must have been even bleaker. But what was the motivation for intelligent and well educated men such as James Dickson, James McGrigor, Walter Henry and William Dent? The more junior staff and regimental posts had little status in society and the monetary rewards were limited. From their letters and memoirs it seems that there were a number of different incentives. One was simply the allure of the uniform, the apparent glamour of army life.

> One of the senior students [at Marischal College], a Mr Farquhar, obtained through his friends the appointment of assistant surgeon to a regiment stationed in Jamaica. The moment he obtained it he exchanged his round hat for a smart cocked hat, mounted a cockade in it, and strutted to the Infirmary, where, at 12 o'clock daily, all the medical students usually attended to accompany the physicians and surgeons of the hospital through the different wards. He attracted the attention of all, and the admiration of some.[36]

Although seemingly trivial, James McGrigor was enough impressed by this episode to include it in his autobiography written over fifty years later. Some sought adventure and, particularly later in the war, the chance to join a British Army with a succession of victories against the French. Of his decision to join up Walter Henry simply says:

> Having obtained from the chirurgical wisdom of Lincoln's Inn Fields an authority to cut up all the King's liege subjects, who chose to permit me, I determined on entering the army and visiting the Peninsula; where Lord Wellington was at the time 'grimly reposing' behind the lines of Torres Vedras, and waiting for a false move on the part of Massena, whom he there held in check.[37]

James Dickson gives no specific reason for becoming a surgeon's mate. In a letter of 1789 it is implied that his father will have considerable influence in his choice of final career, so perhaps the decision was made for him. In a letter to his mother, William Dent felt that his choice of the army needed some justification.

> I hope you dont fret at my entering the army. I am perfectly happy, and I see no reason why you should not be so, for I think the army an excellent School for a young man, who has a desire to excel either in his Profession or to become acquainted with the manners of the World.[38]

It is likely that many joined up because of the difficulties commonly encountered in civilian life. William Dent was well aware that if he set up practice as a doctor in his native Yorkshire, it could be many years before he became fully established. At 21 years old he believed that his youth would count against him. Although a regimental surgeon's pay was not overly generous, there was always the prospect of retiring from the army on half-pay and using this money to supplement private practice earnings.

Doctors entering the army were responsible for kitting themselves out for their first campaign. This involved purchasing the medical officer's uniform, other necessary items of clothing, and some basic medical equipment. Before his departure to Flanders, James Dickson detailed his preparations in a letter home.

> I have laid out some money here . . . It was necessary to have a pair of new boots, spurs, leather breaches, and other articles, also a portmanteau trunk. I shall take very few things with me, only about a dozen of shirts, two or three books and other things in proportion . . . The medicine chest also was taken, and another one has since been

sent out by government. I must however buy a set of amputating and trepanning instruments but the surgeon will take them off my hands afterwards.[39]

The regimental surgeon's uniform was a combination of the medical staff officer's dress and regimental style. Their coats were single breasted with embroidered loops on the breast, but facings in regimental colouring with regimental lace, buttons and epaulettes. They carried a sword suspended from a narrow, black waist belt. The medical staff wore bicorns, whilst the regimental surgeons usually had the head-dress of their unit. The black feather in the hat was worn only by the medical and Judge-Advocate's departments. Not all were enthralled by their new uniform. Hospital mate Walter Henry acquired his from an army tailor in London.

> The awful black feather in my cocked hat was calculated to raise unpleasant ideas, and I considered it scarcely fair for the Horse Guards' people to put me in mourning prematurely and by anticipation for any accidents amongst my patients.[40]

For many medical officers, their introduction to campaigning was their first visit abroad, their first experience of war, and their initiation into army doctoring. Some appear to have coped admirably with these new challenges. William Dent arrived in Gibraltar in the summer of 1810. He thought it a 'strange place', but at least from the evidence of his correspondence he soon settled to his responsibilities. However, others were hopelessly out of their depth, ill prepared by their rudimentary education in both medical and military matters. The hospital mates were even more vulnerable than the regimental assistant surgeons and mates who were at least attached to a particular unit. William Fergusson, a very experienced campaigner, sympathised with the lowly staff doctors who were, 'thrown into a strange army, where they have neither place, nor home, nor experience, nor knowledge how to guide themselves, without even being allowed a servant that could speak their language, but left at the mercy of any native camp-follower'.[41] Fergusson illustrates his opinion with references to inexperienced doctors who were exploited or robbed, or charged under martial law for acting in their own self-defence. One pitiable anecdote was of a Scottish hospital mate who arrived in Lisbon during the Peninsular War and hired the first local who offered himself as a servant. It was hot, and whilst he slept he left all his clothes and baggage at the bedside of his billet. In the morning all were gone and he was left cursing his luck and 'bawling for revenge'.

For those who were able to adapt to life in the army, there was always the possibility of promotion. In general a post might be obtained by purchase, by exertion of influence, or simply on the basis of previous experience and merit. For men without money or influence, advancement could be extremely slow. In the latter part of the eighteenth century it was not unusual for a man to serve as a regimental surgeon for as long as twenty years. When war broke out the prospects for promotion much improved with the formation of new regiments requiring surgeons and the increased hospital establishment and the attendant demand for hospital mates. The various factors at work in the rise through the medical ranks are well illustrated by considering the careers of James McGrigor, James Dickson and William Dent. As we have seen, there were relatively few regulations early in the wars and James McGrigor was able to forego professional examinations and buy his commission as a regimental surgeon for £150. Of course the purchase of rank now appears iniquitous, but on occasion it worked well, allowing very capable men such as McGrigor to make a start in the army. The Duke of Wellington considerably benefited from both wealth and influence early in his career. McGrigor's later rise to the top of the medical department was entirely attributable to his outstanding qualities as a doctor and administrator.

James Dickson was less fortunate than McGrigor, joining the army as a mere surgeon's mate. He hoped for rapid promotion to a hospital mate post which, he informed his father, was both safer than the regimental attachment and also better paid. His efforts to achieve promotion included a personal visit to the Surgeon-General, Thomas Keate, who promised him it in due time. As soon as he transferred to hospital mate in Flanders, his thoughts turned to becoming the surgeon of a regiment. Here, previous service was helpful but there was ultimately no substitute for influence and money. In his letters he asks his father, 'by all means to use interest at home for the surgeoncy in a new Corps'. He adds, 'tho' I am afraid the appointment goes too much if not altogether by interest'. The post of surgeon was largely the gift of the colonel of the regiment, although the approval of the medical board, and particularly the Surgeon-General, was required. Dickson was himself a little uncertain of the complicated etiquette of promotion, asking his father to consult with an influential family friend as to whether it was proper to employ money to procure the surgeoncy of a new corps. The sum he was considering investing was in the region of £ 300–400. Whether Dickson actually paid for his commission as a surgeon in May 1795 is not clear, as his promotion post-dated his last existing letter.[42]

William Dent entered the army in 1810 as a hospital mate for general service. This was a commissioned post, and within three months he obtained promotion to assistant surgeon. He then had to wait until 1824 for his next promotion to regimental surgeon. This very slow advancement was not unusual even in times of war. Often, surgeon vacancies were filled by officers on half-pay rather than by those already in employment as assistant surgeons. Men still remained as assistant surgeons for twenty years, and as late as 1851 there were several regimental surgeons who wore the Peninsula medal and had over forty years' service.[43] The tendency of the medical board to promote officers from home rather than those already in the field was a constant irritation both to McGrigor and the commander of the forces. Wellington, in a letter of September 1812 to Lord Bathurst from the Peninsula, complained vociferously both of the shortage of medical officers and of the methods of appointment.

> I beg to draw your Lordship's attention to the practice of the Medical Board in promoting to vacancies in this army, instead of promoting the officers on the spot, who deserve promotion highly for their merits and services, officers are selected in England, the Mediterranean, or elsewhere, to be promoted. The consequence is increased delay in their arrival to perform their duties, and all who do arrive are sick in the first instance. It would be but justice to promote those on the spot, who are performing their duty; and we should enjoy the advantages and the seniors of the department at least would have experience in the disorders of the climate, and of the troops serving in this country; to which climate they would have become accustomed.[44]

The outcome of this power struggle is not clear, although McGrigor, with Wellington's help, did succeed in promoting several of his favoured officers to senior posts despite the opposition of the board.

Whatever their rank, the medical officers of Wellington's army were in a small minority, surrounded by military officers and the ordinary soldiers. Unsurprisingly, the doctors were not always entirely understood, or appreciated, by the army's officers. There was great opportunity for misunderstanding. In McGrigor's words:

> The army is officered by gentlemen of anything but a studious turn of mind ... A great many of them being well born, and all of them gentlemen, they do not look with much respect to a profession which requires study and close attention, and what they term plodding and drudgery.[45]

He warned his fellow medical officers against being captivated by the lifestyle of the more affluent military officers and falling into 'idle habits'. At worst these differences in outlook led to alienation between the two groups of officers and medical opinion was discounted. William Fergusson bitterly recalled that in the West Indies the views of the army doctor were regarded as less important than the 'convenience of the engineer, the whim of the Quartermaster-General and the profit of the contractor'.[46] Fortunately, this situation was not universal. Over a period of time, the able and conscientious regimental or staff doctor could win over the officers and men and become a respected figure. McGrigor goes as far as saying that 'it is greatly the fault of a medical officer if he become not the favourite of the men and officers of a regiment'. He decries any form of sycophancy to senior officers but emphasises the importance of showing kindness and humanity in the medical management of the men. He further observes that 'the gratitude of the soldier to the doctor lasts longer than that of the military officer'.[47] Many regimental surgeons became immensely proud of their regiment and some even refused offers of promotion elsewhere.

It is of interest to compare the status and role of the army doctor with that of the surgeon in Nelson's navy. We have little evidence that the training or calibre of men was better in the Napoleonic navy than in the army, but there is a definite perception that sailors' medical care was better than that of soldiers. John Hennen, an experienced army surgeon, believed his naval colleagues to have many advantages.

> Their hospitals, their medical stores, their provisions, and all their little comforts are as perfectly within their reach, after the most protracted engagement, as if no such event had taken place; their patients suffer none of the heart-rending privations of a soldier, lying wounded on the field of battle, without bedding, food or shelter; and, when he is removed, torn from his comrades, and sent to distant hospitals by a precarious and uncomfortable conveyance over broken-up roads, or intricate mountain passes. In short, the sailor fights at home.[48]

It is unlikely that the sailor under round-shot fire from an enemy, involved in hand-to-hand combat during boarding actions, or in danger from the falling masts and rigging of his disintegrating ship would have appreciated Hennen's views. Undoubtedly the naval surgeon did have some advantages over his land-based colleagues, but equally he was disadvantaged by the professional isolation inevitable aboard ship. He was entirely responsible for the irreplaceable ship's crew, usually with no senior colleague to turn to. Perhaps it was this need for self-reliance, allied with a freedom from the normal restrictions of medical practice, that explains the probable superiority of the naval doctor.

This comparison returns us to the issue of competence. The professional abilities of the various ranks of medical officers have already been outlined and will be further discussed in later chapters addressing specific practice in surgery and the treatment of disease. At this point it is worthwhile to review the contemporary literature to try obtain a representative cross section of opinion as to their general competence. In addition to the writings of eminent, and no doubt, self-interested, medical men such as McGrigor, Jackson and Hennen, we have the numerous views expressed by military officers and soldiers in their memoirs and diaries. McGrigor comments extensively on the abilities of the men under his supervision. He is not entirely consistent, which most likely reflects a simple reality that, by the standards of the times, a few army doctors were excellent, many were mediocre, and a minority were positively dangerous. A number of his more adverse comments are aimed at the regimental surgeon, who was apparently too often a man who, 'reads less and less every day, makes his hospital duty as light as he can, stops but a short time with his patients, and is in haste to join his brother officers in their plans of amusement'.[49] However, at other times McGrigor compliments the same set of officers, and at the end of a campaign he was quick to applaud their efforts. For instance, after the Corunna campaign he says they showed 'great zeal and humanity', and in his later overview of the Peninsular War he asserted that 'the services of medical officers are of a less brilliant nature than those of the military but in points of utility, talent and zeal, I believe it was acknowledged that the medical was not inferior to any department in the army under the Duke of Wellington'.[50]

Robert Jackson was even more effusive about his compatriots, stating that if medicine were ever to rise from its low position in society 'it is more than probable it will owe its good fortune to the medical officers of armies, and more so to the medical officers of the British Army than to others'.[51] John Hennen was also protective of his fellow surgeons, but he understood that many in military and civilian life had a low opinion of the army's doctors.

> It is a very prevalent idea among the uninformed private soldiers, and some of the junior officers, that the surgeons 'lop off', as their phrase is, limbs by cart-loads, to save trouble; and sorry am I to say, that some private practitioners, whether from ignorance or design, have assisted in propagating the scandal.[52]

Hennen points out that comparisons drawn between civilian doctors and army doctors were often ill-considered, as the military surgeons had to manage many more serious injuries in difficult circumstances than would ever be the case in private practice. He concludes that the only reward that the military surgeon could expect was that of his 'own conscience'.

It is clear from the accounts of officers and soldiers that not all army surgeons lived up to the high standards expected and proclaimed by Hennen and others. There is no shortage of damning anecdotes and adverse opinions to quote from. Lieutenant-Colonel John Moore, later the hero of Corunna, spent the spring of 1790 in Ireland. Here the men found their colonel's medical advice more helpful than that of their regimental surgeon who also acted as paymaster. According to Moore his surgeon was,

> Completely ignorant, devoid of humanity, and a rogue. I have shut up the channels he had of cheating, and have put the hospital upon a tolerable footing, as far as diet and cleanliness; but against his ignorance I have no remedy, tho' I have daily the grossest instance of it.[53]

Similar criticisms persisted during the years of the Peninsular War. John Aitchison, an ensign in the 3rd Foot Guards, fought in several major Peninsular battles. He is a perceptive and outspoken witness in his letters and diaries, on occasion even criticising Wellington. In 1810 he writes:

> In this army there are men in charge of sick now who till they came here had never prescribed in their lives, and there are others who have had no practice beyond answering a prescription in an apothecary's shop in England. Such are the men entrusted with the lives of soldiers, but it must always be the case in a great degree, while the pay remains so small as to induce those only to enter the service who would starve at home. I have myself heard a surgeon say that he had no doubt that two-thirds of deaths in this army were due to the inattention and ignorance of the medical officers.[54]

Cornet Francis Hall's indictment of the hospital mates staffing the hospital at Celerico in Portugal in 1812 is in a similar vein. They were, 'grossly inattentive, and ignorant of the first rudiments of their profession . . . if a few men of talents and information were still to be found among the ignobler band of hospital mates (and my own experience justifies me in affirming there were a few such), it must be ascribed rather to extraordinary good luck than to any merit in the system according to which they were selected.'[55] Hall blames the medical staff for fraudulently seizing hospital comforts intended for the sick. However, he was not entirely unsympathetic to them as he acknowledges that they were much overworked, often without pay, and denied a servant to look after them. He even admits that he probably would have done the same if he had been placed in their situation.

Some of the accusations against doctors arose out of simple misunderstandings and had no basis whatsoever. A good example is the account of Charles O'Neil of the 28th Foot who was wounded in the arm at Waterloo. He was advised by a surgeon in Brussels to have the arm amputated but he refused. 'My readers may perhaps wonder at my obstinacy: but their astonishment may possibly diminish when they learn that for every joint amputated the operating surgeon obtained an enormous price from the government.'[56] O'Neil then gives a graphic description of the large numbers of amputations, carts laden with legs and arms and hundreds of 'poor fellows on the invalid list for the remainder of their lives'. At no stage in the wars were the surgeons rewarded according to the volume of procedures performed.

In the midst of so much criticism, both justified and unfair, it is not surprising that Wellington's doctors were easy targets for the vitriolic caricaturists and satirists of the period. *The Military Adventures of Johny Newcome* was published with illustrations by Thomas Rowlandson in 1816. The author, Lieutenant-Colonel David Roberts of the 51st Foot, was a Peninsula veteran who was wounded during the siege of San Sebastian. The regimental doctor gets a rough ride; the following snippet of conversation between him and the poor new recruit is typical.

'Come,' says the Doctor, 'here's Rum and Segars
This is the way we carry on our Wars,
Here, smoke, my boy, I know 'twill do you good;
And try this country wine, 'twill cool your blood.'[57]

One of the most oft quoted passages used to malign the medical department in the Peninsula was penned by Sergeant Joseph Donaldson of the 94th Foot. Donaldson had strong views and pulled no punches.

> Those medical men we had were not always ornaments of the profession. They were chiefly, I believe, comprised of apothecaries boys, who, having studied a session or two, were thrust into the army as a huge dissecting room, where they might mangle with impunity, until they were drilled into an ordinary knowledge of their business; and as they began at the wrong end, they generally did much mischief before that was attained. The extent of their medical practice in most disorders was to 'blister, bleed, and purge', – what then? why 'blister, bleed and purge again' . . . In the field they did more mischief, being but partially acquainted with anatomy; there was enough of what medical men call bold practice. In cutting down upon a ball for the purpose of extracting it, ten chances to one but they severed an artery they knew not how to stem; but this gave no concern to these enterprising fellows, for clapping a piece of lint and a bandage, or a piece of adhesive plaster on the wound, they would walk off very composedly to mangle some other poor wretch, leaving the former to his fate.[58]

This emotive piece of writing is usually presented in isolation. This is unfair as Donaldson also stresses the scarcity of medical officers in the Peninsula and says that there were many competent doctors who undertook duties that were 'fatiguing and arduous in the extreme'. Elsewhere in his recollections, he pays a touching tribute to the assistant surgeon of his regiment, Joseph Bennett, who died from disease in 1811 whilst attending the sick. Bennett, he says, would always be remembered with gratitude by those who had been under his care. Donaldson cannot have been totally disillusioned with the army medical profession as he himself later qualified as a surgeon.

The most even-handed and commonsensical description of the army's doctors was written by a senior military officer, George Napier, the middle of three famous brothers. He fought extensively in the Peninsula and had first-hand experience of the medical services. George Guthrie amputated his arm after the storming of Ciudad Rodrigo, and he was a friend of Charles Bell, the great anatomist and surgeon. His older brother, Charles, was an experienced Peninsula campaigner and was wounded at Corunna and Busaco. His younger brother, William, also distinguished himself in the Peninsula and later wrote a magisterial history of the war. George Napier's measured opinions were prompted by a visit to his wounded elder brother after Busaco in 1810. The passage in his autobiography contains a number of perceptive insights and is worth quoting in full.

I must say that those medical men whom, unfortunately for him, he came under were all young men just arrived from England, many of them both idle and ignorant; and from the circumstances of the army being on the retreat and closely followed by the enemy, these young surgeons had nobody to give them orders or teach them their duty as military men, so that they were completely left to themselves, which is some excuse for their conduct. And I am bound to state that if one takes the conduct of the whole medical department of the army during the Peninsular War into consideration, one will find few such large bodies of men who are more distinguished for their kindness, skill, and indefatigable exertions for the health and comfort of the sick and wounded; and as to danger, the medical officers of the British army without exception have invariably shown an utter contempt for it, and in the execution of their duty will brave death, either in the field of battle or – which requires a higher mental courage – in the hospitals of the plague and yellow fever!

I am more particular on this subject because it is a very general but erroneous and unjust idea in the army to think slightly of the medical men and to consider their profession as inferior to others, which is a great mistake, for few officers receive so good an education or are so generally acquainted with science and literature; and although I confess one does sometimes meet a ridiculous puppy of an assistant surgeon, or hospital mate, or even a pompous coxcomb in the higher departments, yet (and I speak from thirty years experience) I never met anything but kindness, generosity, and manly honourable conduct, combined with skill and judgement, in those medical gentlemen with whom I have served; and you will generally find the surgeon of your regiment a man whose society will be agreeable to you and whose information, opinions, and experience will be of much benefit to you. I only wish they were better off in pecuniary circumstances, for when I consider the great expense of their education, which they cannot avoid, and the length of time before they obtain the rank of surgeon of a regiment, or staff-surgeon, the pay they receive is very inadequate to their deserts, and not equal to what they would probably have made in private practice, particularly where they have very distinguished abilities. Some of my greatest friends, and men for whom I have the highest esteem and respect, are in the medical department of the army.[59]

If we take into account all the various views expressed on the capabilities of the medical officers, allowing for the inevitable bias of some doctors' accounts and for the overly jaundiced views of some soldiers, it is difficult to disagree with Napier's summation. Of course there were appallingly ignorant and lazy doctors, but others were surprisingly well educated and dedicated, coping admirably in conditions that were hardly compatible with high quality medical care. Many senior doctors, McGrigor above all others, led by example, and the competence of the army's doctors probably improved as the Peninsular War progressed. In a letter to General Thomas Graham in 1813, McGrigor comments, 'We never had so many able surgeons as we have at this moment.'[60] Guthrie, never a man to dispense praise without good cause, noted that after the Battle of Toulouse, the whole medical staff 'worked from morning to evening with assiduity'.[61] Any improvement can be attributed to both better leadership and the unprecedented opportunities to gain practical experience in the field.

Whilst the level of expertise of the army's doctors will remain somewhat conjectural, there is no doubt that many did show the bravery referred to by Napier. Relatively few medical officers perished in battle, but the risks from disease were very real, and all the more frightening as the diseases were so little understood. Contracting a contagious disorder from a sick soldier often meant death for the doctor. Although we have no accurate statistics for disease-related deaths in the medical department, there are plenty of anecdotes from the Low Countries, West Indies, Egypt and the Peninsula to suggest that they were numerous. In the Flanders campaign of 1794 large numbers of doctors fell ill with dysentery and many died. The young Scots surgeon James Dickson was among the victims. In the West Indies the mortality rate amongst the staff and regimental officers was so great that the medical board was unable to find adequate replacements. The dangers in the Peninsula were more uneven, but doctors in the wrong place were unlikely to survive. For instance, in the hospital at Ciudad Rodrigo in 1812, a contagious fever affected all the wardmasters, nurses and orderlies and all the doctors except for a solitary physician. According to McGrigor, at least eleven of the medical officers died.

Probably the most unnerving and dangerous of all hospitals were the 'pest-houses' of Egypt. Bubonic plague attacked the troops and strict quarantine was enforced with a cordon of sentries placed around the hospital tents occupied only by patients and doctors. McGrigor accompanied the expedition as a regimental surgeon and brought attention to the heroism of his colleagues in his *Medical Sketches of the Military Expedition to Egypt from India*, published in 1804.

> From the nature of the prevailing disease, the campaign in Egypt was, in a peculiar degree, a service of danger . . . The zeal, attention, perseverance displayed, particularly by those employed in the plague-establishments, deserves every praise . . . Intrepidity is more than a military virtue; but seldom I believe has there been a greater display of it than among the medical officers in Egypt, whose duty it was to reside in the pest-houses.[62]

How important were Wellington's doctors to the winning of the war? Richard Blanco, McGrigor's biographer, is in little doubt: 'The reformed medical department in the Peninsula and the gradual improvement in the care of the troops were vital factors in explaining Wellington's many victories.'[63] There is evidence to support Blanco's view of the central role of the medical department in Wellington's military machine. Wellington himself was well aware of the crucial role his doctors had to play. This is obvious both from the importance he gave to meetings with McGrigor and also from his dispatches. The following letter to the Prime Minister, the Earl of Liverpool, was written in November 1809.

> It is besides very necessary that some effectual measures should be taken to increase the medical staff, not with gentlemen of rank, but with mates. The duty of the general hospitals in every active army ought to be done by the general medical staff, and the regiments ought to have their surgeons and assistants entirely disengaged for any extraordinary event or sickness that may occur. We have not now one surgeon or assistant with each regiment, instead of three, the others being employed in the hospitals instead of the hospital mates, and we have always been equally deficient. Indeed, one of the reasons which induced me to cross the Tagus on the 4th August, instead of attacking Soult, was the want of surgeons with the army, all being employed with the hospitals, and there being scarcely one for each

brigade; and if we had had an action, we should not have been able to dress our wounded.[64]

The last sentence is worth re-reading. Wellington makes it explicit that a major operational decision was sizeably influenced by the lack of regimental surgeons accompanying the army. Although McGrigor may have had to encourage Wellington to mention the doctors after Badajoz, the Duke already fully understood their importance to his fighting force. Whilst a shortage of doctors could serve as a disincentive to engage the enemy, conversely, efficient medical services could add to the strength of an army and increase the military options. This happened in the latter years of the Peninsular War, when the health of the troops improved in parallel with increased morale and experience in the medical department. McGrigor makes this point in his autobiography when discussing the campaigning of 1813.

> Even during the march, considerable bodies of the convalescents from our far-famed [regimental] hospitals were daily joining their respective corps; and it was said with much truth by an eminent individual, that he thought the extraordinary exertion of the medical officers of the army might be said to have decided the day at Vitoria, their exertions had undoubtedly added a full division in strength to Lord Wellington's army, and without those 4,000 or 5,000 men it is more than doubtful [that he] with all his unrivalled talents, could have carried the day. Perhaps, without that material addition to his force he would not have risked an action.[65]

The 'eminent individual' referred to by McGrigor was William Napier. In his influential history of the Peninsular conflict, he is not universally complimentary about the medical department. However, he fully acknowledged the improvements that were made and pronounced that at Vitoria the 'unremitting attention of Sir James McGrigor and the medical staff under his orders' allowed the army to enter the field at maximum possible strength. The Duke himself was increasingly complimentary to the medical department, comparing it favourably with the commissariat and noting that during the Battle of the Pyrenees, the wounded had received the 'utmost attention' from McGrigor and his officers.

Prior to the Napoleonic Wars, the British Army doctor had a reputation so poor it is now difficult to comprehend. He was excluded from all normal titles and honours and was generally regarded as a second-class citizen. When George III reviewed the troops in 1788, we are told that 'no surgeon was allowed to kiss his hand'.[66] Morale was low and even the army doctors themselves were dismissive of their profession. John Hennen was moved to say that 'he must have been indeed possessed of a most glowing enthusiasm, and an utter contempt for self-interest, who would have buried his talents and his industry in a situation where obscurity, poverty, and neglect spread all their miseries before him'.[67] When Hennen later wrote his classic surgical textbook three years after Waterloo he felt able to declare that 'a brighter day has dawned on military surgery'. It would be overstating the case to claim that twenty years of campaigning had entirely changed the army doctor's image. But the doctors had made a real contribution to the winning of the war, a fact fully recognised by men such as Wellington and Napier. Their status in society had begun to improve.

NOTES

1. McGrigor, J, *Autobiography and services of Sir James McGrigor*,p.95.
2. ibid., pp.278, 412.
3. Drew, R, *Commissioned Officers in the Medical Services of the British Army 1660–1960*, Vol.I, pp.xlviii–l.
4. Chaplin, A, *Medicine in England during the Reign of George III*, pp.77–9; Cantlie,N, *A History of the Army Medical Department*, Vol. I, pp.177–90; Crowe, K E, *The Walcheren Expedition and the New Army Medical Board*.
5. Chaplin, pp.79–80.
6. Chaplin, pp.83–6; Crowe, op cit.
7. *Fifth Report of the Commissioners for Military Enquiry.*
8. Drew, pp.xxxviii–xlii.
9. ibid., pp.xxxvii–xxxviii.
10. Crowe, p.772.
11. Cantlie, p.182.
12. McGrigor, p.176.
13. Fergusson, W, *Notes and Recollections of a Professional Life*, pp.57–8.
14. Chaplin, pp.82–3; Cantlie, p.181.
15. Howell, H A L, *Robert Jackson MD Inspector of Hospitals*; Cantlie, Vol.II, pp.400–6; Crowe, p.773.
16. McGrigor, p.174.
17. Drew, pp.xxxv–xxxvi; Cantlie, pp.427–8.
18. Cantlie, p.180.
19. Henry, W, *Surgeon Henry's Trifles*, p.20.
20. Drew, p.xxxii.
21. Drew, p.xxxiv; Cantlie, p.426.
22. Drew, p.xxxiii; Cantlie, p.427.
23. Cantlie, p.422.
24. Drew, pp.xxv–xxviii.
25. McGrigor, p.175.
26. Moises, H, *An Enquiry into the Abuses of the Medical Department*, p.15.
27. Blanco, R L, *Wellington's Surgeon General*, p.18.
28. Dickson, J, *James Dickson M.A. 1769–1795 Army Surgeon*, pp.13–14.
29. Howell, p.121.
30. Dickson, p.26.
31. Howell, p.121.
32. Dent, W, *A Young Surgeon in Wellington's Army*, p.7.

33. ibid., p.10.
34. Gibney, W, *Eighty Years Ago or the Recollections of an Old Army Doctor*, pp.93–6.
35. McGrigor, p.94.
36. ibid., p.4.
37. Henry, p.19.
38. Dent, p.20.
39. Dickson, pp.35–6.
40. Henry, p.20.
41. Fergusson, p.66.
42. Dickson, pp.66–7.
43. Cantlie, p.435.
44. *Selections from the dispatches and general orders*, p.627.
45. McGrigor, pp.195–6.
46. Fergusson, p.67.
47. McGrigor, pp.152–3.
48. Hennen, J, *Principles of military surgery*, pp.40–41.
49. Cantlie, p.197.
50. McGrigor J. *Sketch of the Medical History of the British Armies*, p.477.
51. Howell, p.138.
52. Hennen, p.58.
53. Oman, C, *Sir John Moore*, p.73.
54. Aitchison, J, *An Ensign in the Peninsular War*, p.95.
55. Hall, F, *Peninsular Recollections*, p.1737.
56. O'Neil, C, *The Military Adventures of Charles O'Neil*, p.254.
57. Roberts, D, *The Military Adventures of Johny Newcome*, p.81.
58. Donaldson, J, *Recollections of the Eventful Life of a Soldier*, pp.165–6.
59. Napier, G T, *The Early Military Life of General Sir George T Napier*, pp.133–5.
60. Blanco, p.141.
61. Guthrie, G J, *Commentaries on the Surgery of the War*, p.146.
62. McGrigor, J, *Medical sketches of the Military Expedition to Egypt from India*, p.ix.
63. Blanco, p.141.
64. *Selections from the dispatches and general orders*, p.318.
65. McGrigor, p.331.
66. Hamilton, R, *The Duties of a Regimental Surgeon Considered*, Vol. I, p.187.
67. Hennen, p.4.

CHAPTER II
In Battle

The wounded were in hundreds without any covering from the
strong sun, lying on every spare space of ground. These the medical
men were attending. The medical officers were quite worn out with
the incessant duty they had been called upon to perform for three
successive nights, and still there appeared no end to their toil.

Captain William Hay of the 12th Light Dragoons at Waterloo[1]

During the Napoleonic Wars the British Army fought numerous battles
against the French. The bulk of these were in Spain and Portugal between
the years 1808 and 1814, although the culmination of this era of
'blackpowder warfare' was at the Belgian village of Waterloo in 1815.
Casualty figures for the whole war are inevitably approximate. Perhaps
there were around 5,500 officers and 85,000 rank and file killed or
wounded between 1793 and 1815.[2] Various sources suggest that in the
Peninsular War approximately 9,000 men were killed and 40,000
wounded. The statistics available for individual battles are probably more
meaningful. Philip Haythornthwaite has calculated the chances of officers
and other ranks becoming a casualty in six Peninsula battles; at Nivelles
and Fuentes de Oñoro there was an approximately one in sixteen chance
of an officer becoming a casualty against a chance of 1:17 for other ranks.
Using the same format, the casualty rates for the other battles were;
Busaco 1:30.5 officers, 1:40 other ranks; Salamanca 1:7.5 and 1:10; Barossa
1:4 and 1:5, and Albuera 1:2.5 and 1:2.5.[3] It can be seen that only at the
shockingly bloody battle of Albuera were officers no more likely than
other ranks to be wounded.

A fascinating article, *On the Mortality and Sickness of Soldiers engaged in*
War by T R Edmonds, written in the mid-nineteenth century, shows
conclusively that officers also had a greater likelihood than the private
soldiers of dying in battle.[4] In the last three and a half years of the
Peninsular War, when the British Army had a field strength of just over
60,000 the total annual mortality from battle, including fatalities on the
field and later deaths from wounds, was 6.6% for officers and 4.2% for the
ranks. Edmonds concluded that in the harder fought battles of the
Peninsula and at Waterloo the mortality rate among officers was more

than 50% greater than that of privates. Even among the officers there were significant differences. Field officers and captains suffered more severely than lieutenants who in turn were more likely to be wounded than ensigns. These mortality differences were significant – an ensign was only half as likely to die in battle as a captain. The differences between the three arms of the service were less striking and reflected the nature of warfare in the Peninsula and at Waterloo. In the major Peninsular battles the death rates among officers in the infantry, cavalry and artillery were 2.1%, 1.3% and 0.4% respectively, whilst the equivalent figures for Waterloo were 8.5%, 10.1% and 3.1%.

These casualty rates mean that after a typical largish battle involving 100,000 combatants, there were likely to be in the region of 10,000 casualties on and around the field and between one and two thousand of these men could expect to die of their wounds. Most of the deaths occurred on the day of action with approximately one quarter of this number dying in the next ten days and then the mortality halving during each subsequent ten-day period. It is obvious that the task that faced the army's medical department was daunting, with every likelihood that the doctors would be overwhelmed by this sudden influx of wounded. The wholly inadequate medical support available can be easily demonstrated by considering the destructive effects of Napoleonic warfare and the medical provision at a regimental level.

In the larger Peninsular battles and at Waterloo the average numerical strength of each regiment of cavalry was 476 men and of each battalion of infantry 831 men.[5] To each infantry battalion were attached approximately forty combatant officers and five non-combatant officers, including one surgeon and two assistant surgeons. In reality, regiments often entered the field severely depleted in men, officers and surgeons. On the second day at Talavera the 24th Regiment had 343 casualties out of a starting strength of 787. At Waterloo the 28th Regiment had 253 casualties from 557 men. In both cases the losses were sustained within a few hours in a relatively small area. This very high density of casualties is a feature of major Napoleonic battles. All the 28th's wounded at Waterloo were theoretically the responsibility of the single regimental medical officer present. Only half of the British battalions in the battle had their full complement of one surgeon and two assistant surgeons. Some help would be available from the medical staff officers. However, at Waterloo there were only fifteen staff surgeons and a solitary physician – the bulk of the work must have fallen on the regimental doctors.

In his seminal work on military surgery, the eminent Peninsular War and Waterloo staff surgeon, John Hennen, has much to say regarding treatment on the battlefield. In an early chapter he advises the regimental surgeon of the preparations necessary before entering an action.[6] Each surgeon had the use of a mule or horse to carry his equipment and stores.

These items were packed in wooden boxes or more usually into field panniers, wicker baskets covered with leather. Hennen recommends that an invoice of the contents of each pair of panniers should be pasted inside the lids to facilitate their use in the field. Essential stores carried in the panniers included 'lint, surgeon's tow, sponges, linen, both loose and in rollers, silk and wax for ligatures, pins, tape, thread, needles, adhesive plaster ready spread, and also in rolls, opium, both solid and in tincture, submuriate of mercury, antimonials, sulphate of magnesia, volatile alkali, oil of turpentine, &c. &c.' The well prepared surgeon would also carry a supply of wax candles with phosphoric matches to allow operations to be carried out in the fading light of the battlefield.

In addition to the panniers, the mule carried a pack saddle and a case for the precious surgical instruments. These were usually preserved by smearing them with oil or wrapping them in lint or paper. The case itself was covered with leather and the whole of the baggage carefully secured with painted canvas. Hennen acknowledges that the combination of panniers, saddle and case was so heavy as to be likely to injure the animal's back and render it useless for the rest of the campaign. He emphasises the importance of lightening the load as much as possible and carefully balancing the panniers. An overall weight of up to 200 lbs, including the animal's forage, was regarded as acceptable. Other items of equipment which the regimental surgeon could usefully take on campaign were a few stretchers ('bearers'), a camp kettle, a camp stool, and a water bucket. The doctor carried his own pocket case of surgical instruments in his clothing and also a canteen of wine or spirits for the 'patient's resuscitation'. Prior to battle, a number of field tourniquets designed to stop haemorrhage were issued not only to the medical officers but also to some of the drummers and other non-combatants. The latter were warned to seek medical advice as soon as possible after the tourniquet was applied. During the action, a reserve supply of surgical materials, medicines, and medical comforts such as tea, sugar, chocolate and soup was the responsibility of the medical staff officer in charge of arrangements. Hennen says that all the medical supplies for a campaign needed to be selected by a board of 'intelligent and experienced medical officers' and not left to the discretion of apothecaries or purveyors. 'For want of this precaution, I have more than once seen whole cart-loads of useless rubbish put in requisition to be forwarded to the army whilst the most necessary articles for the field abounded at the stores of the depots.' In practice the equipment carried was sometimes limited by a lack of transport and there had to be compromises. For instance, during the period leading up to Vitoria in 1813, mules, carts and spring wagons were all scarce and the medical officers carried a haversack for medicines and a small first-aid kit. The contents of the panniers were reduced to the absolute necessities.[7]

The management of battle casualties was not well planned or regulated but often conformed to a familiar pattern. As hostilities commenced, the regimental surgeons accompanied their comrades into action. George Guthrie states that, 'It is quite impossible for a regimental surgeon to be out of fire, if he is to do his duty: and medical staff officers can scarcely be out of cannon shot.' At the beginning of the Peninsular War, at the Battle of Roliça, the post designated to the regimental surgeon and one assistant surgeon at the start of the action was seven paces in the rear of the Colours. Here they were well placed to give initial treatment. The second assistant surgeon remained a little farther to the rear at a regimental dressing station – on occasion this was combined with others to form a brigade dressing station with staff surgeons in attendance. It was the bandsmen's and other non-combatants' responsibility to collect infantry wounded, perhaps apply a tourniquet or some very simple first-aid, and carry them to the waiting medical officers. Farriers performed a similar task for wounded cavalrymen. In the absence of non-combatants in a particular part of the field, the wounded were either ignored or carried to the rear by comrades acting out of altruism or cowardice. As the fighting progressed, most of the regimental surgeons fell back with the wounded to temporary field hospitals. Subsequent treatment was delivered either in the regimental hospitals or in the nearest general hospital to which the wounded were transported in wagons. Overall control was in the hands of the principal medical officer for the campaign who would usually be an inspector of hospitals. Other senior medical staff officers were attached to divisions and brigades. None of this was innovatory. Surgeon to George III, John Ranby, had recommended very similar arrangements for the War of the Austrian Succession in 1744.[8]

Soldiers' accounts of their treatment on the battlefield usually start with their experience of wounding. This was very mixed. Hennen observes that,

> Some men will have a limb carried off or shattered to pieces by a cannon ball, without exhibiting the slightest symptoms of mental or corporeal agitation; nay, even without being conscious of the occurrence; and when they are, they will coolly argue on the probable result of the injury: while a deadly paleness, instant vomiting, profuse perspiration, and universal tremor, will seize another on the receipt of a slight flesh wound.[9]

Many of the accounts by the victims of wounding support Hennen's comments. The initial reaction was often one of confusion and disorientation with pain and even awareness of the wound delayed. Major George Simmons of the 95th Rifles received a musket ball in the thigh during a sharp action on the Coa river in 1810. He later remembered that,

Being wounded in this way was quite a new thing to me. For a few moments I could not collect my ideas and was feeling about my arms and body for a wound, until my eye caught the stream of blood rushing through the hole in my trousers, and my leg and thigh appeared so heavy that I could not move it.[10]

William Green, also in the 95th, received a similar wound in the thigh in the forlorn hope at Badajoz. He says that he 'scarcely felt' the ball go through his thigh, but a musket ball shattering his wrist was 'more like a 6-pounder'. His namesake, John Green of the 68th Durham Light Infantry, received a musket ball wound in the chest at San Sebastian. 'At first, I felt nothing, in about ten seconds however, I fell to the ground, turned sick and faint, and expected every moment to expire, having an intolerable burning pain in the left side.'[11] This initial response to wounding was well known to soldiers. Sergeant Thomas Morris reflected after his experiences at Quatre Bras: 'I was never struck by a ball; but I have often noticed that those who are, do not always feel it at the time.' Morris relates anecdotes from the battle which well illustrate both ignorance of wounds and apparent indifference to very severe injury. An ensign next to him in the line had to be informed by Morris that he was wounded in the arm by a musket ball. "God bless me! So I am," said he, and dropping his sword, made the best of his way to the rear.' A private in the 92nd Regiment had his arm removed close to the shoulder by a cannon ball, but was still able to walk off the field and casually remark to Morris's regiment, 'Go on, 73rd, give them pepper! I've got my Chelsea commission!'[12]

On occasion, soldiers produce remarkably vivid, almost poetic, accounts of wounds. William Keep, of the 28th Foot, was hit in the neck by a musket ball whilst fighting in the Pyrenees.

> The bullet struck me down, and covered me with the crimson fluid, spurting like a fountain from my mouth, whilst I was laying on my back. The blow was severe, it was like a cartwheel passing over my head, but this was instantaneous only, for all pain ceased, and I was left in full possession of my senses, with the warm drops falling upon my face.[13]

Major Thomas Austin had his leg mangled by a cannon ball in Holland in 1814. Immediately after being struck down, he had the presence of mind to examine his wound. 'I found that the bones were laid bare for some distance up the limb, and appeared as white as the finest ivory, the tendons dangling and quivering like so many pieces of thread.' There was little haemorrhage, a fact he attributed to the extreme cold. Soon a burning sensation started in the wound and gradually spread to the rest of his body accompanied by a severe thirst.[14]

Unsurprisingly, the sensation of being wounded has changed little through the ages and the accounts of soldiers from more recent conflicts, notably the First World War, contain all the same elements as those of their Napoleonic predecessors. Whatever his own perception of the injury, the best a seriously wounded man could hope for was to receive first-aid from a regimental surgeon where he fell. Because there was normally a gross mismatch between the number of wounded on the field and the number of regimental surgeons, this was the exception rather than the rule. However, there are some examples in contemporary memoirs of the Peninsula. When Robert Blakeney was wounded in the leg at the Battle of the Nivelle in 1813, his less severely wounded colleagues scrambled away but he was unable to move and lay helpless. After 'some hours' his regimental surgeon appeared. 'I then got what is termed a field dressing, but unfortunately there were no leg splints and so arm splints were substituted.'[15] Edmund Wheatley was wounded during the same action. 'When I recovered myself I found myself on the trunk of a fallen tree surrounded by an Officer of the artillery, two or three men, and a surgeon dressing a large gash in my right thigh. My foot was bound tight between two pieces of flat wood.'[16]

The experiences of Blakeney, Wheatley and others suggest that this first-aid administered by regimental surgeons was normally rudimentary and make-shift. As for many aspects of the battlefield, Hennen's writings give the best medical perspective. He stresses the importance of first giving the frightened, wounded man pain relief and reassurance.

> The tremor, which has been so much talked of, and which, to an inexperienced eye, is really terrifying, is soon relieved by a mouthful of wine or spirits, or by an opiate, but above all, by the tenderness and sympathising manner of the surgeon, and his assurances of the patient's safety.

First-aid was always to be performed in a 'neat and dextrous' manner. He decries the surgeon who, 'roughly, confusedly, and without any apparent interest, hurries over his dressings with slovenliness ill concealed by a prodigality of plaster, lint, and bandages.'[17]

In practice, the wounded who were fortunate enough to receive any help were more likely to be first attended by the regimental bandsmen or their comrades. It was generally accepted that once fighting commenced, the bandsmen would put down their musical instruments and give help to the wounded. This involved collecting them, perhaps giving some very basic first-aid, and then carrying them to the waiting medical officers. The duties were shared by other non-combatants. This might include men who were lightly wounded and regarded as unfit to fight. William Fergusson states that when he was surgeon of a full battalion, he always had thirty to forty men available in the rear for the collection of the wounded.[18] It would be wrong to assume that this was universal. The ad hoc nature of the arrangement is evident from the enormous variation in the number of regimental bandsmen. Some bands had as many as twenty-five men whilst others had fewer than ten, possibly as few as five. It seems very likely that even the bandsmen were thinly spread. This is probably why they are not often referred to in accounts of the battlefield. William Green, wounded at Badajoz, has left a rare description of these men at work.

> In a short time, four men, belonging to the band of some regiment, came up to me and asked me if I was wounded? I said 'Yes.' They had what we call a stretcher, two short poles with a piece of sacking nailed to them for the wounded to lay on, and carried me to the doctor. These band-men were employed in this work, as they are not required to go into action. I asked them 'If they could give me a drink of water?' They replied 'They had none.' One of them said 'There is some a little way off, but there are both dead men and horses in it, you cannot drink it.' I replied 'my good fellow, run and fill your canteen.' It held about three pints; I drank it off. He ran and filled it again; I then got into the stretcher, they carried me shoulder high . . .[19]

Although the stretcher in this account was crude, it was at least recognisable as such. When the army first disembarked in Portugal in 1808, the expedition's medical supplies included twenty-four stretchers. According to Guthrie, these official stretchers were too heavy to be useful and they are rarely mentioned. The most common improvised stretcher, similar to that described by Green, was made using sergeant's pikes as side poles with a blanket as a bed. Alternatively, men were carried from the field in a simple blanket without any other support. This was unsatisfactory. When Robert Blakeney was taken down a steep descent in this manner, his injured leg dropped over the blanket's edge causing him agonising pain.[20] Throughout the wars, almost everything imaginable was used in place of proper stretchers. For instance, in the Pyrenees, George Bell saw the wounded carried on 'branches of trees, on great-coats clotted with blood, and on gory stained sheets taken from the cottages.'[21]

Most of the wounded who have left a record of their experiences were first given help by their fellow soldiers. Circumstances varied. In essence this help might be enforced, for example men ordered to give assistance to the wounded by a senior officer, or voluntary. In the latter instance, the motivation might be to help a personal friend or regimental comrade, or simply any soldier in need. Equally, going to the rear with a wounded man was an effective method of self-preservation. Consider the case of John Green who, as earlier described, was wounded at San Sebastian. As he lay on the ground, the regimental sergeant-major ordered two men to take him to the rear. After carrying him fifty yards, the men became afraid of the ferocity of the enemy's fire and abandoned him. A fellow officer then approached and, with the aid of a stick, accompanied him out of the firing line where he was entrusted to another two soldiers who took him to the nearest dressing station.[22] This incident well illustrates one of the major disadvantages of not having an adequate system for the removal of wounded. Five men were involved in transferring Green a relatively short distance from the front to the dressing station. His wound in effect removed six British soldiers from an active combatant role for at least part of the battle.

The help given to wounded soldiers by their comrades was a contentious issue. Most of the official directives were designed to limit this behaviour rather than to encourage it. The following general order was released by Wellington in Northern Spain in June 1813.

> The commander of regiments and the officers and non-commissioned officers of companies must take care that no man falls out of the ranks under pretence of taking care of the wounded, who is not ordered to fall out by the officers commanding the company, and these officers must take care that no more men are employed on this duty than are absolutely necessary to perform it.[23]

It is reasonable to assume that the better the morale of the troops the more difficult it was to persuade uninjured men to abandon the action and return to the rear. This was certainly true at Salamanca, where an officer in the 43rd Light Infantry says of his regiment: 'Their spirit was so great that I had the greatest trouble to get any men in the midst of the fight to fall out and assist the wounded.'[24] In contrast, at Waterloo, where the Allied Army was less battle-tested and the outcome in doubt for a much longer period, there appears to have been a surplus of willing helpers. A footnote in Wellington's dispatch states that there were 1,875 men 'missing' – many of these must have slipped away with the wounded. Just how many men Wellington judged appropriate to give aid to any given number of casualties is not clear. In his orders to the French Left Corps, Marshal Ney specified that two men should suffice to accompany a man with a fracture and one for a slight wound. He adds that the wounded soldier was not to be carried by his comrades farther than the first hospital.[25] This directive may have been followed in Ney's corps, but much of Napoleon's conscript army was only too willing to return to the rear and they required strict instruction to ignore their stricken comrades. At Lutzen in 1813 even units of the Young Guard drifted back to the dressing stations with the wounded. They were met by unsympathetic gendarmes and at Bautzen, nineteen days later, the troops stayed at the front like veterans.[26]

An inevitable consequence of inefficient evacuation was the risk of re-wounding to those already lying disabled on the field. Much of this was deliberate. At Waterloo, both British and French cavalry attacked wounded on the ground with sabres and lances. This in part accounts for the multiple wounds witnessed by surgeons after the battle. The same occurred in the Peninsula. A British officer lying in the breach at San Sebastian recalls that his attention was aroused by an exclamation from the wounded soldier next to him. 'Oh, they are murdering us all!' French grenadiers were methodically stabbing the wounded. His companion received the same treatment and the officer himself was only saved by the apparent seniority of his rank.[27]

Those soldiers who survived the initial wound, avoided fatal re-wounding, and who were collected from the field, were taken to the nearest dressing station. The stations ranged in size from just a few panniers and other essentials collected together by the regimental surgeons to a major affair with staff surgeons in attendance. In the latter brigade dressing stations more invasive treatment, including early amputation, might be undertaken. The location of the stations depended much on the topography of the battlefield. It was crucial that they were close to the fighting but not overly vulnerable. Hennen says that they should ideally be 'out of the immediate range of shot and shells'.[28] Where possible, natural obstacles were used for cover. At Talavera, the stations were concealed behind the Cerro de Medellin hill in the centre of the British position about 700 yards behind the most advanced troops. At Waterloo, they were placed just behind the ridge of Mont St Jean. Different types of action required different solutions. At the assault landing at Aboukir near Alexandria in Egypt in 1801, the regimental surgeons set up dressing stations on the beach where the more seriously wounded could be transferred by boat to the hospital ships offshore.

William Green, to whom we are indebted for a graphic description of his wounding at Badajoz, was carried by the bandsmen to a large dressing station in a tent manned by about fifty staff and regimental surgeons.

There was a doctor standing by the tent pole, with his coat off, a pair of blue sleeves on, and a blue apron; a large wax taper was burning, and there was a box of instruments laying by his side. The tent was full of wounded, all laying with their feet towards the pole; it was an awful sight to see, and to hear their groans was truly heart-rending. I stepped up to the doctor, he saw the blood trickling down my leg, and tore off a piece of my trousers to get at the wound, which left my leg and part of my thigh bare. He then made his finger and thumb meet in the hole the ball had made, and said, 'The ball is out my lad!' He put in some lint and covered the wound with some strapping, and bid me lay down and make myself as comfortable as I could, saying,

'There are others who need dressing more than you!' I said, 'I have another wound in my wrist,' so he cut the back part of my wrist, about an inch and half, put in an instrument and pulled out a piece of the thumb bone, about half an inch long, which had been broken off by the ball, and driven to the back of the wrist. The ball could not be extracted. He then dressed the wound, and bid me lay down outside the tent as there was no room inside.[29]

That the immediate management of battle casualties was more haphazard than systematic is evident. Whatever the unpleasantness of the dressing stations, it was only the lucky minority who reached them. The central problem was the shortage of all types of resources. Whereas it is not easy to find well documented examples of soldiers receiving first-aid on the field from regimental surgeons, there are numerous tales of men wandering the fringe of the battlefield searching for doctors. At Vitoria, Judge Advocate Larpent rode past numerous wounded who appealed to him piteously. Larpent realised that he had been mistaken for a doctor because of the black feather in his hat and so he immediately removed it.[30] Those medical officers who were on the scene were too often compromised by the unavailability of instruments and the shortage of dressings. At Quatre Bras and Waterloo many of the surgical instruments were left behind by the army.

The difficulties experienced by Assistant Surgeon Haddy James of the First Life Guards were almost certainly not exceptional. When wounded began arriving after Quatre Bras, he admitted frankly, 'I was unable to do anything for their wounds as I had no sort of medical supply with me, and could only watch their painful progress with useless pity.' As wounded passed by he and his fellow medical officers, 'sat lamenting that the medical supplies had not been up the previous day.' James adds, 'I did what I could, but it was woefully little.' On the following day the Life Guards were in action in the town of Genappe as Wellington retreated to a defensive position at Waterloo. Again James was without the vital supplies, and all he could do was speak to the wounded and recommend they make their way to the rear as best they could. On the eve of Waterloo, he was at least able to borrow some rollers and lint from Staff Surgeon Van Millingen, a man of whom we shall hear more later.[31] Even at Waterloo, many of the regimental surgeons had only their small pocket case of instruments available. Without the larger cases of instruments containing the amputation knives, there was little effectual they could do in the first twenty-four hours.

Similar problems were experienced in Portugal and Spain. The sense of helplessness voiced by Physician Adam Neale at Vimeiro is often quoted.

To several, a simple inspection of their wounds with a few words of consolation or perhaps a little opium was all that could be done or recommended. Of those brave men the balls had pierced organs essentially connected with life, and, in such cases, prudence equally forbids the rash interposition of unavailing art, the useless indulgence of delusive hope.[32]

Neale's situation was different to James's as his status as a physician meant that he could not operate. Even so, he was further compromised by the absence of any medical comforts. Army physicians were regarded as being remote from the reality of the battlefield but, to Neale's credit, he enlisted the help of a soldier's wife to make meal into gruel for the wounded. The best regimental surgeons had to be able to overcome these acute shortages. Articles of clothing were frequently used in place of proper dressings. At the Battle of Argaum in India in 1803, there was the usual dearth of medical supplies for the thousand injured men. John Blackiston tells of a surgeon whose bandages had been exhausted taking a long girdle of cotton cloth from the body of an enemy soldier. 'Up sprang the dead man and away ran the doctor. This extraordinary instance of a doctor bringing a man to life, so opposite to the usual practice.'[33]

Whether men lay stricken on battlefields in India, the Iberian Peninsula, or the Low Countries, there was one shortage that caused more distress than even the paucity of surgeons and medical supplies. When Captain Barralier of the 71st received a gunshot wound at Salamanca he was left in a small hut where he was 'surrounded on all sides by wounded and dying men of all nations, some calling out "water"; others, "aqua" and "de l'eau."'[34] On the field of Talavera, there was 'not a trace of shade or coolness or of water', whilst at Waterloo men resorted to drinking stream water tinged with blood. The lack of fresh drinking water was often a problem for Wellington's army and this partly accounts for the routine consumption of huge amounts of spirits and wine.[35] The surgeons were encouraged to carry alcohol to rejuvenate the wounded, but contemporary texts make little reference to the role of water. One of the common symptoms of blood loss is thirst, and dehydration was undoubtedly a major cause of death. It seems that the doctors did not understand the urgent necessity of rehydration. In the modern management of trauma and haemorrhage, the intravenous infusion of clear fluids in the immediate period after the injury is usually more important than the replacement of blood. Even if there had been a better appreciation of this fact, it is unlikely that adequate amounts of drinking water could have been brought quickly to the field by the medical services. The carriage of large quantities of water by the army would have been cumbersome and not militarily acceptable. When the generals selected their ground for battle, a local source of drinking water for the wounded was not a primary consideration.

In the face of all these inadequacies and shortages, there was every need to have an arrangement for prioritising treatment. On a modern battlefield this is referred to as 'triage'. In the Falklands War, British soldiers with shrapnel and gunshot wounds were divided into those requiring urgent resuscitation, those needing early surgery, and those who could wait. The following passage, written by Hennen, could be regarded as an early nineteenth-century description of triage.

> While hundreds are waiting for the decision of the surgeon, he will never be at a loss to select individuals who can safely and advantageously bear to be operated on, as quickly as himself and his assistants can offer their aid; but he will betray a miserable want of science indeed, if, in this crowd of sufferers, he indiscriminately amputates the weak, the terrified, the sinking, and the determined. While he is giving his aid to a few of the latter class, encouragement and a cordial will soon make a change in the state of the weakly or the terrified; and a longer period and more active measures will render even the sinking proper objects for operation.[36]

Hennen similarly expresses the need to prioritise the removal of wounded to the rear. He warns that 'the most clamorous and troublesome among the wounded in the field, or before the walls of a besieged town, are generally the worst characters of the army, and the most slightly injured'. Some feigned injury with the intention of plundering the rations and medical comforts of the genuinely wounded.[37]

Did surgeons practice triage and treat wounded soldiers on the basis of their clinical need alone? The great French military surgeon, Dominique Larrey, claimed to do just this. At Eylau he attended the men of the Imperial Guard, 'faithful to my principles, I began with those who were most severely wounded without regard to their rank or distinction'.[38] Larrey was exceptional in the French Army and made enemies because of his reluctance to delay treatment of ordinary soldiers to attend to officers. In the British Army, all the available evidence suggests that rank was the dominant consideration in determining the likelihood of receiving treatment and its rapidity. At Waterloo, Ensign Howard of the 33rd Regiment makes the telling comment, 'we were charged so furiously that we could scarcely send our wounded officers to the rear and much less the men'.[39]

It is important to remember that it is the officers who have left most of the anecdotes of wounding on the battlefield. Their experiences were not typical of those of the men – indeed, many would probably not have survived to write their memoirs if they had not received the favourable treatment accorded to those of senior rank. Such a case is that of Major George Simmons, who received a musket-ball wound in the leg during the action on the Coa river and was left unable to walk. A fellow officer took off his neckerchief and gave it to a sergeant who wrapped it around the wound to stop the bleeding. He was then put in a blanket by some of the men and carried to the rear. They were remonstrated with by General Robert Craufurd who ordered them back to the action, but they persisted, saying, 'This is an officer of ours, and we must see him in safety before we leave him.' Simmons was then transferred to a horse given to him by a colonel of hussars and taken to a field hospital in a church where there were many wounded strewn about on the stone floor. An ordinary soldier who was lying severely wounded invited him to share his bed. Simmons observed,

> This soldier belonged to the 43rd Light Infantry. I was on the ground, and very ill from loss of blood; he had been placed on a paliasse of straw and was dying, but his noble nature would not allow him to die in peace when he saw an officer so humbled as to be laid near him on the bare stones.[40]

What is noteworthy about Simmons' experiences is that it was the attitudes of his fellow officers, and even more so the men, that expedited his removal from the field to the relative security of the field hospital. In their accounts of battle, regimental medical officers do not generally volunteer the fact that they treated the officers first, but this was the reality. An assistant surgeon of the 7th Hussars found himself in the village of Mont St Jean after Waterloo with a dozen other assistant surgeons in charge of around 500 wounded. The regiment's surgeon had been called to the front to treat the colonel and was not seen again for several days as he accompanied him to Brussels.[41] Regimental surgeons were frequently called away from onerous duties in the field to attend to a solitary wounded officer. Clearly, military considerations of rank much outweighed the medical principles of triage and the well-being of the majority.

The most extreme example of preferential treatment was when the army's commander received a wound. At Corunna, Sir John Moore suffered a very severe round-shot wound which would prove fatal. He was quickly attended by Surgeon William McGill of the 3rd battalion of the Royals (1st Foot) who had been previously working under the cover of a large granite boulder. McGill realised that it was a hopeless case. The left shoulder was shattered, the arm hanging by a piece of skin, several ribs were broken, and the muscles of the chest were badly cut up. McGill started to remove some pieces of uniform from the wound. Moore thanked him but told him, 'You can do me no good, it is too high up.' When he was being carried away in a blanket, two surgeons who had been attending to another senior officer, Sir David Baird, came running up. In a typically selfless gesture, Moore dismissed them with the words, 'You can be of no service to me. Go to the wounded soldiers to whom you may be useful.'[42] Moore was a truly great soldier and these dramatic events have come close to being mythologised. At a more prosaic level, it is clear that at a particularly bloody juncture of the battle at least three surgeons were made available for the treatment of two senior officers.

The assistant surgeon who attended the prostrate Marshal Beresford at Salamanca has left a detailed record of the episode including his thoughts on staying with the great man at the expense of his regiment's own wounded. The doctor does not reveal his identity but he was most likely Alexander Lesassiery of the 42nd Foot. At the outset of the action, he agreed with his regimental surgeon that he would stay near the front to give immediate first-aid. His attention was soon attracted by a Portuguese staff officer shouting for a British surgeon. He responded to the call and found the Marshal seriously but not fatally wounded, lying in a wagon together with a wounded Portuguese sergeant. The assistant surgeon first used his fingers to find a musket ball in the flesh of the left loin and then his knife to extract it. He bandaged up the wound and recommended that later in the day the Marshal should be bled. Beresford, who had remained calm throughout, asked who would perform this.

> From the moment I had recognised the commander-in-chief of the Portuguese army I saw that my being on the spot, at such a moment, might lead to my promotion. A fair, unimpeachable opportunity of tendering fresh services to him on whom the accomplishment of my ambition seemed to depend, was now afforded me. But such is the influence of an unflinching, unaffected firmness of character in a chief over those below him, and such the impression left on my mind by what I had just witnessed, that I felt convinced I should establish a higher place in the marshal's good opinion by remaining in the fight, than by volunteering to leave it, even for the purpose of attending to his own wound. I therefore respectfully submitted to his excellency, that my regiment was then probably in action; that I should be sorry to be out of the way when my friends and comrades might need my assistance, and that I hoped he would be kind enough to permit me to join them. 'Most certainly,' was the reply.[43]

The doctor's calculations may not have been entirely altruistic, but he achieved his ambition as Beresford survived and he was subsequently promoted to staff surgeon in the Portuguese Army. Neither of the generals wanted to waste medical officers' time when there might be others who would benefit more. Beresford invited the assistant surgeon to treat the sergeant first if he was more seriously injured. However, this was not appropriate as the man required amputation and the necessary instruments were not immediately accessible.

The other factor that was likely significantly to influence the quality of medical care received by a wounded man was his nationality. It is natural to think that British troops wounded in the field would be the first to receive attention from their own doctors. One of the many benefits of victory was final control of the field and the opportunity to take decisions regarding the management of the wounded. Many memoirs of the period suggest that the wounded of the losing army were evacuated from the battlefield more slowly than those of the victors. The only likely exception would be a very senior enemy officer, who might be rescued before friendly troops of lesser rank. At Salamanca, Lieutenant Ross-Lewin remembers a French colonel lying badly wounded near the British regiment's Colours. Ross-Lewin's commanding officer directed the drummers to take care of him.[44] At this time there must have been many British soldiers for the bandsmen to collect.

Once the wounded reached the dressing stations and field hospitals, the order of treatment was probably left to the discretion of individual surgeons. The evidence for favouritism is conflicting. After the Battle of Barossa in southern Spain in 1811, Assistant Surgeon William Dent acknowledged that the British wounded were prioritised by their own surgeons. The French were in a wretched condition as their wounds had not been dressed for three days after the action 'on account of our own wounded being so numerous'.[45] Assistant Surgeon Walter Henry tells a different story. When treating a mixture of Allied and French troops in a field hospital in the Pyrenees, he says that the principle was 'first come, first served; without any respect of persons'. In the context of his account it seems more likely that he was referring to nationality rather than rank. This is supported by a later incident quoted by Henry, when a cart containing two wounded soldiers, one British and one French, arrived at the general hospital at Aire. Henry attended the British corporal first, but he was careful to add that this was because he was the 'worser case'.[46]

Both during and after the fighting, all suitable buildings in the area were put to some use by the medical services. A small hut or cottage might provide suitable cover or shelter for a regimental dressing station, whilst larger buildings, perhaps farms or churches, could be brigade dressing stations or field or regimental hospitals. When Sergeant Daniel Nicol of the Gordon Highlanders was wounded in the leg at Talavera, he was fortunate to be able to limp off the battlefield. His account of the places he subsequently visited provides a good illustration of how local buildings were exploited following a major battle. He first struggled through the blazing long grass and brushwood where many of the wounded were burnt to death. He eventually came to a 'large white house' where men were waiting to be dressed.

> Here I found the surgeon of the Gordons, Dr. Beattie, who came at once to me and dressed my leg and put a bandage on it. He then gave

me a drink of water, and told me that I had got it at last. I, smiling, replied, 'Long run the fox, but he is sure to be caught at last'. This made many smile who's bones were sore enough.

Nicol then trudged into the town of Talavera where he received further treatment in a large convent full of hundreds of wounded. 'I lay down and put my head on the dead body of a man of the 61st Regiment and slept amid all the uproar and bustle'. When sufficiently recovered, he was carried to another hospital situated in a church where he was given straw as bedding and used one of the steps of the high altar as a pillow.[47]

This profusion of different hospital buildings accords well with our understanding of the medical arrangements at Talavera. The large white house that Nicol first came to on the battlefield was either a large brigade dressing station or a field hospital. The convent in Talavera was the nearest general hospital to the action, whilst the facility in the church was his own regimental hospital. We have already considered dressing stations, and regimental and general hospitals are addressed in a later chapter. The term 'field hospital' was used rather loosely. It best describes a sizeable building conveniently close to the fighting where staff and regimental surgeons and wounded could be concentrated for the further management of wounds including amputation. The typical field hospital would be larger than a dressing station but would not have the scale or permanency of a general hospital or the particular affiliation of a regimental hospital. Examples of field hospitals are the church at Vimeiro, the convent at Busaco, and the farm of Mont St Jean at Waterloo. It was in the nature of these hospitals that they were quickly flooded with the worst of the wounded. Surgeons worked heroically, whilst the soldiers slumped against the inside and outside walls awaiting their turn.

Some of the grimmest accounts of Napoleonic warfare are from the field hospitals. The best known description, and certainly one of the most keenly observed, is that of William Grattan of the Connaught Rangers, who came across an 'amputating hospital' in a house in the village of Villa Formosa after the battle of Fuentes de Oñoro in 1811.

I was on my return to the army when my attention was arrested by an extraordinary degree of bustle, and a kind of half-stifled moaning, in the yard of a quinta, or nobleman's house. I looked through the grating and saw about two hundred wounded soldiers waiting to have their limbs amputated, while others were arriving every moment. It would be difficult to convey an idea of the frightful appearance of these men: they had been wounded on the 5th [of May], and this was the 7th; their limbs were swollen to an enormous size. Some were sitting upright against a wall, under the shade of a number of chestnut-trees, and many of these were wounded in the head as well as limbs. The ghastly countenance of these poor fellows presented a dismal sight. The streams of gore, which had trickled down their cheeks, were quite hardened with the sun, and gave their faces a glazed and copper-coloured hue; their eyes were sunk and fixed and what between the effects of the sun, of exhaustion, and despair, they resembled more a group of bronzed figures than anything human – there they sat, silent and statue-like, waiting for their turn to be carried to the amputating tables. At the other side of the yard lay several whose state was too helpless for them to sit up; a feeble cry from them occasionally, to those who were passing, for a drink of water, was all that we heard.

A little further on, in an inner court, were the surgeons. Curiosity led me forward; a number of doors, placed on barrels, served as temporary tables, and on these lay the different subjects upon whom the surgeons were operating; to the right and left were arms and legs, flung here and there, without distinction, and the ground was dyed with blood. Dr. Bell was going to take off the thigh of a soldier of the 50th, and he requested I would hold the man down for him. He was one of the best-hearted men I ever met with, but, such is the force of habit, he seemed insensible to the scene that was passing around him, and with much composure was eating almonds out of his waist-coat pockets, which he offered to share with me, but, if I got the universe for it, I could not have swallowed a morsel of anything. The operation upon the man of the 50th was the most shocking sight I ever witnessed; it lasted nearly half an hour, but his life was saved.[48]

Grattan says that the field hospital was close to a pit where the dead from the nearby general hospital were buried. Flocks of vultures hovered overhead. Another field hospital which made a deep impression upon those who witnessed it was the church at Vimeiro. This may have been in part because it was still early in the war and such sights were not yet commonplace. Physician Adam Neale entered the churchyard and saw a large wooden dish filled with hands that had just been amputated and also a heap of amputated legs.[49] Lieutenant Ross-Lewin confirms Neale's account. Rifleman John Harris says that the surgeons had taken two large tables from nearby houses and placed them between the graves. Here they performed the operations 'with their sleeves turned up, and their hands and arms covered with blood, looking like butchers in the shambles'. He also spotted the pile of legs and noted that many of them were still clothed in the long black gaiters then worn by the infantry of the line. The surgeons were too busy to remove clothing before surgery. Harris was asked for his help by one of the surgeons and afterwards was very relieved to leave the churchyard.[50] It was quite common for ordinary soldiers such as Grattan and Harris to be press-ganged into helping in the field hospitals. In another example, Thomas Morris of the 73rd attended the surgeons in a church after the little remembered Battle of Gorde in 1813. His duties included carrying the wounded to the surgeons, holding them down during the operation, and then placing them on straw with an allowance of bread and water. He also buried the dead and the stack of amputated limbs beside the altar.[51]

Field hospitals were used because they were conveniently situated. The suitability of the buildings as temporary hospitals was a secondary consideration. In the Peninsula, many were too small for the number of wounded and lacked any useful facilities. The suffering of the patients was magnified. After the Battle of the Coa, the British wounded were first managed in the local chapel and then moved within hours to Pinhel where they were housed in an unroofed convent lying on the stone floor in wet and bloody clothes. Robert Grant of the 74th Foot said that they were in a shocking state. 'The cries of them would pierce the heart of a slave.'[52] Similar problems were encountered at Waterloo, where the accessible buildings were soon saturated with the casualties. In the field hospital in the farm of Mont St Jean, about a third of a mile behind the fighting, an eyewitness says that the three rooms in the lower part of the house and even the stables and cow-houses were filled with wounded British officers. Field hospitals were also established in other villages and hamlets around the battlefield.

In the British Army's campaigns outside Europe the same general arrangements for casualty evacuation and field hospitals applied, although there were variations dependent on the local topography and culture. In India, where the young Wellesley successfully waged the Second Mahratta War, the typical field hospital was quite an elaborate affair equipped with 200 beds. It was maintained by a small army of sentries, followers and baggage animals in addition to the medical staff, some of whom were withdrawn from the regimental medical organisation. At the Battle of Assaye in 1803, a tented field hospital was set up a distant twelve miles from the battlefield with doolies, elephants, horses and bullocks used to convey the 300 wounded from the field. Each corps provided one tent for every ten wounded and the battalions furnished dressings. Twenty pioneers were made available to the chief surgeon. The future Duke of Wellington made a personal visit to the hospital, a habit he was to keep in the later Peninsular War. In Egypt, it appears that field hospitals were formed in a more sporadic manner than in India. For instance, at Aboukir, a field hospital in a local mosque was only opened following problems in transferring wounded to the general hospital. The mosque was very close to the field and the staff and regimental surgeons manning it came under fire.[54]

In the American War, the best documented battle with respect to the medical arrangements is that of New Orleans in 1815. Here the British suffered around 2,000 casualties and the Deputy Inspector of Hospitals, John Robb, won praise for his management of the wounded. According to Major Harry Smith, 'The number of wounded was three times what the Inspector-General Robb was told to calculate on, but never did an officer meet the difficulties of his position with greater energy, or display greater resources within himself.'[55] Despite Robb's best efforts, the conditions in the temporary field hospitals were no improvement on the Peninsula. Lieutenant George Gleig of the 85th wandered into one where,

> Every room was crowded with mangled wretches, and apparently in the most excruciating agonies. Prayers, groans, and, I grieve to add, the most horrid exclamations, smote upon the ear wherever I turned. Some lay at length upon straw, with eyes half closed and limbs motionless; and incoherent speech of others indicated the loss of reason and usually foretold the approach of death.[56]

The officers were housed in a separate room but this was little better.

The only other significant theatre of war was the West Indies. Here the chance of perishing from wounds was slight compared with the constant threat of disease. However, there was some fighting and we have an account of what it was like to be wounded in the tropics from Captain Thomas Henry Browne, who received a musket ball in the left elbow at Fort Desaix on Martinique in February 1809. Following his wound, he was taken to a field hospital which had been formed in a sugar plantation a short distance to the rear. Browne says that the hospital was subsequently converted into a 'regular' military hospital, implying that it acquired some permanency. He occupied a small hut near the main house which was thatched with dried-out sugar cane. As in the Peninsula, the army's doctors were forced to make the best of the local architecture. Browne was apparently well nursed by locals with the main threat to his recovery being the tarantula with which he shared his accommodation.[57]

From the preceding discussion, we can visualise the regimental surgeons and their assistants at the beginning of the action either hurriedly giving first-aid on the field or waiting tensely at the dressing stations for the inevitable flood of casualties. Later, they would have to fall back and gather in the overcrowded field hospitals where they would be joined by the staff surgeons. This gives an impression of quite restricted movement, but this was not always the case. Indeed, what is most striking about the two best memoirs of battle by British regimental surgeons, Walter Henry's of Vitoria and William Gibney's of Waterloo, is how mobile they were on the battlefield. Both these accounts are exciting eyewitness descriptions of two of Wellington's greatest victories. They also give an invaluable insight into the work of the army doctor in battle and are worth quoting in full.

At the time of Vitoria, Walter Henry was a regimental assistant surgeon. However, during the battle, the 22-year-old doctor did not accompany his own regiment but was instead attached to a staff surgeon at divisional level. This meant that Henry was liable to be called to the point of greatest need, for instance the village of Subijana de Alava where there was particularly fierce fighting. At the commencement of hostilities, he was in the south of the battlefield as General Hill stormed the Heights of La Puebla.

On that celebrated Sunday morning there was a little light rain about day-break, followed by some mist and fog; which, however, did not last long, and were followed by a remarkably fine clear day. Having, from the commencement of the campaign, been attached as assistant to Staff-Surgeon Wasdell, in medical charge of the Second Division, I moved with the Head Quarters, and thus always occupied a house when they were stationed in any village. On this occasion, as we all anticipated something to do this day, I awoke before day-light and looked out of the window at the camp of the Division, half a mile below – but nothing was to be seen but the dense vapour – after another hour the mist was clearing away – the men were striking the tents and getting under arms – in half an hour more the whole was in motion towards the village of Puebla, where there was a bridge over the River Zadorra, a branch of the Ebro about two leagues from Vitoria . . .

As we were crossing the clear stream of the Zadorra at Puebla . . . bye and bye the fighting thickened – we passed one or two dead bodies of French soldiers on the road, and the whole column moved towards the table land above the river in compact order. When we reached the top a grand and spirit-stirring spectacle met our view. We saw the extensive line of the whole French army posted on a range of heights about two miles off, in order of battle, with Vitoria in the centre. The position appeared to be nearly four miles in length – the greater part of the troops were in column – some in line; and the Artillery was disposed in batteries on the most commanding points. Numbers of mounted officers were moving about slowly from one part of the field to another. This was the first time I had seen a powerful army prepared for battle; and the sensation was exciting, exhilarating and intoxicating. I was young and ardent, and felt strong emotions in anticipating the approaching combat and the probable discomfiture of the imposing masses. I longed to join in the struggle and 'throw physic to the dogs'.

When our Division had advanced along the high road to Vitoria, within long cannon-range of the enemy's position, we were ordered into a field to the right, and then halted. The word was then given,

'With ball-cartridge prime and load!' In the meantime, Sir Rowland Hill and a large staff, including the staff-surgeon and myself, rode forward to a small height where there was a better view; but the crowd of mounted officers having attracted a shot from one of the enemy's nearest batteries, the greater part of us were ordered away, and only Sir Rowland and two or three of the senior officers remained. The contrast between the aspect of the two armies at this part of the field was striking enough. On one side the dark and formidable masses were prepared at all points to repel the meditated attack – the infantry in column with loaded arms, or ambushed thickly in the low woods at the base of their position – the cavalry in line with drawn swords – and the artillery frowning from the eminences with lighted matches. While on our side all was quietness and repose. The chiefs were making their observations, and the men walking about in groups, amidst the piled arms – chatting and laughing, and gazing; apparently not caring a pin for the fierce hostile array in their front.

Soon after, the Brigade of Colonel O'Callaghan, consisting of the 28th, 34th, and 39th Regiments, attacked the village of Subijana d'Aliva, and having there suffered a heavy loss, I was ordered to the assistance of their surgeons. We collected the wounded in a little hollow, out of the direct line of fire, but within half musket-shot – unpacked our panniers and proceeded to our work. This brigade had, I believe, between four and five hundred men put hors de combat in the course of an hour; so, we were fully employed. A stray cannon-shot from a distant battery would drop among us occasionally, by way of a hint to inculcate expeditious surgery. Spring wagons were in attendance, in which we placed our patients and sent them to Puebla, the nearest town, where Dr. McGrigor, then at the head of the medical department of the army, had made the most judicious arrangements for their reception and comfort. When we had attended to all the wounded of this Brigade that we could find; including the large proportion of officers – several of the latter hit mortally – a message came to the staff-surgeon from the heights on our left; for a long time the scene of a bloody struggle: that there were a large number of wounded, and that they required more medical aid. There, the 50th, 71st, and 92nd regiments had been sent early in the day to assist Morillo and his Spaniards; but, strong reinforcements having joined the enemy on the hill, those gallant Corps were hard pressed and suffered great loss. I was again detached and ordered up the hill on this urgent requisition. I had been so entirely occupied, professionally, for three hours, that I was quite in the dark as to the state of the engagement; except that, latterly, the sound of the firing appeared louder and closer than at the beginning. As I galloped up the hill, a round shot passed so near my head as to make me bob instinctively . . . After working hard for two hours with the medical officers of the Brigade, I returned according to my order to the depot of the wounded near Subijana, whence I had set out. Every thing now appeared changed – the firing was far advanced towards Vitoria – the enemy had abandoned several points of his position and seemed to be in full retreat.

In front of the village of Subijana d'Aliva, which had been taken early in the action, by Colonel O'Callaghan, there was a wood, about four hundred yards off, which was full of French Tirailleurs. Between this wood and the village was a large cornfield, without any hedges or enclosures, or cover of any kind more than the green wheat: and here I could not help thinking then, (and I am of the same opinion still;) that there had been very needless exposure and wanton waste of life, without the possibility of any good being derived from it. I saw myself, early in the action, parties detached from the village, where they had good cover, and there fruitlessly and fatally contending with the fire of the Voltigeurs from the wood and the Artillery from the main French position. So ignorant, even, did these brave men appear of the true danger of their situation, that they enhanced it a hundred fold, by absolutely grouping themselves, in little masses through the field for mutual protection; each of which objects formed a target not to be missed by covered Infantry, and scarcely by Artillery. Such was the loss sustained in this point, that in one part of the field, not more then about two acres square, I counted one hundred and fifty men either killed or very badly wounded. Here the staff-surgeon, two other surgeons and myself, set to work afresh, after swallowing some wine and biscuit; and here we remained collecting, dressing, amputating and sending to the rear, till seven o'clock.

When our work was done and we had picked up every wounded man in the neighbourhood of Subijana, we mounted our horses, that had been regaling themselves all the time in the wheat, and pushed on for our own Division, now, with the whole army far in front . . . After such a day's work there was a great deal of confusion at nightfall – soldiers and officers straggling about unable to find their Corps. The staff-surgeon, a Mr. Frith, Chaplain to the Forces, and myself, strayed about the country three hours after dark, fruitlessly endeavouring to find the Second Division. Regiments, Brigades, and even Divisions, became intermingled; and it was at least mid-day after the battle before this confusion was remedied. In the course of our wandering that eventful evening we also got our humble share of the plunder; for we picked up a sheep, a keg of cognac brandy, and I stumbled over a piece of superfine cloth that made me afterwards a pair of inexpressibles [trousers], of which I was sorely in need. After wandering till midnight to no purpose, we fell in with some stragglers of the Buffs and 57th, who kindled a fire, skinned and dressed our sheep, and broiled us a chop upon the coals. They divided their biscuit with us, and we gave them a share of our cognac. After this we wrapped ourselves in our cloaks and slept profoundly after a good days work.[58]

Unlike Henry, Assistant Surgeon William Gibney did not have such a free-ranging role at Waterloo but was attached to his regiment as was more usual. However, the 15th Hussars, part of Grant's cavalry brigade, took up several different positions in the course of the battle. At the outset the main body of the regiment was placed on the right of the British position on the Nivelles road to the rear of the château of Hougomont. Early in the conflict, squadrons were moved farther to the right to meet what turned out to be a diversionary attack by French Lancers. Subsequently, they successfully charged a unit of Grenadiers à Cheval but were then predictably repelled with heavy casualties by a square of French infantry. Lieutenant Henry Lane later wrote to the historian William Siborne: 'In short, during the day we were constantly on the move, attacking and retreating to our lines, so that at the close of the Battle, the two squadrons were dreadfully cut up.'[59] The regiment entered the action with twenty-four officers and around 400 troops – Gibney, who was accompanied by the regimental surgeon and another assistant surgeon, says that by the end two officers were killed and seven others wounded and that nearly half of the sergeants and men were killed or wounded. Gibney's account of Waterloo commences when the Hussars received orders to redeploy. Like Walter Henry, his first emotion was of resentment.

> Suddenly disgust took possession of me, my regiment was ordered to another part of the field, and I was forbidden to accompany them. I was to remain where I was. For the first time in my life I hated my profession; my heart was with the old regiment. I had tasted a bit of fighting and rather liked it, and to remain alone, a mere spectator of passing events, was most unpalatable. If battle had any terror for me, it had passed away and almost its novelty. I looked on at the struggle raging round me, more as a spectator at a field day than as one seriously interested in it. I believe that all my thoughts were concentrated in the fate of my own regiment; it was away in the thickest of the fight, and naturally I was anxious to know how all was faring. I was not left long in doubt, as before a quarter of an hour had passed several wounded men had discovered my whereabouts, and after attending to their injuries I inquired concerning the regiment

generally, but few knew much beyond what concerned themselves, they had had hard hand to hand fighting, but thought none of the officers had been killed and wounded. Whilst thus occupied an order came for us medical officers to shift our quarters, as there was no shelter for us whilst dressing the wounded; shot, shell, and bullets flying about us in all directions. Indeed, we were exposed to the fire of the French artillery and their infantry, so were directed to take up our quarters in the village of Mount St. Jean.

It was neither an easy or pleasant task to undertake, for the shot were flying about us in every direction, though in the sunken road we were somewhat protected. The huge cannon balls hissing and whistling over our heads, lodging with a terrible thud into the opposite bank, or striking the surface and rebounding, committed havoc and destruction in most unexpected quarters. Many of these missiles would have done comparatively little damage had the road not been paved, but on striking these stones the shot not only rebounded, but caused large fragments of rock to fly about, killing and wounding many who would otherwise have escaped . . . On reaching the village we found our services at once put into requisition. It was full of wounded, and among them many of my own regiment, which report said had suffered heavily. We lost no time in doing our duty; but whilst thus occupied an order came from Colonel Dalyrymple for us doctors to join the regiment, and so the surgeon and I again essayed the detestable paved highway. The shot and shell flying about us were if possible worse than before; but, thank the merciful Creator, we escaped, and proceeded onwards to where we expected to find the regiment, but it was not there, and no little difficulty attended our discovering its whereabouts, with fighting, cannon roaring, bullets whistling, and dense smoke all around.

At last we got up to them, and were informed that the services of only one medical officer were required, and, being the junior, it fell to my lot to remain, Mr Carson [actually Thomas Cartan, Surgeon of the 15th Hussars] returning to Mount St. Jean. The regiment was halted and we were sheltered from all but shell firing by hugging the bank of a sunken road or lane, and here I received orders as to how I was to act when they engaged the enemy, and was informed of all that had occurred since we parted. It was a terrible role of killed and wounded; but the violent death of so many of their comrades did not seem in any way to affect the spirits of the men . . . As the day went on the roar of cannon seemed to increase, and any termination to the fight unlikely to occur. Both sides fought desperately, and were resolved to win; but as the regiment moved about, I was told to return to Mount St. Jean, where I could be more useful, and to which village most of the wounded made their way.

Nothing could exceed the misery exhibited on this road, which, being the highpave, or I might say the stone causeway leading to Brussels, was crowded to excess with our wounded and French prisoners, shot and shell meanwhile pouring into them. The hardest heart must have recoiled from this scene of horror; wounded men being re-wounded, many of whom had received previously the most frightful injuries. Here a man with an arm suspended only by a single muscle, another with his head horribly mangled by a sabre cut, or one with half his face shot away, received fresh damage; but what made the scene more depressing was the knowledge that it was impossible to afford relief to all or even a goodly proportion of the sufferers, added to the conviction that for very many, their cases being utterly hopeless, time could not be spared on their behalf. It was a cruel task to be obliged to tell a dying soldier who had served his king and country well on that day, that his case was hopeless, more especially when he was unable to realise the same for himself, and then to pass on to another, where skill might avail.

. . . About seven o'clock in the evening I was again ordered to rejoin the regiment, and doing so, it was with no little sorrow that I observed how terribly its numbers had diminished and that many a dear friend of mine among the officers was killed or wounded. The contest seemed to me to me nothing diminished, but more general and desperate . . . During much of this time I accompanied the regiment, riding by the Colonel's side, only quitting them or halting when they were charging, or opposing other cavalry. Again I was directed to return to Mount St. Jean, and succeeded in arriving safely notwithstanding every difficulty and increasing horrors.

I had not been ten minutes in the village, indeed, had hardly commenced giving my assistance, when the colonel of my regiment was brought in desperately wounded, he telling me it had occurred almost immediately after I had left his side. A round shot had shattered his leg, and entering the horse's abdomen, killed it on the spot. As the wounded limb was on the side near which I had been riding, it is not improbable that had I remained I also should have suffered. The leg was only suspended by a few muscles and the bone in splinters. Amputation, and that at once, was the only chance. I got the Colonel placed in a room where there were several other wounded officers, and separating the foot from its connections, told him he must undergo the operation of amputation. Then after obviating all danger from haemorrhage, I endeavoured to get him removed to a more suitable place for the operation; so removing a door from an outhouse, we placed him upon it, and as we were leaving the dreadful room I came across Mr. Carson, who suggested him being taken to Waterloo, there being more accommodation . . .

With the aid of my door and six men we got the Colonel to the village of Waterloo, about one mile distant, and sought for accommodation, but every house and cottage was crowded.[60]

Gibney says that the provision for the wounded in the villages around the field was 'hideously bad'. He comments frankly, 'Of course aid could not be given to all. The numbers lying about were too considerable for even a fair proportion to receive relief, and doubtless not a few perished from want of immediate assistance; though this last is applicable chiefly to the French prisoners, as our own countrymen naturally claimed first attention.'[61] There was little use of the 'first come, first served' principle at Waterloo.

Both Henry and Gibney were very close to the fighting and were fortunate to avoid injury and even death. It was not unusual for medical officers to be as exposed as this. In his writings James McGrigor vigorously opposes the view that they should not be in the front line, emphasising the importance of quickly suppressing haemorrhage, extracting balls and applying splints.[62] McGrigor was used to danger. Early in his career at Nijmegen he came under cannon and shell fire in a field hospital in a church and had to move the wounded to a safer area. A white flag on the steeple gave little protection.

How many medical officers were killed and wounded whilst working on the field and in nearby hospitals? We have some anecdotal information but few reliable figures. At Quatre Bras and Waterloo the doctors appear to have escaped remarkably lightly with only the principal medical officer of the 3rd Division and the assistant surgeon of the 92nd Foot wounded. There was probably a large element of good fortune in this as we know from memoirs of the campaign that many were in the thick of the fight. In the Peninsula there are similar isolated incidents documented. At Albuera, George Guthrie's assistant surgeon was killed and at Talavera, the assistant surgeon of the 10th Foot had his left leg carried away by a cannon ball. The most precise figures are found in John Hall's recent compilation of officers killed and wounded in the course of the Peninsular War.[63] This is not comprehensive but it makes very interesting reading. Among the approximately 3,000 entries there are eighteen medical officers; fifteen infantry regimental surgeons, one cavalry regimental surgeon, and two staff surgeons. Most officers were only wounded once, but Thomas Fiddes of the 9th received wounds at Corunna, Salamanca and Vitoria. The majority of wounds were relatively minor, only three were definitely severe and none proved fatal (the fatality at Albuera is not included). Drew's roll of army medical officers, again not entirely comprehensive, indicates that about 600 doctors served in the Peninsular War. This allows the very rough estimate that only one in thirty received wounds. Compared with other officers, it was only a slight risk. The doctors were far more likely to die from the diseases of their patients than from the musket balls of the enemy.

Although they could be optimistic of surviving a major battle, most medical officers found it a traumatic and exhausting experience. They were grossly overworked with little chance of respite either during the battle or for several days after. Some performed Herculean labours. At the bloodbath of Albuera, Staff Surgeon George Guthrie had responsibility for 3,000 wounded men with just four wagons for their removal and the only equipment for treatment in the panniers of the regimental surgeons. In the nearby village of Valverde, he and the regimental surgeons laboured from five in the morning until eleven at night for days on end. Undoubtedly, the most remarkable physical 'tour de force' after a battle was that of Dominique Larrey who, according to his memoirs, performed about 200 operations in the first twenty-four hours after Borodino. This works out as an operation every seven minutes! Whilst the celebrated military surgeons of the era such as Guthrie and Larrey performed these near miracles, the ordinary army doctor had to cope as best he could. Following the Battle of Lundy's Lane in Canada in 1814, 21-year-old Assistant Surgeon William Dunlop had sole responsibility for 220 wounded men as his regiment's two other surgeons were sick. His difficulties were exacerbated by the intense heat, swarms of flies and the proliferation of maggots in the wounds.

> Long before I could go round dressing the patients, it was necessary to begin again; and as I had no assistant but my serjeant, our toil was incessant. For two days and two nights, I never sat down; when fatigued I sent my servant down to the river for a change of linen, and having dined and dressed, went back to work quite refreshed. On the morning of the third day, however, I fell asleep on my feet, with my arm embracing the post of one of the berths.[64]

The arduous nature of the work undertaken was often exacerbated by the lack of warmth and light. At the siege of Ciudad Rodrigo in January 1812, the freezing conditions added to the misery of the wounded. Assistant Surgeon Samuel Good of the Guards worked through the night. Two amputations were performed 'by the light of a miserable candle, the flame of which was perpetually agitated by the wind'.[65]

Medical officers had to face the possibility that the battle could be lost and that they, their field hospitals and patients could all fall into the hands of the enemy. The fog of war affected all – in their accounts of Vitoria and Waterloo, Henry and Gibney acknowledge that for much of the time they had little idea of the likely outcome. This possibility of enemy capture gave an extra urgency to the medical work. When the British made a rapid tactical retreat across the Coa river, the temporary field hospital was set up on a hill overlooking the fighting. Rifleman Edward Costello says that he did not have to wait long for treatment as the French were expected any minute and 'everything was done with the greatest dispatch'.[66] On the rare occasions that British doctors and wounded were overtaken by the French, for instance after Talavera, they were mostly well treated. Experienced campaigner John Hennen gives the following reassurance to prospective army surgeons.

> Should a reverse take place, it then becomes the duty of a certain proportion of the hospital staff to devote themselves for their wounded, and become prisoners of war along with them; and it may be an encouragement to the inexperienced, while it is grateful for me to observe, that I have never witnessed, nor traced, on enquiry, an act of unnecessary severity practised either by the French or English armies on their wounded prisoners; while, on the contrary, the contending nations have, in numerous instances, vied with each other in acts of tenderness and humanity to those whom the chance of war had thrown into their hands.

He adds that when an army was retreating it was more sensible to leave the severely wounded men to the enemy rather than attempting to drag them along with appreciable loss of life.[67]

Siege warfare was a crucial part of the Peninsular conflict and it is appropriate to consider briefly the medical arrangements and attendant problems that were peculiar to a siege. According to Guthrie, a surgeon's post was initially at the gorge of the trenches and then, during the final assault, it was at the foot of the breach. Usually, a number of locations to which the wounded could be carried were identified. The general orders for Ciudad Rodrigo simply state that a 'place will be fixed' but do not specify where. We have more information for Badajoz, where the main dressing station was established in a quarry which was well within musket range. This was almost certainly the dressing station described by William Green. Assistant Surgeon James Elkington was attached to a staff surgeon at Badajoz in the same way that Walter Henry was at Vitoria. When at the dressing station, he says that the fire was tremendous with musket balls flying by and grape landing on the ground. It was a frustrating day for the medical officers. 'As medical men we were useless; the badly wounded would not come to us and the slightly hurt would not remain under fire to be dressed.'[68]

When the siege was over, the enormous task of retrieving the wounded from the debris of the breach began. The three days of debauchery that followed the successful assault at Badajoz made this task doubly difficult. When Walter Henry arrived on the scene he expected to find 'everybody occupied in attending to the wounded and preparations for burying the dead', but instead all he saw was 'dreadful drunkenness, violence and confusion.'[69] Those who tried to help the wounded were impeded by men intent on butchery and pillage. The memoirs of Badajoz well illustrate the horrific nature of the Peninsular War. A grim humour provided the only relief. Sergeant William Lawrence recalls the incident of a soldier who was requested by his wounded colonel to carry him from the breach to the dressing station. He acquiesced, but the night was dark and the noise so intense that he did not notice when a cannon ball took the colonel's head off. On arrival the surgeon enquired why he had brought in a headless trunk. The man indignantly pointed out that the colonel had a head when he had found him, how else could he have asked to be taken from the breach? The story rapidly spread and the unfortunate soldier was often asked, 'Who took a headless man to the doctor then?'[70]

Whether after a siege or pitched battle, the reality of the Napoleonic battlefield was far removed from the glamorous portrayals of nineteenth-century salon painters. The civilians who flocked to Waterloo were appalled by what they saw. One eyewitness says that on the following morning there were thousands of wounded who 'could not help themselves, were in want of everything; their features, swollen with sun and rain, looked livid and bloated'. Another, visiting Quatre Bras, saw forty wagons of wounded coming from the village of Waterloo: 'The men had been in cottages and not able to be removed before. Many died instantaneously, others were in a putrid state – a kind of living death.'[71] The wounded were tortured by thirst and the French wounded, many of whom received little attention, sustained themselves by eating the flesh of the dead horses that surrounded them. James Elkington rode over the field three days after the battle. At this stage, he says, peasants had been employed to bury the dead, their noses covered with handkerchiefs to mitigate the stench. The local inhabitants were still unable to re-enter their homes as they were filled with wounded.[72] The last British wounded were not removed from the field until four days after the battle, and, according to Sir Charles Bell, the French wounded were still being collected from the woods at the beginning of July.

Similar sights were encountered after Peninsular War battles. The normal mechanism for collecting the wounded once the fighting had stopped was the formation of 'fatigue parties'. These were small groups of men, usually arranged on a regimental basis, whose job was to give succour to the wounded and remove them to the nearest medical attention. This was an onerous and unpleasant duty and was not always willingly performed, particularly when the troops were distracted by the booty of war. At Badajoz, Elkington noted that each fatigue party would bring in a certain number of wounded but would then go off plundering.[73] Sergeant William Surtees of the 95th rifles volunteered for fatigue duty after the siege, but a captain of his regiment had to use a stick to coerce many of his comrades to help. It was not a satisfactory arrangement.

> Many who, from the nature of their wounds, required great care and attention in carrying them, the half-drunken brutes whom we were forced to employ exceedingly tortured and injured; nay, in carrying one man out of the ditch they very frequently kicked or trod upon several others, whom to touch was like death to them, and which produced the most agonising cries imaginable.[74]

Where possible the wounded were carried from the field on spring wagons or on pieces of artillery – the use of wheeled transport is the subject of the next chapter.

A recurrent theme of the wars is the apparent callousness of many soldiers towards their wounded comrades in the hours and days following battle. Whereas appreciable numbers of men were all too ready to retreat to the rear with casualties during the action itself, later there was a general attitude of indifference. A number of diarists acknowledge as much. After Vimeiro, Subaltern George Wood reported: 'We now returned to our former ground, and immediately fell to work making first to boil our kettle; for, though the killed and wounded presented shocking sights on all sides, this did not take away our appetites.'[75] Seven years later, in the words of Lieutenant Hamilton:

> Upon entering a house at Waterloo, we found every room in it filled with dead or dying. I was glad to get a chair, and sat down at a table in a large room, in every corner of which were poor creatures groaning. The master of the house having brought us a piece of bread and a bottle of wine, we began to talk over the events of the day . . . after we had finished our bread and wine, which we enjoyed very much, notwithstanding the room was full of poor wounded human beings, we retired to a hayloft for the night, which we passed in perfect repose.

Hamilton's unapologetic account is quoted by John Keegan in his wonderfully evocative interpretation of Waterloo. Keegan attributes the indifference to the sufferings of the wounded to a collective defence mechanism rather than to fatigue alone.

> Heartless as this sounds, it accords with what we know of much human behaviour in disaster situations, where the greater the scale of the devastation and loss of life, the more profound is the survivors' feeling of helplessness and frustration, from which they seek escape by inactivity.[76]

It was fortunate for the wounded that those who had not actually participated in the battle were, at least on some occasions, not overwhelmed by such feelings of inadequacy. Civilian help was especially valuable at Salamanca and Waterloo. After these battles, the most effusive praise is reserved for the local people. Within twenty-four hours of Salamanca, the inhabitants of the city sent carts loaded with provisions including fruit, water and dry wood. Women prepared lint and rags as wound dressings and local girls were seen escorting the wounded who were able to walk. They also carried their equipment. Spanish doctors came to the field and treated the wounded by torchlight. Ensign John Aitchison's tribute is typical.

> When their assistance was most wanted, they came forward both high and low as became them, and even ladies of birth went to the field of battle and lent all their delicate assistance at removing the wounded into their houses and administering every comfort in their power – this lasted the whole night and they have since assisted at the hospital. But let the rest of Spain follow the example of Salamanca and they shall be equally protected![77]

Similar generosity was shown to British and Allied soldiers by the citizens of Brussels after Waterloo. Much of this help was actually administered in the city, but there are also instances of aid on the battlefield. In a rare civilian account of the care of wounded in battle, a schoolboy in Waterloo recalls the wounded entering the village in steadily increasing numbers along the path from Mont St Jean. His father, the village schoolmaster, provided them with dilute beer and willingly gave shelter to a severely wounded officer.[78]

The reliance on civilian help underlines the overall inadequacy of the medical arrangements for battles such as Salamanca and Waterloo. During the wars, some lessons were learnt and expertise in battlefield medicine was acquired – there is reason to believe from contemporary accounts that the medical department performed best at the Battle of Toulouse at the end of the Peninsular War. Even here there were persisting deficiencies and basic problems were not solved. The most fundamental, which it would be difficult to over emphasise, was the entirely insufficient number of medical officers to cater for the casualties of a major battle. As John Hennen wryly observes: 'However superfluous the number of professional men may appear before a battle or a series of movements, it will very seldom be a source of complaint after the operations.'[79] Any extra medical officers needed to be part of a better organised medical service with a proper mobile field medical unit with stretcher bearers, ambulance wagons, and trained orderlies for efficient evacuation. It was this combination of lack of personnel and an inadequate infrastructure for casualty evacuation that caused the unnecessary level of suffering and loss of life wherever the British Army fought.

Some army doctors were well aware of the potential solutions. Notable among them was John Gideon Van Millingen who, in his *Army Medical Officer's Manual* published in 1819, made detailed suggestions for a more efficient method of coping with the casualties of battle.[80] Van Millingen's views were based upon his experiences as a regimental and staff surgeon in the Peninsula and at Waterloo, and his work was commended by Hennen and others. His plan centred on a 'Hospital Corps of Ambulance'. Each ambulance field company would be on a scale of twenty men for every thousand soldiers in the field or sixty for an infantry brigade. Each man carried one half of a stretcher which could be quickly assembled in the field. Two types of ambulance were provided, a 'long car', where the more lightly wounded could sit sideways, and a spring wagon for the more severely wounded. There was still reliance on drummers and pioneers to carry the wounded to the regimental aid post, but then the Hospital Ambulance Corps, with a regimental assistant surgeon in charge, would rapidly transfer them in a hand carriage to a brigade hospital out of musket range. Here, the regimental surgeons and assistant surgeons would dress wounds and control haemorrhage before the ambulances took the wounded on to a larger divisional hospital out of artillery range where operations could be performed.

Van Millingen's scheme was not perfect. In the long periods of inactivity, the ambulance corps personnel were to be employed as orderlies in general hospitals. When a major battle was fought, they would have to be suddenly withdrawn, leaving the hospital manned by untrained staff just when they were about to be filled with wounded. However, his proposal of systematic management of casualties from the point of wounding to their admission to a large hospital with involvement of considerable numbers of trained staff was a significant advance in thinking. This was too much too soon for a post-Waterloo army characterised by financial restraint and reductions in manpower. It would be nearly half a century before an ambulance corps similar to that described by Van Millingen was adopted. Britain's reticence to provide the best possible care for her wounded soldiers was in stark contrast to the initiatives already taken by her greatest enemy.

NOTES

1. Hay, W, *Reminiscences 1809–1815 under Wellington*, p.202.
2. Hodge, W B, *On the mortality arising from military operations*.
3. Haythornthwaite, P, *The Armies of Wellington*, p.28.
4. Edmonds, T R, *On the Mortality and Sickness of Soldiers engaged in War*.

5. ibid.
6. Hennen, J, *Principles of Military Surgery*, pp.40–45.
7. Cantlie, N, *A History of the Army Medical Department*, Vol.I, p.359.
8. Ranby, J, *The method of treating gunshot wounds*.
9. Hennen, p.48.
10. Simmons, G, *A British Rifleman*, p.78.
11. Green, J, *The Vicissitudes of a Soldier's Life*, pp.188–9.
12. Morris, T, *Thomas Morris: The Napoleonic Wars*, p.69.
13. Keep, W T, *In the Service of the King*, p.192.
14. Austin, T, *Old Stick Leg*, pp.141–2.
15. Blakeney, R, *A Boy in the Peninsular War*, p.324.
16. Wheatley, E, *The Wheatley Diary*, p.17.
17. Hennen, p.52.
18. Fergusson, W, *Notes and Recollections of a Professional Life*, p.8.
19. Green, W, *Where My Duty Calls Me*, p.36.
20. Blakeney, p.324.
21. Bell, G, *Soldier's Glory*, p.89.
22. Green, J, p.189.
23. *Selections from the dispatches and general orders*, p.695.
24. Muir, R, *Tactics and the Experience of Battle in the Age of Napoleon*, p.204.
25. Ney, Marshal, *Memoirs of Marshal Ney*, Vol.II, p.356.
26. Elting, J R, *Swords Around a Throne*, p.285.
27. Fletcher, I, *The Peninsular War*, p.117.
28. Hennen, p.45.
29. Green, W, pp.36–7.
30. Larpent, F S, *The Private Journal of F Seymour Larpent*, pp.158–9.
31. Haddy, James J, *Surgeon James's Journal*, pp.21–8.
32. Neale, A, *Letters from Portugal and Spain*, p.17.
33. Weller, J, *Wellington in India*, p.196.
34. Barralier, Capt, *Adventure at the Battle of Salamanca*, p.276.
35. Howard, M R, *Red Jackets and Red Noses: Alcohol and the British Napoleonic Soldier*.
36. Hennen, p.57.
37. ibid., p.45.
38. Dible, H, *Napoleon's Surgeon*, p.73.
39. Keegan, J, *The Face of Battle*, p.173.
40. Simmons, p.80.
41. Cantlie, p.389.
42. Oman, C, *Sir John Moore*, pp.595–6.
43. Maxwell, W H, *Peninsular Sketches*, Vol.II, pp.341–2.
44. Lawford, J P and Young, P, *Wellington's Masterpiece*, p.265.
45. Dent, W, *A Young Surgeon in Wellington's Army*, p.25.
46. Henry, W, *Surgeon Henry's Trifles. Events of a Military Life*, pp. 82, 95.
47. Nicol, D, *The Gordon Highlanders in Spain*, pp.102–3.
48. Grattan, W, *Adventures in the Connaught Rangers*, pp.75–7.
49. Neale, p.18.
50. Harris, Rifleman, *Recollections of Rifleman Harris*, pp.61–3.
51. Morris, p.23.
52. Horward, D D, *Napoleon and Iberia*, p.215.
53. *Selections from the dispatches and general orders*, p.92.
54. Cantlie, p.268.
55. Smith, H, *The Autobiography of Sir Harry Smith 1787–1819*, pp. 239–40.

56. Haythornthwaite,139.
57. Browne, T N, *The Napoleonic War Journal of Thomas Henry Browne 1807–1816*, pp.102–3.
58. Henry, pp.67–71.
59. Siborne, H T, *The Waterloo Letters*, p.144.
60. Gibney, W, *Eighty Years Ago, or the Recollections of an Old Army Doctor*, pp.189–201.
61. ibid., p.207.
62. McGrigor, J, *Autobiography and Services of Sir James McGrigor*, pp.333–4.
63. Hall, J A, *The biographical dictionary of British Officers killed and wounded*.
64. Dunlop, W, *Tiger Dunlop's Upper Canada*, pp.35–6.
65. Maurice, F, *The History of the Scots Guards*, p.357–8.
66. Costello, E, *Edward Costello. The Peninsular and Waterloo Campaigns*, p.34.
67. Hennen, p.61.
68. Elkington, J, *Some episodes in the life of James Goodall Elkington*, p.92.
69. Henry, p.43.
70. Lawrence, W, *A Dorset Soldier*, pp.68–9.
71. Cantlie, p.390.
72. Elkington, p.99.
73. ibid., p.92.
74. Surtees, W, *Twenty Five Years in the Rifle Brigade*, pp.144–5.
75. Wood, G, *The Subaltern Officer*, p58.
76. Keegan, p.199.
77. Aitchison, J, *An Ensign in the Peninsular War*, p.77.
78. Brett-James, A, *The Hundred Days from Eyewitness Accounts*, pp.196–7.
79. Hennen, p.45.
80. Millingen, J G Van, *The Army Medical Officer's manual Upon Active Service*.

CHAPTER III
Transport

Ye invalids, stretched on your beds of down, comfort yourselves;
submit to your pains with Christian philosophy, and bless your
lucky stars that you did not belong to the army of Portugal! Rejoice
that you are not dragged along by bullocks, sometimes forced into
a run owing to the steepness of the adamantine roads, that your
lives are not shaken out of you by ups and downs, first over one
rock, then over another.

Lieutenant John Cooke, 43rd Light Infantry[1]

In their attempt to transport sick and wounded men, the British Army's doctors were entirely overshadowed by their French counterparts. The first major French initiative was taken in 1792 when Pierre François Percy, the army's Surgeon-in-Chief, designed his 'wurst'. This was a four-wheeled vehicle drawn by six horses. It was able to carry eight surgeons and contained adequate instruments and dressings to deal with 1,200 casualties. The surgeons were accompanied by orderlies who were responsible for manoeuvring the vehicle to the rear of any action to collect the wounded. These wursts were ultimately too heavy and cumbersome to allow very efficient casualty evacuation, but Percy deserves credit for this early attempt at a mobile field ambulance.

It was Percy's more illustrious junior colleague, Dominique Jean Larrey, who developed these formative ideas into a fully functioning organisation for casualty evacuation. Larrey's ambulance had two great advantages which now appear commonsensical but which at the time were highly innovatory. Firstly, the light mobile ambulance wagons were able to keep up with the troops of Napoleon's army and allowed the French surgeons to work in the actual area of fighting. Secondly, the vehicles could be used to collect the wounded on the battlefield and transport them out of immediate danger to receive early treatment behind the lines. It is important to appreciate that Larrey's 'ambulance' was much more than a simple carriage for the sick and wounded. Each ambulance unit had a strength of 340 men under the direction of a chief surgeon. These were divided into three divisions of 113 men, each in charge of a surgeon of the first class, aided by two assistant surgeons of the second class and twelve partly trained assistant surgeons of the third class. The other personnel were a mixture of drivers, orderlies, clerks and military officers. The last were important as the medical staff of the army had no military rank and therefore no real authority. To each division were attached eight two-wheeled ambulance wagons, four four-wheelers, and four ordinary transport wagons. The light two-wheeled ambulances were designed for flat country and were well-sprung, box-like vehicles into which two stretchers could be easily slid. The larger four-wheeled ambulance wagons were used in more mountainous country and were designed to take four men who could be lifted in through sliding panels on each side. The light ambulances were drawn by two horses and the heavy by four. If necessary, the ambulance division could be split into smaller units under the direction of a mounted medical officer. Larrey accepted that in rugged mountain country mules and pack-horses were also needed to carry panniers containing dressings, surgical instruments and medicine. A macabre but necessary duty of the ambulance, usually performed by the medical orderlies, was the collection and burial of the dead.[2]

Medical officers of other European armies cast covetous glances at Larrey's great achievement. Neither the British nor the French were quick to acknowledge the superiority of the other in any part of their military arrangements, but, to their credit, the British Army's doctors praised the French ambulance system. William Fergusson admitted that the French method of transport was 'greatly superior' and added 'it contains much that we might copy with great advantage . . . Our means of transporting sick and wounded have ever been deficient and cruel.'[3] John Hennen also applauded the success of the French system, 'an establishment of that kind, duly modelled, would no doubt be of important service in our field arrangement'.[4]

In the Peninsula, the British arrangements fell far short of Larrey's humanitarian vision. As has been described, the removal of wounded soldiers from the battlefield was at best haphazard. Beyond the battlefield, the difficulties involved in moving large numbers of wounded and sick men over long distances through inhospitable terrain would be hard to overstate. Although later in the Peninsular War regimental hospitals were increasingly used, for much of the conflict men who required significant medical treatment had to be removed from their regiments and taken to the general hospitals behind the lines. Those who recovered would later have to make the return journey to rejoin at the front. The number of sick and wounded in transit at any one time was considerable. This accounted for the substantial difference between the army's records of the number of sick men, the 'sick states', and the returns of the sick in hospital. At any given time, the divisional sick states were greater because many of the men absent sick from their regiments were not actually in the hospitals, but were either on the road to the hospital, in convalescence elsewhere, or on the road back to their regiment. This discrepancy was noticeable enough for Wellington to write to the Earl of Liverpool in July 1810 to explain its cause.[5] With admissions and discharges at the general hospital in Lisbon alone averaging between 600 and 1,000 per week, it is evident that in the whole of the Peninsula there were usually thousands of sick and wounded on the move. Efforts were made to track these men by giving them 'tickets' to present on arrival at the general hospital. However, this was not universally successful. In a general order of April 1813, Wellington felt it necessary to remind the regimental officers of the importance of this policy.

> The omission to make out and transmit these tickets has, besides, occasioned other inconveniences and irregularities (in addition to loss of arms), and it has become almost impossible to account for the soldiers supposed at their regiments to be in general hospital, owing to the frequency of the omission on the part of their officers to send tickets with them, and the men being unable from sickness to tell their own names, or the state of their necessaries, and frequently concealing both purposely.[6]

When the sick were few in number, they might simply be left in a town or village in the charge of a non-commissioned officer and under the care of a local civil magistrate awaiting the arrival of the general hospital. Where there was a need for evacuation, the majority of soldiers were transported through Portugal and Spain in 'sick convoys'. These were small groups of men gathered together at some convenient point for transfer to the general hospital, or assembled at the hospital station for return to active duty. They were most likely to be formed at the front in the weeks after a battle when there were numerous wounded, during periods of widespread disease, and when the army was moving forward rapidly and unable to carry the sick with it. The best description of the organisation of these convoys can be culled from the general orders issued by Wellington. During active operations there was a need for flexibility with constantly changing hospital stations and routes of evacuation. We have a good example of this in the medical orders issued during March and early April 1811 when Wellington drove Masséna's famished army out of Portugal towards Salamanca. The cumbersome general hospitals had little hope of keeping pace with the army, and orders in early March direct that the wounded be left at Santarem or sent back to Pombal on commissariat mules. Following the Battle of Casa Nova in mid-March, the wounded were collected and brought to the Condexia road to facilitate their further movement. At this stage a general hospital was opened at Coimbra and it was directed that all sick and wounded were to be sent to the town. Another hospital was later opened at Celerico, sixty miles to the north-east. The establishment of these hospitals allowed the transport arrangements to be consolidated with, at first, a sick convoy to Coimbra once a week, and later once a fortnight. Within a short time there were a thousand British and Portuguese patients in Coimbra. Further arrangements were made to periodically send transport ships to Figueira, at the mouth of the Mondego river, to evacuate sick to Lisbon. These details well illustrate that the evacuation to the rear hospitals was complex and much dependent on the military situation. In general, Wellington was loath to carry sick with the army and urged his officers to immediately send to the general hospitals all their men who were unable to march. In an order of July 1811, he reminds them that the transport available was unlikely to be sufficient if sick were allowed to accumulate and only sent back when the order to march arrived.[7]

The opposite movement of convalescents from the general hospitals to their regiments required consent from headquarters. Instructions issued from Abrantes in June 1809 specify that a convoy was to be formed whenever forty men at the hospital were sufficiently recovered to be able to march by 'easy stages'. Each soldier carried with him three days' supply of bread and biscuit as a reserve, and they were fed at each halting place on the route. Every convoy was under the supervision of military officers. The Abrantes order states that an officer should be in command of a body of forty men (with two officers for eighty men, etc.) and that there must be a non-commissioned officer for every twenty sick.[8] These officers had to regularly report their progress to headquarters. When the sick were numerous, an assistant surgeon might also be attached to the convoy to supervise treatment.

Responsibility for these convoys offered little reward. In the Peninsula, the distance between the front and the general hospitals could be hundreds of miles and the rate of progress was only around fifteen to twenty miles a day. The anonymous author of the introduction to Wellington's general orders gives an officer's perspective.

> There is no duty so vexatious as the detachment of wounded to the rear. The eternal screeching of the ungreased wheels of the Portuguese bullock carts which too often irritate the sick man into a fever, if he has not one already, the breaking down of the cars or the escape of the drivers with the bullocks belonging to others, the upsetting of the wagon train wagons from the badness of the rocky roads, the assembly of the sick in the morning, the only novelty being some new misery, such as to become sexton and bury a man who died during the night or on the road, are daily occurrences.[9]

Not only did officers receive little thanks for leading the convoys, but their reasons for doing the job well could be misinterpreted. When Sergeant

John Douglas was put in charge of sick on the road to Celerico in 1812, he encountered the usual frustrations of inadequate transport, poor roads and lack of shelter. The convoy became lost, but finally arrived at the hospital where Douglas promptly handed over his charge. The assistant surgeon requested him to take over further sick. Douglas refused:

> I retained in my memory the epithets that are thrown out on those who were too eager to fill such situations, and in general in no great hurry to rejoin the Regiment, and who could spin a yarn far superior to those who were already present with their Regiment and no way affected with that terrible disorder well known in the army by name of cannon fodder.

Even when he was faced with a shortage of rations he told the doctor that he would rather beg his way back to his regiment than remain behind.[10]

The medical officers' role in a convoy was to give medical treatment, but there were instances when there was no military officer present and the doctor was in charge. They were no more likely to be thanked than their military compatriots. Assistant Surgeon James Elkington commanded a convoy of sick and wounded on the road to Coimbra in May 1811. The wounded suffered so much they frequently requested to be shot. On arrival he was berated by the commandant for not keeping account of the kits of the men who had died on the journey. Elkington retorted that there was no military officer with the convoy and that his time had been entirely taken up with attending the wounded.[11] In the same year, Assistant Surgeon John Murray of the 39th Foot had responsibility for the carriage of 170 wounded men in bullock carts between Elvas and Lisbon, a journey of one hundred miles. The men with broken limbs and amputations suffered severely, whilst the less badly wounded were 'the greatest rascals I ever met with'. Their numerous misdemeanours included the theft of a lady's petticoat. Murray concluded, 'It is hard to say which are to be most pitied, the doctors or the wounded.'[12]

Convalescents might have been able to march, but most sick and wounded returning to the rear required some form of transport. There was nothing to match Larrey's meticulously designed ambulance wagons, and the medical department had to rely on the same forms of transport used by the commissariat to supply the Peninsular army with food and other necessities. This was mostly a mixture of mules, local bullock carts and army spring wagons. The choice of vehicle was determined largely by availability, but also by the terrain and the state of the roads. The road system in large parts of Portugal and Spain was crude and often disrupted. Heavy rain could easily destroy the existing roads and paralyse the army. In the Pyrenees, many of the vital communication routes were little more than mule and mountain tracks.

The most frequently used wheeled transport in the sick convoys was the ubiquitous Portuguese or Spanish bullock-cart or ox-wagon. These were resorted to because of the lack of anything better and soon became notorious among the soldiers. Few Peninsular diarists fail to mention these primitive vehicles. Surgeon Henry Milburne gives one of the better descriptions.

> A more inconvenient, ill-constructed, clumsy carriage cannot be well conceived. The body of the carriage is merely a platform of rough boards, which is placed upon two wheels, rather lower than the front ones of an English wagon, composed of pieces of timber, pinned together, and secured by others nailed across – these do not revolve on the axle-tree but are fastened to it, the whole of which turns in grooves, sometimes secured with iron. The pole, passing between the oxen, is fastened to a yoke bound to their horns, so that the poor animals draw by their head, or rather it may be said that they pull the machines forwards. The shocking inconvenience of such a jolting conveyance for sick and wounded persons may easily be conceived; added to which the noise they make is the most disagreeable possible, the revolution of the axle-trees producing a kind of humming monotonous sound, something similar to the drone of a bagpipe, which may be heard at the distance of a mile or upwards.[13]

Joseph Donaldson described the noise as like the grating of an iron door on rusty hinges.[14] Apparently, the Portuguese did not grease the wheels as they thought that the excruciating sound frightened away the devil. The normal jolting motion was often increased as pieces broke off from the circumference of the wheels. Progress was intolerably slow, usually about two miles an hour.

The ox-carts were either used in convoys or attached to individual regiments as 'sick-carts' to gather men and their arms when they became ill on the march. Those sick or wounded who survived a long journey in them were unlikely to forget the experience. Several journeys are related in graphic detail by Peninsular veterans who were well used to the normal hardships of campaigning but were shocked by what they endured and witnessed in the carts. In July 1810 Edward Costello of the 95th Rifles was wounded whilst skirmishing on the Coa river. He was put into a bullock cart with six others, although he judged it barely adequate to accommodate more than two. Following a journey through the night, he was so cramped and fatigued he was unable to move at all. When a dead man fell across him, he was too weak to push the body off and his calls for help were ignored by the Portuguese driver.[15] John Spencer Cooper, ill from malaria, underwent a similar ordeal on the road to Villa Vicosa in a cart he variously describes as 'rubbishly' and an 'abominable vehicle'. According to Cooper, the slowness and noise was enough to 'wear out the patience of any healthy man'. He was soaked with rain and suffered from violent nose bleeds, no doubt exacerbated by the persistent jolting.[16] After Joseph Donaldson had witnessed a convoy of sick in bullock carts the screeching noise of the wheels was forever associated in his mind with the 'pallid faces and piercing groans of the wounded'.[17]

Although the ox-carts were castigated by all those soldiers unfortunate enough to have to use them, they did have certain advantages. They were light, relatively easy to repair, and specially built to withstand the poor roads of the country. The local peasants were able to drive them and could be encouraged to mend them. Most importantly, they were available in much greater numbers than any other form of wheeled transport. An immense amount of them were brought into service, some on long-term hire as part of the permanent transport of the army, others on a more temporary basis by requisition from the district. The latter process was fraught with difficulty as not all peasants were willing to surrender their carts for the carriage of British supplies and sick, and many were no more happy at the prospect of accompanying the carts far from their own homes. Local magistrates often laboured diligently to provide the necessary vehicles, but contretemps between British soldiers and Portuguese and Spanish peasants were inevitable, particularly where the transport was urgently needed for sick and wounded men. Harry Smith recalls an incident in Portugal when he threatened to hang the local village magistrate unless bullocks were found to draw the carts carrying his wounded comrades.[18] This threat of force was not unusual. During the retreat to Vigo in January 1809, another officer resorted to desperate measures to obtain carts for the sick when a group of peasants failed to accede to his request.

> We produced our pistols, one of which I gave to Lieutenant F_____, and girded on my sabre; and at my recommendation, he ordered out a file of men, though they were principally feeble and in a convalescent state, and ordered them to load before the mob. Then we proceeded to the fields, and after a chase of two hours, we procured a significant number of bullocks and carts.[19]

Because of unresolved problems in requisitioning sufficient local carts, Wellington ordered the construction of additional carts of an improved pattern which were entrusted to drivers employed directly by the commissariat. It is not clear to what extent this 'commissariat car train' was used for casualty evacuation. The only real alternative form of wheeled transport were the spring wagons of the army. These formed part of the Royal Wagon Train which had a chequered history and a less than illustrious reputation. The wagon train was formed in 1799 and, although its wagons were unsuitable for the roads of Portugal and Spain, it appears that that it did play its part during the Peninsular War, chiefly transporting wounded and sick. Patchy though the wagon train was, it became a target for further reductions. Politician William Huskison, who has a place in transport history as the first man to be killed by a railway engine, stated that, 'The Wagon Train is an annoyance on foreign service and useless at home.'[20] The House of Commons insisted that the train be reduced from twelve troops to seven, but Wellington, already desperately short of transport, summarily ignored the order to disband them.

As the Peninsular War progressed, the Royal Wagon Train became increasingly used for sick transport. A general order issued in October 1810 directed that three spring wagons should be attached to each division of infantry for the carriage of sick soldiers and their equipment. Each accommodated eight sitting or two lying cases, and were designed to be drawn by four horses with two drivers. In the Peninsula, the horses were often replaced by oxen, mules or asses. A staff surgeon was to oversee them and ensure that they were not used for any other purpose. By May 1813 there were four medical officers actually attached to the different companies of the train. Although this was all better than no provision at all, it would be wrong to portray these spring wagons as a major advance. Any similarity to the French ambulance organisation was entirely superficial. Firstly, the number of spring wagons was hopelessly inadequate, in William Fergusson's words, 'not a tithe of what an army on actual service would require'.[21] When the quartermaster general inspected the corps in October 1812, it consisted of no more than eighty-seven horses and eleven wagons and all in very poor condition. Secondly, the drivers of the Royal Wagon Train had inherited some of the habits of their predecessors, the Royal Corps of Waggoners, a collection of ruffians commonly called the 'Newgate Blues' with reference to the famous prison. In a letter of June 1812, Wellington states that all the spring wagons at this time were being used for removing sick to the rear, but he admits that, 'the drivers are very irregular, and take but little care of their horses'.[22] Finally, the wagons were unsuited to the roads and terrain of the Peninsula. It seems that their use as ambulances was in large part due to their failure as supply vehicles. In his seminal work on Wellington's army, Charles Oman comments that 'Wellington finally gave up all idea of relying on them for load-carrying, and mainly employed them for his sick and wounded.'[23]

Like many of his comrades in the 95th Rifles, Major George Simmons was wounded at the Coa in 1810. He later shared a spring wagon with three others.

> The springs of this machine were very strong, and the rough ground we passed over made them dance us up and down in an awful manner. Bad as the movement of the bullock cars was, this was ten

times worse, if possible. I felt happy when I was put under cover for the night upon the ground floor of a dilapidated house.[24]

By the following morning the mules drawing the wagons had disappeared and Simmons was relieved to be transferred back to a bullock cart. Not all agreed with him that the spring wagons were more uncomfortable than the local carts, but the diaries, letters and memoirs of the period leave no doubt that a journey in either vehicle was a form of purgatory. The only other means of wheeled transport used for wounded were artillery carriages. Quartermaster William Surtees remembers that at the Battle of Barossa, near Cadiz, a senior officer emptied the artillery carriages of all the spare ammunition in order to make room for the wounded.[25] They were quite well suited for the purpose but were only occasionally accessible for casualty evacuation.

The mules, asses and horses pulling these vehicles were also forms of transport in their own right and were all used to carry sick and wounded. In the Peninsula, each regiment was accompanied by thirty to forty 'private' mules carrying the officers' baggage. There were about thirteen 'public' mules, including one for each company's camp kettles or tents, one for entrenching tools, one for the paymaster's books, and one for the surgeon's medical panniers. In addition, large numbers of mules were employed by the commissariat to move supplies. In times of need, at least some of these mules could be pressed into service by the medical department. They were especially valuable when other transport was not feasible. A general order issued from Frenada in 1811 directed:

> When it is necessary that soldiers should be removed to the hospitals, and that the roads are of a description that the spring wagons cannot be used, the mules returning to the magazine for supplies must be employed to carry them to the hospitals, which have been stationed on the roads to the magazines with a view to this convenience.[26]

Animals were always in short supply. An artillery officer, writing in early 1813, noted that the artillery department was short of 900 mules, and the commissariat were wanting 3 to 4,000.[27]

For soldiers wounded in the Battles of the Pyrenees, mules were the mainstay of evacuation to the hospitals. Ensign George Bell was given the responsibility of escorting the wounded of his brigade during fighting in the mountains in June 1813. He had to get them to the hospital at Elizondo on the Spanish-French border.

> The only conveyance for the poor cripples with broken arms and legs and shattered shells were some mules sent up by the Commissary. Two men were placed on each mule, with their broken limbs

75

bandaged up in a way and dangling down. No help for it; no cart-roads in the Pyrenees, and the poor fellows were groaning with their sufferings all the way.[28]

Bell implies that even the jolting ox-carts would have been preferable. For the more seriously sick and injured the difficulties of riding a mule were considerable. The animals were supposedly managed by gangs of local muleteers, who, through the course of the war, acquired notoriety among the men and officers of the British Army. Many of the best of the Portuguese were with the army, and the muleteers were all too often of low quality. In a single paragraph, Oman variously refers to them as 'ruffians of the lowest sort', 'the scum of a great harbour city' [Lisbon], 'rascals', 'undesirables', and 'villains'.[29] Many were interested only in absconding with army stores, or in plundering the wounded and dead on the battlefield. Wellington wrote wearily to Lord Liverpool in 1812 that, 'after every allowance is made, we must expect disappointments when we have to deal with Portuguese and Spanish carters and muleteers'.[30]

Invalids were especially vulnerable to the unsavoury behaviour of muleteers and bullock-cart drivers. In 1812 John Green of the 68th Durham Light Infantry, weakened by a fever, fell behind his division. He was put on a mule to carry him to Nisa, in central Portugal, a distance of nine miles.

> Of all the men I ever saw, the Spanish muleteer who accompanied me was the most unfeeling; for he drove his mule before the rest, making the poor animal trot all the way; and if the mule slackened its pace, he would run at and kick it on the legs and hams, crying, in the Spanish language, 'cursed, cursed', this was because he had a sick soldier to carry.

The muleteer ignored pleas to slow down and Green says that if he had had the opportunity he would have shot him.[31] Others did resort to violence. When Lieutenant William Swabey caught a bullock driver hitting with a stick a wounded soldier who was too weak to leave the cart to walk up a hill, he took immediate revenge on the miscreant. 'I actively beat him till I could not stand over him.'[32]

It would be unfair to suggest that all the muleteers and drivers behaved in this way. August Schaumann had plenty of dealings with them in his role as commissary and he witnessed their shortcomings. Nevertheless, he praised them for being tough and devoted. 'More than once on retreats and marches, while in charge of my baggage and public funds, and when everything was in confusion, they were separated from me, and might easily have escaped and made their fortune by so doing, but they always turned up sooner or later.'[33] Oman also acknowledges this characteristic but attributes it to their wish to avoid conscription into their own army and their hatred of the French rather than to any real loyalty to the British.

Of the other forms of land transport used for casualty evacuation in the Peninsula, the most distinctive was the local sedan chair. Harry Smith rode in a Portuguese chair slung between two mules after the Battle of the Coa. He sat in one seat and laid his injured leg on the other and apparently travelled in relative comfort.[34] William Tomkinson of the 16th Light Dragoons was wounded in the neck and arms whilst skirmishing near Oporto in 1809. He refused a bullock cart for the journey to the city and a sedan chair was procured. It took about two and a half hours to cover the eight miles. Tomkinson was much fatigued and kept asking the carriers to stop to allow him to rest. 'I was dreadfully irritable and wished the dragoon to shoot the Portuguese who held up the curtain of the sedan windows to look at me, which they repeatedly did on my entering the town.'[35] The sedan chair had its detractors and was not often employed, but it seems to have had some advantages. It gave a relatively smooth ride, had adequate space for one wounded soldier, and provided protection from the sun.

Stretchers were little used beyond the immediate confines of the battlefield, although there is the occasional reference to them. Private William Wheeler says that in September 1813 'bearers' were used to carry wounded officers from the Biddasoa to the hospital at Passages, and Edward Costello remembers being stretchered to the hospital in Lisbon by men of the Portuguese militia.[36] Few wounded or sick men could be expected to travel far on foot. After the Battle of the Coa, there were no mules or wagons immediately available and about seventy disabled soldiers set off on the road to Pinhel using their rifles as crutches and helping each other to hobble along. The worst of the wounded were transferred to bullock carts at the nearest village. According to William Grattan, some of the wounded after Badajoz preferred walking 'from a disinclination to bear the jolting of the carts, or the uneasy posture of sitting astride a horse'.[37] For men who were unable to walk, almost any alternative was welcome. Ensign Robert Dallas disembarked at Portsmouth after the retreat to Vigo and was so sick he had to be carried to an inn in a wheelbarrow.[38] This was not an isolated incident. After the Battle of Bautzen, there was a shortage of proper vehicles and Dominique Larrey organised a convoy of the local wheelbarrows to transfer the French wounded the fifteen miles to Dresden.[39]

If the coast was accessible or rivers navigable, there was always the possibility of transporting the sick by water. In the Peninsula, river transport was regarded as much preferable to the appalling roads, but there was limited navigable inland waterway. The Tagus river was normally navigable as far as Abrantes, about 100 miles upstream from Lisbon, and the Douro for about fifty miles above Oporto. The Mondego was also useable, although this route did involve being transferred to a sea-going ship at the river mouth. When Wellington's campaigning extended into northern Spain his major seaports were at Santander and Passages. After the horrors of land transport, a journey by water had much to commend it. Mrs Fitzmaurice, the long-suffering wife of a soldier in the Rifle Corps, shared a voyage with soldiers wounded at Badajoz.

> I have often heard described the luxury of sitting on the gunwale, with a broken leg in the water, eating delicious oranges; – luxury dearly purchased at the expense of much previous suffering. During three days the boat glided down the beautiful stream.[40]

It was not always so idyllic. Surgeon James Elkington accompanied a sick convoy on the Mondego river in late 1811, when he was buffeted by a terrible storm, 'every flash of lightning caused the man at the wheel to let go and cross himself calling on St. Antonio'. The boat was often aground.[41] Edward Costello's experiences on the Mondego involved the best and worst of river travel. Sick though he was, he enjoyed the exquisite scenery that passed as the boat floated towards Figueira on the coast. As the journey progressed the intense heat began to affect the wounds which were soon alive with maggots. There was a scarcity of doctors and many men either died on board or needed later amputation of limbs.[42]

On arrival at Figueira, Costello, like many others, was transferred to a sea vessel for the final journey to Lisbon. There is little doubt that for sick soldiers a voyage in a 'transport', the term used for these vessels, could be just as unpleasant as a stretch in an ox-car or spring wagon. Many of the ships used for sick evacuation, and indeed for transfer of healthy men and supplies, were unseaworthy. As the demand for vessels rose, the quality of the timber used fell, and transports could be little better than rotting hulks with a life-expectancy of only a few years. An admiral, serving in Lisbon in 1811, commented that if the army had been aware of the quality of the ships that carried its men there would have been a mutiny.

Ill soldiers were normally embarked onto ships that were too small, had no facilities for their care, and only sporadic medical cover. In January 1809 around 4,000 sick soldiers were hurriedly boarded after the Battle of Corunna. Surgeon Henry Milburne describes the chaotic intermixing of regiments, with many of the sick deprived of any medical assistance. He embarked on the transport *Alfred* with two other surgeons and over 250 sick and wounded men. In Milburne's words they were 'very uncomfortably accommodated and destitute of every necessity their condition required'.[43] In the rough but rapid passage to the south coast the men experienced a renewal of the sufferings endured during the earlier retreat. Vermin crawled through their ragged bloodstained clothes. For many there was no respite at journey's end as, because of the shortage of hospital beds on land, they were kept cooped up in the transports. Physician Adam Neale, aboard one of these vessels, described men kept in filthy surroundings without adequate food and water. He blamed the conditions for the unnecessary loss of a thousand lives.[44] The debacle after Corunna was well publicised, but the death of sick men in the transports was not unusual. On one passage from Portugal a year later, sixty-four patients perished. Even relatively short voyages around the Portuguese and Spanish coastline caused considerable mortality. Sergeant James Hale of the 9th Foot, wounded in the left arm, set sail for Bilbao from Passages in 1813. Despite the pleasant weather, he says that it was a miserable trip for the wounded as there were no beds or hammocks and the rolling of the ship caused them to cry out with pain. Several died and their bodies were committed to the sea.[45]

Among Peninsular War journals and diaries there are several epic narratives of long journeys made by men disabled by disease or wounds. One of the most vivid is that of Colonel Neil Campbell who travelled from near Almeida to Lisbon during June and July 1811 whilst debilitated by a severe bout of malaria. Campbell's account illustrates how many different modes of transport might be resorted to in a single journey.

> I found myself so weak as scarcely to be able to articulate, or to turn in my bed. Although it was not likely that the French would send any party twenty miles in advance from Ciudad Rodrigo, it was not pleasant to think that I was on the great road from that, and not a British or Portuguese soldier within fifty miles of me. I was carried in my bed, on peasants' shoulders, to Pinhel on the 20th [June]. What I suffered in conveyance from thence to Coimbra is beyond description – a distance of more than 100 miles, part of it rough road, and no inns. I first tried a liteira. This is a very large sedan-chair, but instead of men, there is a mule before, and another behind, with the poles fixed on their sides. Conceive their unequal movements, sometimes at a slow trot, but generally a walk. The liteira, besides jolting up and down, possesses a motion backward and forwards like a sedan-chair, but to a much greater extent. I had no alternative but my horse, exposed to the sun, in very hot weather, and on white glaring roads. I was lifted out and in, off and on, twenty times, trying both conveyances in turn – obliged to go on, in order to reach some village where I could find shelter, perhaps ten or twelve miles off. Unable in my weak state to endure this suffering and fatigue for more than one day, my attendants hired a cart of the country, which is very clumsy, and mounted on two solid wooden wheels (the noise of which may be heard a mile off), and drawn by two oxen. Having then no bed, I was placed in it, lying at full length upon straw. I could have borne this had the roads been good, but when we came to some places,

where the cart was jolted and thrown in all directions, I really felt sometimes as if I must give up. After two days' trial, I was obliged to discharge the cart, the motion was so violent. The rest of the journey, I made on horseback at a walk; and so feeble was I, that I could not move two paces without a supporter. I generally managed to travel five miles in the morning, and again from two till seven in the afternoon and evening, frequently resting for twenty or thirty minutes under the shade of a tree, to slumber on my cloak. In most of the villages the houses were full of filth and vermin, and in many instances the French had burned everything, down to the very doors and flooring, so that it was impossible to enter them. When this was the case I generally went into the church for shelter.

My attendants were numerous: my assistant surgeon, a subaltern of my regiment, an orderly corporal, four servants and two of their wives, three riding and four baggage horses, an ass, and two goats. Whenever we came to a town or large village for our night halt, the civil magistrate gave us a billet on one of the principal inhabitants, who was thereby obliged to provide accommodation for myself, my servants and horses, as well as the use of a kitchen and table utensils; and also a bed for me, with clean linen and lights. If there is no commissary, the magistrate must likewise furnish rations of fresh beef and mutton, bread and wine. If the inhabitant on whom the billet is given be rich, he frequently sends in a dinner or supper. In the course of my journey this happened to me three or four times . . . If you refer to the map, you will see that my route from Pinhel lay by Vizeu, on the right bank of the Mondego. About twenty-five miles from Coimbra I went by water to Figueira, at the mouth of the Mondego, and by the same mode, a few days after, to San Martinho, and thence to Caldas, where there is a hot chalybeate spring, and a very fine public establishment.[46]

Colonel Campbell will have regarded his retinue, including a regimental surgeon, as appropriate to his senior rank. Of course, from a medical perspective, the attachment of an indispensable medical officer to one sick man made little sense. Most similar accounts are by officers who received privileged treatment. For the ordinary soldier the agonies of such a journey must have been even greater and the chance of survival reduced. Apart from the obvious risk of death from wounds or sickness, long journeys were associated with other dangers. Although a very senior officer like Campbell could expect to be well fed, for those without servants to provide for them the threat of starvation was real. The officer overseeing a sick convoy was responsible for drawing rations from the commissary's mule train but this was not always possible. In the Pyrenees, Ensign George Bell was unable to procure food, or even 'a spoonful of water' for the wounded and dying men in his care. He could not sleep at night because of their groaning.[47]

The combination of poor roads, unreliable drivers and rickety vehicles made accidents common. Where streams crossed the roads it was not unusual for the wounded to be pitched into the water and left to fend for themselves. John Green describes just such an incident between Nisa and Abrantes, where he fell off an ass into a ford and owed his survival to the following man who grabbed his coat.[48] George Simmons recalls a similar narrow escape in Portugal when the bullocks became unmanageable, trampled over his servant, and tipped him out of a cart onto the roadside. He fortunately missed the surrounding rocks and landed on a patch of soft ground. Simmons also survived a threatened attack by peasants who were attempting to steal the bullocks. His servant and some artillerymen, who happened to be close by, came to his rescue, taking a peasant prisoner and forcing him to drive the vehicle.[49] The Peninsula was a dangerous environment and being a British soldier incapacitated by disease or injury was no guarantee of protection from elements of the local population.

Perhaps the greatest fear of the sick and wounded was of being abandoned by their comrades. There are several examples of this, mainly during the army's forced retreats. On the road to Corunna near Villafranca, in the words of Commissary Schaumann:

> At the entrance of a certain defile we all marched higgledy-piggledy or rather pushed each other forward through the darkness in one compact mass. Never shall I forget the heartrending cries of some wounded men, when their cart broke down, and they were deposited in a shed and left behind. The poor devils implored us fervently not to leave them to the mercy of the French advanced guard; but the whole procession marched on unfeelingly.[50]

The reason for these 'breakdowns' was usually the bullocks dying of famine and exhaustion. When, at Mayorga, it became necessary to dump the French wounded, they were guarded for as long as possible to prevent them being massacred by the peasantry.

Some British wounded were fortunate enough to receive constructive help from their fellows. Edward Costello gratefully acknowledges the assistance that he and other wounded Riflemen received from the Guards of the First Division en route to Lisbon in 1810. Forty Guardsmen and an officer escorted them to their final destination. A private soldier of the 11th Light Dragoons witnessed the damaging effect of a long journey on wounded men in southern Spain a year later. They had received little attention to their injuries and through prolonged exposure to the sun they were in a sorry state.

There was no lack of willingness on our parts to assist them. We soon cleared out the best houses in the place; spread straw, and, where we could find it, linen, for them on the floors, and gave ourselves up to the business of cleansing their hurts – the smell proceeding from which was fearful. Over and over again we were forced to quit the miserable patients in a hurry, and run out into the open air, in order to save ourselves from fainting; while they, poor fellows, reproached us, with a degree of bitterness which none of us cared, even in thought, to resent for a moment.[51]

Transport of invalids was equally dogged with problems in other theatres of war. Indeed, in some campaigns, the dangers to the sick on the road appear to have been even greater than in the Peninsula. In Ceylon between 1803 and 1805, the British were decimated by a virulent form of 'jungle fever'. Columns of troops crossing the island became, in effect, giant sick convoys which were terrorised by the enemy. The native bearers soon deserted, and the sick and wounded who could not be carried fell into the enemy's hands. According to one officer: 'Many were taken, their hands and feet bound, their mouths stuffed with grass to prevent their cries, slung upon a bamboo pole, and thus borne off to be butchered like sheep.' Some were rescued by their comrades charging with the bayonet.[52] Prior to their desertion the natives in British employment had carried the disabled men on 'doolies'. These were a form of hammock or bed suspended from a bamboo pole which was carried by four bearers. The conveyance was also extensively used for sick transport in India, where they were either attached to individual units or under the orders of the superintending surgeon.

There is little need to consider each campaign in detail as there was considerable overlap with the Peninsula. The army's medical department was generally short of suitable transport and was forced to exploit any available local vehicles in a way analogous to the use of ox-carts in Portugal and Spain. In the Flanders campaign of 1794, sick men were dragged across the frozen wastes in country wagons, some of which had been adapted to make them more comfortable. The local two-masted trading vessels (billanders) carried sick on the canals. Most were horribly overcrowded, and when they came to a halt they effectively changed from transports into floating hospitals. In Egypt, the local narrow lateen-rigged vessels (feluccas) were commandeered for casualty evacuation. The debacles of Buenos Aires (1807) and Walcheren (1809) were both characterised by a dearth of transport. On Walcheren there were inadequate vehicles for carriage of fever cases to the hospitals. The embarkation of the sick was a repeat of the mistakes of Corunna. Invalids were mixed with the healthy and there were not enough medical officers to man all the transports.[53] In another unsuccessful British venture, the American War of

1812–14, British and American wounded were variously moved on litters made of blankets hung between poles, on wagons and sleighs, and by water.

Despite repeated cases of ineptitude in transport arrangements and the unnecessary suffering and deaths caused among the medical department's patients, there was no great public recrimination. Contemporary memoirs of the wars contain complaints but little direct criticism. Most victims were apparently resigned to another unpleasant truth of army life. There were a few discordant voices. Captain William Swabey made the following observations in December 1812, after the army had completed its miserable retreat from Burgos to Ciudad Rodrigo.

> I am obliged once again to cry shame against the regulations for the transport of the sick. The unfortunate beings, more fit for their death beds than for being moved from one place to another, are daily passing through here [San Payo] on cars without springs; every jolt of which is sufficient to fracture a limb; others dying are left neglected and unpitied by the road side, two hundred probably having only one hospital mate to dress their wounds or minister to their diseases.[54]

Ensign John Aitchison wrote to his father only three days after William Swabey penned his comments on the transport system. Aitchison was also bitter at the treatment of his wounded and sick comrades during the retreat. Little escapes Aitchison's critical eye. He especially stresses the lowering of morale that poor medical services caused. His letter is, by the normal standards of Napoleonic diarists, a vilifying attack on the authorities.

> By the end of the 3rd day's march the scene was indescribable melancholy. I never saw so many dead animals in so short a distance – independent of this, however, our route was sufficiently marked by the bodies of men who had died from wounds and sickness and others left to become prisoners, perhaps a worse fate from want of means to bring them off. The above is no exaggerated statement, written to excite compassion or impose on credulity, it is the unstudied statement of an eyewitness ... I have marked with particular emphasis the want of transport for the sick in this army, because it appears to me to be so shamefully deficient that nothing can palliate, much less excuse it. After passing the Agueda [river] when an enemy pressing the rear could no longer be urged in extenuation, I have seen sick soldiers rolled up in their blankets, lying by the roadside, left for want of conveyance, perhaps to die: and within a few miles of Ciudad Rodrigo, I had one from my own

company left to his fate (having lost the use of his limbs from cold in the retreat) and this after exhausting my own means, by carrying on my private mules another in the same state – I shall also mention while on this subject that from the same deficiency of transport, wounded soldiers were abandoned on the field, and this too at a time when by their valour, they had so far driven back the enemy as to render their comrades safe from being molested. Will such enormities as these be believed in Britain? In that country so renowned for the devotion of her sons – held up to the world as an honourable example of pious charity and riches!!

What must be thought of a government so stinting in comfort – nay bare justice – to the defenders of their country, as to deny a General the means of easing the suffering of the Soldier when worn out, probably of restoring him to the service; and this the government of a country which is compelled to adopt every plan which human ingenuity can suggest could keep full the ranks of her army? . . . The means of carrying sick attached to this army in the field is only six wagons to a division; a division consists of 5,000 men and a wagon will hold 7 men – conveyance is thus provided for 42 men, which is quite enough for casualties on ordinary marches, but on extra-ordinary occasions (such as a skirmish) what of necessity is resorted to? – why, that men who are unfit to march by sickness only, are turned out to make room for the wounded!! What becomes of these men? – they make exertions to follow till nature at last is exhausted, and they fall down and die; or perhaps are picked up singly by the enemy, who in pursuit have neither the power or inclination to give comfort. Is the soldier rendered unfit for service by sickness not equally entitled to be taken off as the one who has had the misfortune to be wounded? Nobody, one would think, will deny this? Yet Ministers by their conduct do![55]

Aitchison later applauds the French transport arrangements, saying that the enemy lost and abandoned far fewer sick men during retreats in the Peninsula than did the British. He was able to make these strident remarks as the post home was not censored. His opinions did not prevent him later becoming a general and a knight.

The man who took on the responsibility for remedying the deficiencies of the medical department in the Peninsula, including the lack of transport, was James McGrigor. In January 1812 McGrigor replaced the largely ineffectual James Franck as Inspector-General of Hospitals to the army. The new medical chief, then 40 years old, had served his time as a regimental surgeon, before being appointed superintending surgeon to David Baird's force during the Egyptian campaign of 1801. He later had charge of military hospitals in the Southern Division of England and had visited Walcheren to reorganise the medical services there. By the time of his arrival in the Peninsula, he was widely recognised as a skilful physician and, perhaps more importantly, as a strong and capable administrator. He had respect from his military superiors, including Wellington, and from his medical subordinates. Although a hard taskmaster he led by example.

Of his relationship with Wellington, McGrigor was later to write in his autobiography.

> He [Wellington] said he wants such an officer as me, who thoroughly understood the duties, who was acquainted with the habits of soldiers, and who would prevent the malingering propensities of both officers and men at the hospital stations, where all sorts of irregularities prevailed, and he promised me his utmost support, which from that moment I fully experienced.[56]

McGrigor reported to Wellington every morning, giving him details of the hospital state, the number of dead, the number fit to march and convalescent, the prevalence of diseases and their causes, and any other matters relating to the health of the army. The regularity and detail of these reports underline the importance Wellington gave to an efficient medical department. However, although the two men had a good working relationship, Wellington was not slow to reject McGrigor's proposals whenever he felt that they might interfere with military operations. This was to prove the case with medical transport, the formal provision of which McGrigor quickly realised was hopelessly inadequate. Whilst travelling between Coimbra and Celerico in February 1812, he witnessed for himself the wounded carried in uncovered bullock carts without food or comfort. Not only did many die on the road, but the survivors suffered so much from the transport that many lived only a few days when they finally arrived at the hospital, '. . . the medical officers at these stations had not fair play with them. They received these patients in that state when it was impossible to do anything with them'.[57]

Not all the sick needed to undergo arduous journeys to the rear or to be left at the hospitals en route. In his conversations with the regimental surgeons and their commanding officers, McGrigor understood their desire to carry their slightly wounded and sick men with them. Although there was no authority from headquarters, he supported the practice of ox-carts accompanying the regiments to carry the less severe cases and prevent them being sent to the rear. This was better than nothing, but McGrigor was eager to replace these makeshift arrangements with a proper ambulance service with larger numbers of ox-carts and spring wagons under direct medical supervision. It was at this point that Wellington expressed his disagreement. He 'at once exclaimed against it, and said he would have no interruption to the movements of the army which my plans would clog. On my further explaining, he warily said he would have no vehicle with the army but for the conveyance of the guns; so that for the time I was obliged to give up my plan, I saw that he was strongly opposed to it.'[58] Wellington did admit that McGrigor's ideas 'were excellent if they had been practicable'. The matter was dropped but McGrigor was almost as stubborn as Wellington and, whenever the opportunity arose, he reminded his commander of the need for additional sick transport. In June 1812:

> I am sure that when I recommend any change in the mode of conveyance of sick to the rear, I risk the recommendations of what may be unpopular, but it is my duty to state that if any steady and regular mode could be secured to each brigade, it would greatly diminish the mortality, which has sometimes been very great.[59]

Wellington remained insistent that he had authorised the maximum possible number of vehicles for casualties.

McGrigor had to strike a difficult balance between, on the one hand, providing the best possible evacuation of the sick and wounded under his care, and on the other, doing nothing to counteract Wellington's orders, impede the movement of active units, or overstep his authority. After the Battle of Salamanca, he journeyed to join Wellington in Madrid and, en route, discovered considerable numbers of sick on the road, many without any provisions or medical attendance. Accordingly, he sent instructions to the principal medical officer in Salamanca asking for medical officers and purveyors to be sent to the appropriate places. He also alerted the deputy commissary-general, recommending the supply of provisions and carts and the movement of commissariat officers. When he arrived in Madrid, he reported what he had done to Wellington, who at the time was sitting for a portrait by Goya. On hearing his senior doctor's account of events the Duke lost his temper.

> 'I shall be glad to know,' exclaimed his Lordship, 'who is to command the army? I or you? I establish one route for the army, you establish another, and order the commissariat and supplies by that line. As long, as you live, Sir, never do so again; never do anything without my orders.'[60]

The famed Spanish artist, who knew no English, looked on aghast, wondering what could have provoked such an outburst. McGrigor tried to argue that after the retreat from Talavera when the sick and wounded had been abandoned to the French, there had been severe criticism in England. He pointed out that if lives were to be saved, there had been no time for consultation. When a chastened McGrigor finally left the room, Wellington, in a more conciliatory manner, gave him an invitation to dine.

There was a sequel to this rare admonition for McGrigor. Several months later, Wellington informed him that the army would have to retreat from Burgos. He asked the doctor what was to become of the sick and wounded. McGrigor replied that he had anticipated the situation and had taken the precaution of already sending many of the wounded and disabled by ox-carts and mules to Valladolid. As a result, there were only a handful of more seriously wounded left in the city in the care of six surgeons. 'Admirable,' was Wellington's response. When the army reached Valladolid, where there were more than 2,000 sick and wounded, Wellington again approached his senior doctor, saying of the hospital, 'I fear our numbers are very great. What is to be done, for you see, we must be off from this place, and conveyance there is none?' McGrigor again reassured him that the number of sick remaining was small as he had previously used all the available carts and mules to send them on to Salamanca. Wellington commented, 'And you have made Salamanca chock full, I cannot stop there.' McGrigor, undaunted, replied that he had put in place a chain of hospitals running through Ciudad Rodrigo to Oporto and that the flow of wounded to the rear would not impede Wellington's retreat. 'This is excellent!' exclaimed the Duke. By this stage McGrigor was unable to resist reminding his chief of the earlier incident.

> My Lord, you recollect how much you blamed me at Madrid for the steps which I took on coming to the army, when I could not consult your Lordship, and acted for myself as I had done. Now, if I had not, what would the consequence have been? He [Wellington] added, 'It is all right as it has turned out; but I recommend you still have orders for what you do.'

McGrigor was left to conclude that, 'This was a singular feature in the character of Lord Wellington.'[61]

Wellington's earlier loss of temper and his rather lukewarm acknowledgement of McGrigor's actions should not disguise his genuine affection for his surgeon general. Later in the year, when McGrigor was incapacitated by a kick on the knee from a horse, Wellington provided him with his own carriage, the only one with the army. The Duke was not always quick with compliments, but he did show his regard for McGrigor and the medical services. When, in late 1812, the commissary ineptly handled the ration problem, Wellington compared them directly with the medical department which, he said, 'is the only one which will obey orders; on them I can rely for doing their duty'.[62] It would also be wrong to assume that Wellington's reluctance to provide a more formal ambulance service arose out of callousness. There are numerous anecdotes suggesting that he much regretted the suffering caused to his sick and wounded by inadequate transport and took local action whenever this was possible. Edward Costello remembers that after the Coa, Wellington and some of his staff galloped up to the convoy of wounded.

> Glancing his eye at us for a moment, and seeing our crowded condition in the carts, he instantly gave an order to one of his aides-de-camp to obtain additional conveyance from the Juiz de Fora [local magistrate], and also bread and wine.[63]

Largely because of Wellington's unwillingness to approve an ambulance service, there was no fundamental difference in transport provision for the sick at the end of the Peninsular War compared with at its outset. Procurement of vehicles was still opportunistic and the quality of conveyances left much to be desired. McGrigor, however, made the best of a difficult situation and undoubtedly in the final years of the war there were a few more spring wagons available, and the local carts and mules were better organised. The most benefit arose not from better transport but from the increased use of regimental hospitals, which allowed many sick and wounded to be treated nearer the front and, in part, avoided the need for them to be transferred large distances to the rear. The aftermath of the Waterloo campaign reflected the truth that the experience of the Peninsular War had led to no real solution to the problems of casualty evacuation. Each regiment now had a spring wagon to carry its wounded. Just as in the Peninsula, they were inadequate in number and little suited to the quagmire of a road between the field and Brussels. The wounded were forced to make the journey on foot, on horseback, or in any kind of local vehicle. James Elkington commented:

> The transport was not sufficient to remove the British; the different pieces of French artillery as they were brought to the rear were loaded as well as possible with these unfortunate beings – a day or two after a general action is the period to gain a fine idea of the miseries of war.[64]

Because of Larrey's achievements there has always been a tendency to eulogise the French army's ambulance arrangements. However, it would be naive to think that Napoleon's ill troops were immune from the miseries that afflicted British soldiers on the road. Larrey could not be omnipresent and it is evident from contemporary memoirs that French sick convoys could be as horrific as in any other army of the period. For instance, Pierre François Percy's description of eighty wagon-loads of wounded from the Battle of Espinosa arriving at Burgos in November 1808.

None had left the wagons for five days, their straw was fouled, some lay on mattresses covered with pus and excrement. They were covered with rags and pieces of carpet. We got them out as best we could and as many wished to relieve themselves, we had to hold them suspended for the purpose. These manoeuvres took a good two hours in a frightful stench.[65]

The failings of the British Army were not unique. Larrey's groundbreaking concept was only realised in part.

In the period immediately after Waterloo, little attempt was made to correct the deficiencies in the British system. In a set of instructions issued in 1827 for medical arrangements on active service, Director General McGrigor makes it clear that wagons were to be made available for the evacuation of wounded. The misappropriation of these wagons was commonplace and medical officers were urged always to examine them closely to ensure that no unauthorised baggage was carried.[66] These transport arrangements were well intended but seem to have evolved little since the end of the Peninsular War. Even during the Crimea, basic lessons had not been learnt. The British, without ambulance facilities, frequently had to request help from the French. It was sixty years after Waterloo before Britain finally followed Larrey's example and formed a proper field organisation including a trained ambulance corps.

NOTES

1. Cooke, J, *A True Soldier Gentleman*, p.92.
2. Richardson, R, *Larrey. Surgeon to Napoleon's Imperial Guard*, pp.34–8, 92–3; Dible, H, *Napoleon's Surgeon*, pp.16–17; Howard, M R, *In Larrey's Shadow. Transport of British Sick and Wounded in the Napoleonic Wars*.
3. Fergusson, W, *Notes and Recollections of a Professional Life*, p.62.
4. Hennen, J, *Principles of Military Surgery*, p.42.
5. *Selections from the dispatches and general orders*, p.370.
6. ibid., p.678.
7. ibid., p.498.
8. ibid., p.264.
9. Kempthorne, G A, *The Medical Department of Wellington's army*, p.72.
10. Douglas, J, *Douglas's Tale of the Peninsula and Waterloo*, pp.63–6.
11. Elkington, J G, *Some episodes in the life of James Goodall Elkington*, p.90
12. Murray, J, Letter to his father, 29 June 1811.
13. Milburne, H, *A narrative of circumstances attending the retreat*, pp.94–5.
14. Donaldson, J, *Recollections of the Eventful Life of a Soldier*, pp.91–2.
15. Costello, E, *Edward Costello. The Peninsular and Waterloo Campaigns*, pp.35–6.
16. Cooper, J, *Rough Notes of Seven Campaigns*, p.32.
17. Donaldson, p.92.
18. Smith, H, *The Autobiography of Sir Harry Smith*, p.32.
19. Anon, *Operations of the British Army in Spain by an Officer of the Staff*, p.58.
20. Glover, M, *Wellington's Army in the Peninsula 1808–1814*, p.18.

21. Fergusson, p.62.
22. *Selections from the dispatches and general orders*, p.600.
23. Oman, C, *Wellington's Army 1809–1814*, p.314.
24. Simmons, G, *A British Rifleman*, p.81.
25. Surtees, W, *Twenty-Five Years in the Rifle Brigade*, p.122.
26. *Selections from the dispatches and general orders*, p.542.
27. Rogers, H C B, *Wellington's Army*, p.99.
28. Bell, G, *Soldier's Glory*, p.81.
29. Oman, p.29.
30. Haythornthwaite, P, *The Armies of Wellington*, p.121.
31. Green, J, *The Vicissitudes of a Soldier's Life*, pp.78–9.
32. Swabey, W, *Diary of Campaigns in the Peninsula*, p.151.
33. Schaumann, A, *On the Road with Wellington*, p.224.
34. Smith, p.32.
35. Tomkinson, W, *The Diary of a Cavalry Officer*, p.12.
36. Wheeler, W, *The Letters of Private Wheeler*, p.128; Costello, p.37.
37. Grattan, W, *Adventures in the Connaught Rangers*, p.220.
38. Atkinson, C T, *A Subaltern of the 9th in the Peninsula and Walcheren*, p.62.
39. Richardson, p.193.
40. Brett-James, A, *Life in Wellington's Army*, p.256.
41. Elkington, p.90.
42. Costello, p.37.
43. Milburne, p.72.
44. Cantlie, N, *A History of the Army Medical Department*, Vol.I, p.307.
45. Hale, J, *The Journal of James Hale*, p.119.
46. Campbell, N, *Napoleon at Fontainebleau and Elba*, pp.24–7.
47. Bell, p.81.
48. Green, pp.79–80.
49. Simmons, pp.84–5.
50. Schaumann, p.118.
51. Anon, *Reminiscences of a Light Dragoon*, III, p.363.
52. Kempthorne, G A, *The Army Medical Services at Home and Abroad*, pp.224–5.
53. Howard, M R, *Walcheren 1809. A Medical Catastrophe*.
54. Swabey W, p.151.
55. Aitchison, J, *An Ensign in the Peninsular War*, pp.219–20.
56. McGrigor, J, *Autobiography and Services of Sir James McGrigor*, p.261.
57. Blanco, R L, *Wellington's Surgeon General*, p.121.
58. ibid., p.123.
59. ibid., p.129.
60. McGrigor, p.302.
61. ibid., pp.310–11.
62. Cantlie N, p.351.
63. Costello, p.35.
64. Elkington, p.99.
65. Blond, G, *La Grande Armee*, p.208.
66. Cantlie, p.448.

CHAPTER IV
Hospitals

It is at a hospital station and not on a field of battle that the calamities of war are best estimated.

Cornet Francis Hall, 14th Light Dragoons, 1811[1]

Hospitals as we know them today are a surprisingly recent development. One hundred years before Waterloo there was hardly any hospital provision in England. Even after a surge of philanthropic hospital opening in the eighteenth century, only a very small proportion of the sick could expect hospital care. The number of beds available in voluntary general hospitals in 1800 in England was approximately 4,000, serving a total population of nine million. Half of these beds were in London. The facilities were open only to the 'deserving poor', those who could not access other types of medical care and who were also in work. Any prospective patient had to find a 'subscriber' who was willing to certify him 'a proper object of the charity', and also enough money to defray the cost of his burial if he were to die in the hospital. These regulations might be relaxed to allow admission for the effects of a serious accident or for symptoms needing immediate relief. In general the hospitals provided some treatment, rest and convalescence, but restricted themselves to complaints that would respond to treatment. Conditions inside the hospitals were often little better than in the surrounding urban areas. For instance, the Westminster Hospital was established in a place particularly prone to flooding and it became notorious for fevers, malaria, typhoid and 'infectious diarrhoea'. All the hospitals were perfect settings for the spread of the infectious diseases common in civil life, such as tuberculosis.[2]

In the army several types of hospital were in use during the eighteenth century. Each regiment had its own hospital run by the regimental surgeon and mate. The medical staff officers were attached to larger general hospitals which were opened in towns a short distance from the fighting. In peacetime permanent general hospitals at home treated the troops and veterans in garrison. Around a battlefield temporary field hospitals coped with the immediate casualties and any overflow from regimental hospitals. On campaign there were also 'Flying' or 'Marching' hospitals designed to transfer wounded men from the field to the fixed or general hospitals at the base. Any seriously sick or wounded soldiers were likely to end up in the general hospitals. These institutions had no proper medical corps and the wounded were usually nursed by soldiers deemed unfit for other duties.

In the years before the Napoleonic Wars, several eminent army doctors expressed definite views on the best management of the army's hospitals. Best known amongst these is John Pringle whose *Observations on Diseases of the Army*, published in 1752, is a pioneering work in military medicine. Pringle was an army physician during the War of the Austrian Succession and served in Flanders, Scotland and central Europe. He was one of the first to suggest that any hospitals be designated havens for the wounded and be formally removed from the line of fire. He was an enthusiastic supporter of regimental hospitals, declaring that only those sick and wounded who could not be accommodated in the regimental system or moved with the army should be transferred to general hospitals. He emphasised the importance of using large, well-aired buildings for hospitals – apparently churches were ideal. By avoiding overcrowding and maintaining good ventilation, he was convinced that the spread of disease could be minimised. Pringle was supported in many of his opinions by David Monro, a physician who served in the Seven Years War. He is remembered for his *Observations on the Means of Preserving the Health of Soldiers*, published in 1780. Monro proposed numerous regimental hospitals near to the action. He specified large, well ventilated, clean buildings with good drainage. His book contains much advice as to the appropriate conduct of medical staff and patients. Rapid discharge was encouraged 'because recovered men are always the most riotous'. Also influential was Richard Brocklesby, another army physician. His *Economical and Medical Observations tending to the Improvement of Military Hospitals*, published in 1764, is a vigorous attack on the state of army hospitals. He criticises the design of the army's general hospitals which he blamed for the spread of 'hospital fever', now known to be typhus. Brocklesby's alternative design guaranteed the flow of fresh air through the wards. He also recommended the practice of commandeering cottages for use as regimental hospitals to accommodate forty sick men. One of his more controversial views was that, as most of the disease in the army was medical rather than surgical, only physicians should have supreme control of hospitals.

The organisation of the British Army's hospitals in the Napoleonic era shared many characteristics with the system just described. As we will see, it also shared many of its shortcomings. It seems that the hard-learned lessons penned by Pringle, Monro and Brocklesby in the second half of the eighteenth century had to be gradually relearnt during the prolonged campaigning in the Low Countries and the Peninsula. At the outset of the wars, the major division of the general hospitals, permanent at home and semi-permanent on campaign, and the more mobile regimental hospitals persisted. Between the general and regimental hospitals were brigade, divisional and passing (or intermediate) hospitals. Their roles were often ill-defined. The final type of semi-permanent hospital was the convalescent depot, where the recuperating men often fully justified Monro's dictum that well soldiers caused the most trouble. The transient field hospitals created on the edge of battlefields for the immediate treatment of casualties have been described in Chapter II.

Uncertainty about the relative importance of different hospitals and the inter-relationships between them, particularly the dominant general and regimental types, was to fuel the most acrimonious medical debate of the war. Even the most hardline advocate of regimental hospitals had to concede that during a major campaign large hospitals needed to be established behind the lines. These 'general' hospitals, often at intervals of thirty to forty miles, were usually located in the larger villages or towns in make-shift buildings such as convents, churches and schools. They were always necessary after a large battle, although casualties were usually first treated in field hospitals. A typical general hospital catered for 300 patients, although this could be increased to 500 if circumstances dictated. Equipment for the hospitals, such as trestle beds, bedding and hospital clothing, was supplied from the purveyor's store or by requisition from the local inhabitants. When a soldier was admitted to hospital, some money was stopped from his pay to cover the cost of his diet and any additional medical comforts. The Inspector of Hospitals supplied the medical stores and the staff. Hospitals were administered by principal medical officers overseeing the medical staff – a physician, staff surgeon, any available regimental surgeons and assistant surgeons, and the hospital mates. All other subordinates such as wardmasters and orderlies were enrolled from combatant men and a regimental officer acted as commandant. The medical officers had no disciplinary powers and were not expected to assist in keeping order.

General hospitals were far removed from the well equipped military hospitals of the present day. In essence they were buildings in the locality judged large enough to house the sick and wounded. Other than crude cleansing of the rooms and the gathering together of available medical staff and stores, there was little attempt to render the hospitals suitable for use in any modern sense. The poor state of the British general hospitals, both on land and afloat, during the Flanders campaign in 1794 unfortunately set a precedent for much of the rest of the wars. The nature of campaigning in the Low Countries highlighted the deficiencies of the general hospital system. Rather than a static campaign, which would have allowed the formation of fixed general hospitals, the army was forced into a fighting retreat with the removal of the numerous casualties to constantly changing hospital stations behind the battle lines. The civilian physicians placed in charge of these military hospitals had little or no relevant knowledge and were entirely unable to exert the necessary authority. They were little helped by the military commanders, equally inexperienced in hospital management, who had responsibility for maintaining discipline. Even when a more competent military officer was appointed, he rarely remained long enough in post to make a difference.

The situation was exacerbated by a shortage of buildings suitable for hospital use. The British Ambassador at The Hague unsuccessfully pleaded with Britain's Dutch allies to provide the necessary accommodation. The existing hospitals were subject to vehement criticism from all sides. Sick and wounded were crowded together on straw on the floor in cold churches and warehouses. The medical officers were described as ignorant and callous, and the orderlies were apparently a rabble. The morale of the soldiers, already low in the face of the army's forced retreat, was further undermined by their fate if they were unfortunate enough to fall sick. When a man was ordered to the hospital his comrades would exclaim, 'Ah, poor fellow, we shall see thee no more for thou art under orders for the shambles!'[3] To try and relieve the overcrowding men were sent back to England and transport vessels used as hospitals.

James Dickson served as assistant surgeon on a hospital ship at Dordrecht in November 1794. His correspondence to his father is initially optimistic, but he is forced to acknowledge the cramped conditions and lack of supplies which affected all the army's hospitals.

> There are upwards of twenty transports, besides other vessels, 15 of which are fitted up as hospital ships, none of them to contain less than 70 patients, so that there are about 1,050 sick soldiers here, exclusive of convalescents amounting to about 300 more; yet great as you may think this number, there are as many more at each of the hospitals at Gorcum, Rhennen, and the field hospital at Nimeguen. I have about 70 patients in my ship, which has been lucky in being one of the healthiest, not having more than 4 at an average dying weekly; though most of the other ships have had twice that number. In this however I claim no merit, as for weeks together I have not had a single article of medicine to give them.[4]

Although Dickson appeared genuinely devoted to his duties, the hospital ships were condemned as much as the hospitals on land. One inspector described them as filthy, with intolerable food, and doctors who 'jogged along in their own errors'.[5] At the end of the campaign there was inevitable discontent at the performance of the general hospitals. In addition to all the shortcomings already described, they were also denounced for their excessive cost, for their inaccessibility to wounded men, and for being a continual drain on the regimental surgeons who many felt would have been better employed in their own regimental hospitals. Many able regimental surgeons became disillusioned at having to serve under the command of less experienced staff surgeons and physicians. The mortality in the general hospitals was very high – possibly over 60% of men admitted died in the hospital wards. Overcrowding encouraged the spread of diseases such as typhus and hospital gangrene. William Fergusson, an experienced inspector of hospitals, delivered a thunderous verdict:

> Regimental hospitals were all but unknown and in the general hospitals there was neither system, or code, or rule of management. As soon as circumstances pressed, every hospital consequently became a pest-house – a deadly drain upon the effective strength of the army. The evils of accumulation, that mighty fount of human disease, became aggravated from month to month, until at the last I verily believe no army ever exhibited in its hospitals a more lamentable spectacle of indiscipline and abuse.[5]

The young Arthur Wellesley, the future Duke of Wellington, commented of his experiences in the Flanders campaign, 'I learnt what one ought not to do, and that is always something.' The campaign had given the army's medical officers every opportunity of learning how not to manage general hospitals.

In the early years of the Peninsular War, James Franck, the army's Inspector of Hospitals, was a strong supporter of the general hospitals, preferring them to the regimental facilities. The reliance on general hospitals was increased by the difficulty of providing reliable transport for the bedding and other equipment of the regimental hospitals. General hospitals were again located in larger towns or villages where there were suitable buildings. The decision to open a hospital in a particular place was generally taken by the Inspector of Hospitals following consultation with Wellington and the quartermaster-general.[7] Owing to the nature of the early war in the Peninsula several of the general hospitals acquired a permanent character, notably those at Lisbon, Abrantes, Coimbra, Elvas and Oporto. By the end of the war, hospitals had been opened for at least a short period in over fifty locations in Portugal and Spain.

The standards of care in these hospitals were supposedly determined by the Standing Instructions for Hospitals issued by the medical board in 1800. These detailed the hospital routine, the administration of the wards, and the payment of subordinate staff. The latter were provided from the regiments, the number of officers, NCOs and privates being determined by the number of men from their unit under treatment. Where possible, slightly wounded men were chosen to avoid denuding the army of fit combatants. With the subordinate staff drawn from many different regiments, it was crucial to have firm discipline and good supervision from an experienced senior officer. Normally one wardmaster and six orderlies were provided for each 100 beds. Soldiers acting as stewards were entitled to draw 1s.a day, wardmasters 6d.a day, and ward orderlies 3d.a day. It is doubtful that soldiers' wives were routinely employed in the general hospitals. At least some of the medical officers were much opposed to this, one commenting, 'The employment of females is one of the great sources of irregularity . . . every species of excess, idleness and plunder is carried on under their auspices.'[8]

Although the regulations in the early years of the Peninsular War were well meaning, the day-to-day running of the general hospitals remained largely in the hands of untrained personnel. Unsurprisingly, the hospitals were soon being criticised in a way reminiscent of the Flanders campaign fifteen years earlier. Thus they were overcrowded and insanitary. There was little attempt to separate the sick according to the type of disease, with the consequent rapid spread of contagious disorders. Discipline was lax, the quality of treatment was perceived as being poor, and the hospitals were remote from injured men at the front. Because of a shortage of hospital mates, the regimental surgeons were removed from their regiments, where they were sorely needed, to staff the wards. The eye-witness accounts of soldiers admitted to the hospitals give credence to these accusations.

Few soldiers can have had more personal experience of the general hospitals than John Spencer Cooper. Whilst campaigning with the Royal Fusiliers, Cooper was plagued by a recurrent fever, probably malaria, and during the years 1809 and 1810 required several hospital admissions in Portugal and Spain. An account of his experiences is included in an appendix to his memoirs.

The Hospital at Olivenja was a long low room, with another at a right angle to it; crowded with fever patients; the ventilation bad; many deaths daily. The hospital at Villa Vicosa was in a convent; about 150 patients in the four corridors; next to no ventilation; small windows; great barrels or tubs for all purposes; the stench horrible; logs of fir burning at the four corners of the building, to drive away the infection; smoke blinding . . . My case was really pitiable; my appetite and hearing gone; feet and legs like ice; the three blisters on my back and feet untreated and undressed; my shirt sticking in the wounds caused by the blisters; my knapsack and necessaries lost; and worse of all, no one to care a straw for me.

The Hospital at Elvas; Into bomb proof barracks again. No ventilation, twenty sick men in the room, of whom about eighteen died. In this place there was one door, and one chimney, but no windows. Relapse again; deaf as a post; shirt unchanged and sticking to my sore back; ears running stinking matter; a man lying close on my right hand with both his legs mortified nearly to the knees, and dying. A little sympathy would have soothed, but sympathy there was none. The orderlies (men who acted as nurses to the sick) were brutes.

The hospital at Guarda, miserable like the above. The hospital at Celerico; After arriving at Celerico I had another severe relapse of fever. The infection was dreadful: nearly all in the room where I were at one time insensible, bawling out the most incoherent jabber. I had my turn of that also. Although there were about twelve of us in two small rooms, there was not a single chamber utensil. A blanket was spread on the floor instead. Some made use of the window for every purpose. I saw neither bason, soap, nor towel. Such was the place and such our condition.[9]

One of the largest hospital stations in the early years of the war was at Elvas in southern Portugal. Here there was a general hospital in a convent and the smaller hospital in a barracks referred to by Cooper. The latter was in large part for convalescents. Several other eyewitnesses concur with Cooper in suggesting that Elvas incorporated most of the despised features of the general hospital system. It was widely accepted that nearly a hundred men a day died in the hospitals and that the final death toll ran to several thousand. Edward Costello of the 95th Rifles was admitted to Elvas in 1810.

In our regiment, alone, the flux and brain fever reigned to so frightful an extent, that three hundred men died in hospital. I myself was seized with the prevailing fever shortly after our arrival, and was sent to the Convent of St.Paul, the general hospital at Elvas. I could not help remarking the manner of cure adopted by our doctors; it principally consisted of throwing cold water from canteens or mess kettles as often as possible over the bodies of the patients; this in many cases was effectual, and I think cured me. I, however, had a narrow squeak for my life, though I fortunately recovered after an illness of nearly six weeks, thanks to my good constitution, but none to the brute of an orderly, who, during the delirium of the fever, beat me once most furiously with a broom stick. On leaving the hospital with other convalescents, I was sent to the Bomb proof barracks, where it frequently became our duty to see the dead interred. This was a most horrible office, and obliged us to attend at the hospital to receive the bodies, which were conveyed away in cart loads at a time to the ground appointed for their burial. This lay outside the town beneath the ramparts, and was so very small for the purpose required, that we were obliged to get large oblong and deep holes excavated, in which two stout Portuguese were employed to pack the bodies, head and heels together, to save room.[10]

Costello is not the only Rifleman to have left an account of Elvas. His comrade, William Green, was fortunate not to be admitted as a patient but he assisted in the administration of treatment. Green's grim description of the hospital agrees so closely with Costello's to allow no doubt that this was the true state of affairs. He also helped with the burial of the numerous dead, noting that this was done at night without any formal honours or even the simplest burial service. The following anecdote illustrates the cheapness of life in the hospitals.

> A young man in the same company as myself, a native of Hinckley, fell ill of the fever, was taken to the dead-house, laid on a plank, with his feet tied together; he was to have been buried the same night. As the sentinel was on his post he heard a noise in the dead-house; he called the corporal of the guard, the door was opened, and the poor fellow had fell off the plank, and was trying to get the string off his feet. He got well and joined in the ranks with me after that.[11]

At this time the sick rates in the army varied between 20% and 30% and the number of men in the general hospitals was around 5,000. A major battle added large numbers of casualties to the steady flow of sick and put a major strain on the nearby hospitals. This was the case after the Battle of Talavera in July 1809 where there were 4,000 British casualties. A general hospital was opened in a large convent in Talavera with the subordinate staff chosen from men who were only lightly wounded. The hospital became the scene of frenetic activity, as was witnessed by Commissary August Schaumann.

> While on an errand in the town I passed a convent where the wounded were having their limbs amputated and dressed. Never shall I forget the heartrending cries which could be heard coming from the windows in the front of this building; while from one of the windows the amputated arms and legs were being flung out upon a small square below. In front of the door lay the wounded, who had been deposited there as fast as they arrived, awaiting their turn. Many of them were already dead.[12]

When Wellington withdrew from Talavera, the hospitals with their staff and remaining 1,000 patients fell into French hands. This led to some interesting comparisons between the standards of medical care provided by the two enemies. Certainly the British hospital was too small for its purpose and there was overcrowding with patients lying on the floor in the corridors. Despite efforts by the purveying staff to procure beds and other equipment from army stores and local sources, there was also a shortage of these vital supplies. Doctors visited the wards but the wounded were, in at least some cases, expected to dress each other's wounds. When the French forces entered the town, they found provisions secreted by the Spanish and mattresses, blankets and food were liberally distributed amongst the English wounded. Sir John Fox Burgoyne, a senior engineer officer, was moved to comment.

> After the battle of Talavera . . . our wounded were put up as well as we thought they could be, in some large buildings in the town, and laid on the ground in their blankets. They were necessarily left to the mercy of the enemy . . . When the French entered, a general officer visited the hospital and said the accommodation was not at all sufficient for 'de brave soldats'; and before evening, the town was ransacked for mattresses, and the condition of these poor patients was greatly ameliorated in every respect.[13]

When Marshall Mortier visited the hospital a week later he commented on its cleanliness, which he apparently compared favourably with French hospitals. The view shared by some British military officers (Burgoyne was perhaps one) that the French hospitals during this period were superior to the British is not borne out by the experiences related by patients and doctors. Andrew Jordan of the 91st Foot was admitted to two French hospitals in the Pyrenees whilst suffering an attack of fever. In the first he was left in 'a most deplorable situation' with no medicines or attention by a surgeon, whilst in the second, a converted chapel, he lay in the aisle on a little straw. The hospital was unguarded and he eventually recovered sufficiently to escape.[14] Many French soldiers fared no better. A lieutenant in the Chasseurs à Cheval of the Guard says of a general hospital in Calabria:

> The poor patients were all laid on the bare floors without blankets, water, and without hope. Three hundred died the first day, sixty-five every day thereafter.[15]

Surgeon Pierre François Percy describes another French hospital:

> The courtyard is poisoned by the substances emptied into an open ditch, which overflows. Corpses are piled at the foot of the stairs leading to the main rooms, where they empty themselves, spreading a frightful odour. The stench is general in the wards, each mattress having harboured ten or twelve patients without ever having been washed.[16]

According to Percy, Napoleon despaired at the state of his hospitals, '. . . he swears, rants, and the evil continues'. French historians have also damned the Emperor's hospitals. One described them as the 'tombs of the Grand Army'. Another has said of the hospitals in Spain:

> They were antechambers to death; the sick were tended by Spanish nurses who were waiting for an opportunity to kill them, and by French auxillaries, soldiers who had often inflicted their own wounds and, at the first opportunity, would vanish into the human scum of both sexes which followed the columns.[17]

Throughout the years 1810 and 1811 the number of British general hospitals in the Peninsula fluctuated, depending on the military situation. For instance, when Wellington occupied the Lines of Torres Vedras, the number of hospitals was quickly reduced from thirteen to four. Some convalescents were of necessity housed in ships in Lisbon harbour. When the British later pursued Masséna's retreating army out of Portugal, new general hospitals were set up at various stations on the Tagus river. This allowed hospital supplies and medical attendants to be sent to the hospitals along the river. As the army advanced farther, sick men were evacuated from these hospitals to Lisbon, allowing them to be closed and new hospitals were formed in even more forward situations, for example at Coimbra and Celerico in northern Portugal. By the end of 1811 the army had dispersed into winter quarters over a wide area and all men unfit to march had been sent to the general hospital at Celerico.

Celerico was a wretched place without suitable accommodation, the buildings being crowded and insanitary. Sickness in the army was at an unexpected high with over 17,000 in the hospitals. Wellington described the number of sick at Celerico as 'astonishing'. He added that he had seen no 'bad cases' there, but this is contradicted by Cornet Francis Hall who witnessed not just the overcrowding but also a high mortality.

> During the autumn of 1811, at Celerico only, from 50 to 100 men were buried daily, and even after I arrived in the winter, from ten to twenty corpses were carried daily through the streets with scarcely the fragment of a tattered cloak, or a few boughs, to shroud their ghastly remains, and in this state were flung into a hole, which constituted a common receptacle without the town. Death was too common a guest to be treated ceremoniously. During the sultriest part of the season the crowded state of the hospitals (an evil irremediable, perhaps, considering the means of accommodation) tended greatly to increase the virulence of the contagion. Two patients occupied each bed, and when one died another was brought in to fill his place, and share in mind as well as body, the infection of his disease.[18]

100

In these conditions vermin and insects abounded. Lieutenant John Cooke, also a visitor to Celerico in 1811, says that so many flies settled on the faces of the sick that those who were still strong enough were 'obliged to tear them off their faces and squeeze them to death with their hands'. He saw the medical officers overwhelmed with work and falling sick themselves.[19]

When superior accommodation was available, there was at least the possibility of a hospital being better ordered and more hygienic. A case in point was the pleasant university town of Coimbra, where in 1811 the general hospital was located in large convents. Assistant Surgeon Walter Henry arrived in Coimbra in the summer, when there were approximately a thousand sick in the town.

> I was directed to cross to the other side of the Mondego and take charge of a ward of about a hundred poor wounded fellows, lately brought in from the front, and now quartered in the Francisco convent . . . The long corridors of the convent were occupied by a double row of beds containing the sick and wounded, classified into wards according to the nature of the case, with a medical officer, ward master, and sufficient number of orderlies to each (1 for 8 or 10 patients), a common kitchen for the whole, a purveyor to provide supplies, and an apothecary to prepare medicines. Often I have stopped on entering to admire the picturesque perspective of the long corridors . . . now appointed to the solace of pain, the preservation of life, and the best duties of humanity and benevolence.[20]

Henry's favourable account of the medical services at Coimbra is supported by Captain George Napier who received treatment there. The medical staff, he says, 'were indefatigable in their endeavours to make every officer and soldier under their care as comfortable as they could'.[21] When one considers the contrasting conditions in the hospitals in 1811, it is not suprising to learn that in December Wellington himself ordered 400 men to be transferred from Celerico to Coimbra.

What was needed in the middle years of the war was systematic change in the general hospitals to ensure that the high standards that were occasionally attained at hospitals such as Coimbra became routine. This, like the transport arrangements, was a major challenge facing James McGrigor when he arrived in the Peninsula in 1812. Typically, he wasted no time in assessing the medical situation. Although he was a strong supporter of the regimental hospitals, it was obvious that one of his first tasks was to improve the general hospitals. Accordingly he undertook a tour of inspection, travelling on horseback through incessant rain through the Portuguese countryside which had been ravaged by the French. Predictably he found Celerico to be an unhealthy location with an excess mortality in the dilapidated houses which served as hospitals. At Coimbra, where he spent a full week, he commended the choice of buildings which were well ventilated, but even here there were problems with some irregularities in the hospital stores, and a high rate of typhus and hospital gangrene in the wards. When he inspected the medical registers, he discovered that many discharged patients had quick relapses of disease and had to return to the hospitals. McGrigor instituted immediate improvements at Coimbra, further dividing and classifying the sick by disease and degree of recovery, and ensuring their placement in separate wards and buildings. This simple measure was later duplicated in other hospitals and did much to limit the spread of contagious disease.

Under McGrigor's influence, the medical activities in the Peninsula's hospitals became better documented and more regulated. As has been alluded to, there had been previous attempts to raise standards by the issue of regulations. Notably in 1801 recommendations pertaining to the responsibilities of the hospital's medical and subordinate staff had been circulated. However, during 1812 and 1813 a list of recommended treatments and a more detailed set of hospital directions and regulations appeared. It was again stipulated that there should be separate wards for different diseases. Patients with 'continued fever', dysentery, and surgical problems were to be kept apart, ideally in a separate building. Each ward was to have good ventilation and overcrowding was to be avoided. Each patient was to have at least five feet of space allocated. Subordinate staff were to be employed so that there was one orderly for every eight patients and an assistant wardmaster and nurse for each floor or compartment of the hospital. Wards were to be fumigated with nitric acid under the direction of the principal medical officer. The plaster walls were to be whitewashed and wooden pallets scoured with soap and water.

The medical staff had to visit the wards at least twice a day, at nine o'clock in the morning and at seven o'clock in the evening. Each medical officer was to keep a case book detailing the name, age, disease and treatment of each patient. When a new patient was admitted to the hospital, he was to be examined by the principal medical officer or other doctor. He was also to be washed with warm water and soap, to have his hair combed and cut, and to be provided with a 'well-aired shirt' and other hospital dress. The wording of the regulations hint at the poor state of discipline in some general hospitals. For example, 'Swearing, indecent conversation and every species of gaming are most strictly prohibited', and later, 'No poultry, pigeons, pigs, rabbits, dogs, or other animals likely to breed vermin, or create dirt, are to be kept by any person whatsoever within the precinct of the hospital.' Recreational alcohol consumption on the wards was also strongly discouraged.[22]

It is reasonable to assume that the regulations reflected the contemporary views of the army's senior medical officers. Certainly, John Hennen, who worked long hours in general hospitals in the Peninsula and in Belgium, supported the measures. In his textbook he stresses the importance of choosing a suitable building for the hospital – ideally something high, dry and detached with sufficient doors and windows to allow good ventilation. Sizeable public buildings, churches, granaries, convents, barns or unusually large private houses might be used. He stipulates that ideally the individual rooms should have open fireplaces to further encourage the free flow of air, and be big enough to hold from twelve to sixteen beds, a number observable by the wardmaster and easier to keep clean than a larger contingent. Also the accumulation of 'animal effluvia' was diminished. Hennen gives considerable details of the allocation of space he considered reasonable but essentially each bed was to stand alone, away from the walls and raised from the floor in at least thirty-six square feet, more if the ceilings were low. Where enough soldiers could not be found to ready the hospital for the wounded, Hennen suggested hiring local labourers. He was mindful of the need to keep discipline in the hospitals, commenting that, 'there is no body of men more troublesome when left to themselves than soldiers: they have so long acclimatised to have all their wants supplied or anticipated, and have in fact been completely transformed into machines, activated and directed by their superiors that if uncontrolled they are entirely helpless or degenerate.'[23]

Not all the new rules were welcomed by either the medical staff or the patients. When Sergeant William Lawrence was admitted to the general hospital at Estremoz in 1812, alcohol was strictly forbidden. According to Lawrence, 'this was more of a hardship than our wounds'. He and his comrades resorted to lowering a kettle on a string out of the hospital window so that it could be filled by the owner of a wineshop on the opposite side of the street. When he was subsequently admitted to Ciudad Rodrigo, he encountered a more relaxed regimen. He says the doctors and attendants were kind and he was permitted an unrestricted diet and also alcohol.[24]

McGrigor worked tirelessly to improve the medical services, and whenever possible he personally supervised the hospitals under his control. He makes frequent brief appearances in the military and medical memoirs of the wars. At Vera in northern Spain, Judge Advocate General Larpent tells of McGrigor's disgruntlement when the large public room he had directed to be cleaned for use as a hospital was used for a religious service. Walter Henry witnessed McGrigor's efforts in the hospital at Aire, '. . . he generally gave his officers plenty of work when humanity and the public service required it; and he made them do their work well too'.

In January 1813 McGrigor went on a further exhaustive general hospital tour. He particularly wanted to get information first hand from the hospital staff. Although Celerico remained problematic with a high incidence of strange fevers, there were no other major problems. In a later medical article on the Peninsula, McGrigor praised the general hospitals, saying that 'several' were in excellent order.[25] Wellington also visited some of the hospitals and reported his 'perfect satisfaction with the whole of them'. The commander in chief was particularly pleased at the large number of men being discharged for duty. He applauded the exertions of the hospital staff. Undoubtedly, from this time in the war there was an improvement and Fortescue's wholesale condemnation of the general hospitals as 'hotbeds of waste and dishonest dealing' was no longer applicable. However, it would be equally wrong to believe that all hospitals in the later years of the war were well equipped and organised. Despite his best efforts, McGrigor could not be always on the scene and some hospitals were still housed in unsuitable accommodation and inadequately supplied. A major battle still caused intolerable over-crowding. After the Battle of Vitoria Larpent visited the general hospital in the nearby city.

> I have been over the hospital and the scene which I there witnessed was most terrible; seventeen or eighteen hundred men, without legs or arms, or with dreadful wounds, and having had nothing to eat for two or three days, their misery extreme, and not nearly hands sufficient to dress or take care of the men – English, Portuguese, Spaniards, and French altogether, though the Spaniards and Portuguese had at first no provision at all for their purpose. Half the wounded have been scattered around the villages in the neighbourhood: and there are still many to come in, who arrive hourly, and are lying in all the passages and spare places around the hospital.[26]

General hospitals were most suitable for a static campaign and they remained vulnerable to the rapid movement of the army through northern Spain when the hospital stores were left behind and locally purchased drugs and dressings were of poor quality. This happened at Bilbao in September 1813. James Hale of the 9th Foot was admitted to the hospital after being wounded at San Sebastian and surviving a traumatic sea journey from Passages.

> . . . our hospital was about half way between the sea and that town, and had been formally built for the purpose of a rope walk, but to all appearance it had not been much in use. It was two stories high, and having a good boarded floor on the second story, it made a middling good hospital. This was such a hospital as is seldom to be seen; for there were about thirteen hundred men in it, all wounded; and what

is most remarkable, about twelve hundred were in one room, for there was no partition to divide us from one end of the hospital to the other, which was of a great length.There we lay for nearly two months without any beds or bedding.[27]

According to Hale most of the men had lost their belongings and only owned the soiled clothes they were admitted in. There were no utensils in the hospital except for a few buckets and kettles purchased locally to boil food in.

Private William Wheeler of the 51st Regiment was wounded in the Pyrenees in late 1813 and was originally admitted to the hospital at St Jean de Luz before being successively moved to the convalescent hospital at Santander and then the general and convalescent hospitals at Fuenterrabia. John Green of the 68th was wounded near San Sebastian and experienced the general hospitals at Santander and Passages. Both men are reliable witnesses and are generally complimentary about the hospitals, although in the general hospital at Fuenterrabia Wheeler noticed there was still a high incidence of disease and the scene in the 'incurable ward' was one of 'continued misery and woe'.[28] In the general hospital at Santander there was evidence of the judicious measures in medical administration which had substantially improved the care of the sick and wounded. The hospital was located in a large, well ventilated building and newly admitted men were sent to different wards and provided with a bed and bedding. All regimental clothing was taken and stored and the men were given a set of white hospital clothes including a long coat, a flannel waistcoat, a pair of trousers, a shirt and a flannel cap.[29]

Similar measures were in place at Passages where, in September 1813, the surgeons attended twice a day to dress wounds and 'every medical officer was attentive to his charge and did all that could be done for our recovery'. Each man was provided with a 'hardened bed-tick filled with straw, two blankets, one pair of sheets and one rug'. However, until hospital stores arrived from England, the men had previously had to make do with bedding fashioned out of biscuit bags sewn together and filled with fern.[30] Availability of adequate supplies was undoubtedly one of the major factors determining the quality of general hospitals. Wellington's thrust into northern Spain in 1813 had the advantage of liberating the coastal area and allowing the hospitals to be opened in seaports where the provision of supplies was much easier than for centres inland. In Passages, a special depot for medical stores was opened. The change in the nature of the campaign also had the advantage of shortening the line of evacuation for sick and wounded.

Wheeler's account gives a number of interesting insights into hospital life. At Santander, he helped the doctor with 'the books', illustrating how less severely wounded or sick patients were liable to be used for routine hospital tasks. At Fuenterrabia, where evidently there were problems, he criticised the army's chaplains for the lack of spiritual support available to the sick.

> There was no minister of religion to cheer the dying sinner . . . if these revered gentlemen were stationed at the sick depots and made to attend to the hospitals, they would be much more usefully employed than following the army with their brace of dogs and a gun.[31]

An issue which has been little explored is the attitude of the local population to the opening of British military hospitals in their towns and cities. The number of pre-exisiting hospitals in Spain was limited. The main city hospital in Madrid was apparently well constructed and able to accommodate 3,000 patients. French army doctors installed water cisterns and latrines and set aside wards for the use of the Grand Army. However, the sharing of a Spanish hospital was exceptional and the British Army generally relied on being able to use large civic and religious buildings. Understandably, the arrival in their midst of sizeable numbers of soldiers with contagious diseases caused anxiety amongst local doctors, dignitaries and the general populus. Even healthy troops frequently commented that they were not made as welcome in Spain as in Portugal. The uneasy relationship between the locals and the British medical services came to a head in Santander in early 1814, when there was a concerted effort by the Spanish to close the general hospitals which totalled 4,000 beds in local buildings and temporary accommodation. Santander was a particularly suitable location as it had a large harbour and abundant shipping to move supplies. A Spanish physician regularly visited the hospitals and declared that there was a 'dangerous malady' which necessitated a state of quarantine. This restricted the movement not only of the sick but of the medical staff, the hospital attendants and the supervising military officers. It was also requested that the British not use the harbour for any purpose.

Wellington consulted with his own doctors, who acknowledged a few cases of typhus but denied that any serious epidemic of illness justifying quarantine affected the hospital station. He then wrote a stinging letter to the local board of health pointing out that the inconvenience to the town's people had been alleviated by the importing of prefabricated buildings from England for hospital use, and by the full payment of all hospital expenses. He observed that, '. . . the inhabitants of the town have always manifested an extreme sensibility to the inconvenience which was the natural result of the fortunate circumstances of the war, and have made many indirect efforts to remove the hospitals'. He acknowledged the disturbance caused but reminded the local officers that 'it will appear extraordinary to the world that the British troops, after having rendered such services to the Spanish nation, should be obliged to go to England to look for hospitals'. The Duke's intervention was timely and the hospitals stayed open.[32] The prefabricated buildings referred to by Wellington were portable wooden huts sent out from England. McGrigor had previously seen them used as hospitals in the West Indies. In early 1813 he suggested their adoption in Spain to Wellington, who wrote to the government requesting shipping of the necessary timber and carpenters. The largest collection of these temporary hospital buildings was located near Castello Rodrigo where 4,000 convalescent patients were housed.[33]

After the last major battle of the Peninsular War at Toulouse, the general hospital in the city was well provided with medical staff, supplies and medicines. By May 1814 the hospitals at Toulouse and those on the coast of northern Spain had been closed, their patients embarked for home, whilst many of the hospital stores and a number of the portable hospital buildings were dispatched to the forces fighting in America. However, little more than a year later, the army medical department faced a fresh challenge at Waterloo. Wounded were transported the nine miles to Brussels where six general hospitals had been hurriedly opened – the Jesuits, Elizabeth, Annonciate, Orpheline, Notre Dame and Gendarmerie. British wounded who could not be accommodated in Brussels were sent by canal to Antwerp where a further five hospitals were established – the Minimes, Façon, Augustines, Hôtel de Nord and La Corderie. Spare hospital beds at Bruges, Ghent and Ostend could not be used for lack of transport. In total the Brussels hospitals housed 2,500 allied patients and there were a similar number at Antwerp.[34]

The only detailed surviving account of the organisation of the general hospitals is by John Thomson, Professor of Military Surgery at Edinburgh. Although there is little reason to doubt his general observations, he had little first-hand experience of military hospitals and he only arrived in Brussels three weeks after the battle. Here he spent twelve days making a detailed inspection, before passing a further several days in Antwerp. He was impressed by what he saw.

> The wards of the hospitals in which the wounded were placed were large and well-aired, their beds, in general, excellent, and the supply of bedclothes such as to allow of their being changed as often as necessary. Provisions of every kind were good, cheap, and abundant.[35]

He noted that, wherever possible, similar cases were brought together in the same wards to minimise the spread of contagious diseases.

Thomson's observations suggest that many of the organisational improvements made in the hospitals in the latter years of the Peninsular War were retained in the hospitals after Waterloo. He portrays the general hospitals in Brussels as a great success. However, others who visited the hospitals before him were less impressed. John Hennen was in Brussels immediately after the battle. He agrees with Thomson that the Jesuits and Elizabeth hospitals were clean and well ventilated, but he says that the Gendarmerie, the last of the hospitals to be opened, was filthy.[36] It had originally been a police barracks and was unfavourably situated on low ground. The 300 unfortunate patients were mostly French prisoners of war. In Antwerp, Thomson was accompanied by James Simpson, an advocate. Simpson is complimentary about the Façon hospital which housed 800 British wounded. The large barracks were ideal for a general hospital and the men were well cared for and doing well. In contrast the hospital at La Corderie, a building 1,300 feet long originally constructed as a rope-walk, was a more depressing scene. The 1,500 French wounded were arranged in four long rows of beds and were faring much worse than their British counterparts in other hospitals. However, Simpson, like Thomson, makes no criticism of hospital management in Antwerp.[37]

It is reasonable to say that the British general hospitals after Waterloo ultimately provided high quality and well regulated care for many of the wounded – hence Thomson's laudatory comments – but that immediately after the battle they were inadequate for the number of wounded entering Brussels. In the event, only considerable help from the local inhabitants of the city prevented the army's hospitals being completely overwhelmed. The houses and churches of Brussels became temporary hospitals and attention was lavished on the wounded. On the eve of the battle, the mayor of the city invited his fellow citizens to send him every type of bedding they could spare. Anyone who had old linen or lint was requested to give it without delay to the parish priest. Local ladies dressed the wounded, in part compensating for the lack of a trained hospital corps. The comments of Edward Costello, who injured his hand at Quatre Bras, are typically generous.[38]

> In the morning [the day after Waterloo] the scene surpassed all imagination and baffles description: thousands of wounded French, Belgians, Prussians, and English; carts, waggons and every other attainable vehicle were continually arriving heaped with sufferers. The wounded were laid, friends and foes indiscriminately, on straw, with avenues between them, in every part of the city, and nearly destitute of surgical attendance. The human and indefatigable exertions of the fair ladies of Brussels however, greatly made up for this deficiency; numbers were busily employed – some strapping and bandaging wounded, others serving out tea, coffee, soups, and other soothing nourishments; while many occupied themselves stripping the sufferers of their gory and saturated garments, and dressing them in clean shirts and other habiliments.[38]

The experience of the Flanders campaign, the Peninsular War and Waterloo was repeated wherever the British Army campaigned and opened hospitals. The quality of hospitals always largely depended on the nature of the campaign, the local geography and climate, the quality of the medical staff, and the influence of military officers. In the West Indies in the last years of the eighteenth century, the hospitals were scattered through the islands over a distance of 600 miles. The medical board was determined not to have a repeat of the Flanders debacle and vast quantities of hospital stores were shipped to the forces. Initially there was some success and, in Cantlie's words, 'the troops were annihilated in spite of good hospital treatment'.[39] However, it would have been difficult to sustain even a modern hospital system in the face of rampant insect-borne diseases such as malaria and yellow fever, and the accommodation was soon regarded as being overcrowded and insanitary. Senior medical officers, including William Fergusson, suggested that hospitals be built at higher altitudes where the frequency of fevers was noticeably reduced. This advice was not necessarily valued by commanding military officers.[40]

Another example of a severe epidemic of disease flooding the general hospitals occurred at Walcheren in 1809. The British invasionary force was decimated by a lethal combination of infectious diseases.[41] The main town, Flushing, had been destroyed during the earlier British siege and there was a disastrous shortage of surviving buildings to serve as hospitals. Private houses, churches and warehouses were used and conditions were appalling. Men were 'packed together in hovels, such as would be thought unfit for dogs, exposed to the noxious night airs, and in some cases with only damp straw to lie on'.[42] In the town of Veere, every morning several hundred feverish men crept out of the hospital, which had been installed in the immense cathedral-like church, and crawled along to the town square where they drank a mixture of port wine and bark from barrels. Medical officers also fell sick and civilian help was sought. An inspection of the hospitals in late 1809 was recalled by an officer in his diary, '. . . the miserable, dirty, stinking holes some of the troops were of necessity crammed into were more shocking than it is possible to express'.[43] By the time James McGrigor arrived on the scene, the shortage of some supplies had been partly rectified, but there were still cases of two soldiers having to share one bed. At a later public enquiry the hospital arrangements were criticised as being overly complacent with inadequate supply of vital stores and personnel.

In a situation analogous to the Peninsular War, the general hospitals of the American War of 1812 were very mixed. After the Battle of New Orleans in 1815, the arrangements were commended, but after Lundy's Lane a year earlier, the greatest battle on Canadian soil, the hospitals left much to be desired. According to Surgeon William Dunlop of the 89th Foot, the hospital at Fort George was a 'ruinous fabric built of logs'. The small buildings were inadequate and wounded lay on the floor on straw or in cramped berths. It was even impossible for the doctors to reach them to dress wounds.[44] The American hospitals of the war were afflicted by the same problems. Dr James Mann, in charge of the American medical services in upstate New York, was a pioneer in the mould of McGrigor. He had well developed views on what constituted the ideal military hospital which mostly agreed with his British colleague's. He emphasised the importance of good ventilation, stating that rooms should be at least twenty-four feet by thirty feet in size with ceilings at least eleven feet high. Such a ward would be large enough to hold twenty patients under the attention of at least two nurses. He also suggested a separate room where patients about to be admitted could be washed and dressed in clean linen. He agreed with McGrigor that it was essential to keep good hospital records relating to the patients and their medical treatments.[45]

Throughout the war, there was a necessity for general hospitals in England to serve the home battalions and also to receive wounded and sick soldiers from overseas. The latter function was particularly important after a campaign associated with high levels of sickness requiring large-scale evacuations. Examples include Sir John Moore's Corunna campaign, where the troops disembarked on the south coast, and the Walcheren campaign where the landings were in south-east England. Unfortunately, many general hospitals, notably those at Deal, Gosport and Plymouth, were closed between 1806 and 1809 in order to save money. Unsurprisingly, the regimental hospitals were unable to cope with the 11,000 sick of the Walcheren expedition and temporary accommodation was hastily created between Harwich in the north and Dover in the south. These hospitals received almost as bad a press as the facilities in Walcheren. Thomas Wright, a physician and former hospital mate during the American War of Independence, described the barracks at Harwich, which housed 400 patients.

> On a cheerful hill over Harwich has been constructed a barrack for infantry etc., the soil forms a natural declivity by which the drains of rain water, of damp and filth are provided for, should the artificial drains and sewers be obstructed. The houses or huts are of wood and disjunct, with wide intervening ways, every apartment opening to the street without communication with any other, every room ventilated through the ceiling so that the light non-respirable airs must be perpetually borne up while the heavier flow off below, at least during summer, so that if, with due attention to cleanliness and fumigation, contagion could not be obviated, yet the insulated state of each ward would prevent the progress of it.

Although some thought appears to have been given to the design of the hospital, Wright can say little positive of the patients and staff.

> The pallid look of the breathing spectres was so ghastly, they exhibited a type of the resurrection, and their unhappy attendants, too few to administer relief to half the number through fatigue, little calculated to communicate hope or confidence in the sick.[46]

John Harris of the 95th Rifles fell sick on Walcheren and was later sent home and admitted to the temporary hospital at Hythe. He was in a ward of eleven men which 're-filled ten times, the former patients being carried out to the grave'. Many of the men died on the floor in the night, others in the baths which were used for treatment.[47] A civilian visitor was horrified: 'I have been through civil hospitals but never saw anything like it in them . . . gaunt spectres of men, some half-dressed, tottering along between rows of beds. Others, still weaker, lounged on their beds, attenuated, pale, acute of feature, balanced between relapse and recovery.'[48]

An officer of the 71st Regiment originally wanted to be an actor but joined the army impulsively after an attack of stage fright. When sick after Walcheren, he was admitted to the hospital at Braeburne in Kent, where the orderlies appear to have been no better than at Elvas and elsewhere in the Peninsula.

> All the time I was in the hospital, my soul was oppressed by the distress of my fellow sufferers, and shocked at the conduct of the hospital men. Often I have seen them fighting over the expiring bodies of the patients, their eyes not yet closed in death, for articles of apparel that two had seized at once; cursing and oaths mingled with the dying groans and prayers of the poor sufferers. How dreadful to think, as they were carried from each side of me, it might be my turn next! There was none to comfort, none to give a drink of water, with a pleasant countenance.[49]

Similar scenes of overcrowding and inadequate staffing occurred in the hospitals receiving the remnants of Sir John Moore's typhus-ridden army after the retreat to Corunna. James McGrigor was at this time Inspector of Hospitals in Portsmouth and he did his best to house the 6,000 sick by using all the ordinary hospital accommodation in the town, converting barracks into hospitals, and by taking over the previously unused part of the large naval hospital at Haslar. The hospital's medical staff included regular medical officers, officers of the militia, local civilian practitioners and London medical students. Despite McGrigor's efforts, the available space was insufficient and he had to resort to floating hospitals, which, by his own admission, were of very low quality. It was not only the patients who died, and the shortage of doctors and orderlies was in part due to the relentless spread of contagious disease. In the appallingly overcrowded converted barracks at Ramsgate, only five out of thirty-eight orderlies escaped and twelve out of the fifteen doctors contracted typhus, one dying. At Portsmouth, out of 116 medical officers in the hospitals, twenty-one suffered severe attacks of fever and six died.[50]

The events after Walcheren and Corunna confirmed the impossibility of coping without a significant number of well established general hospitals at home and, following vitriolic correspondence between the members of the army medical board, some hospitals were reopened. The largest of these were at Plymouth and Gosport with a depot hospital on the Isle of Wight. All were well placed to receive sick from the Peninsula and other stations abroad. A further large establishment in Chelsea, the York Hospital, was used in the training of the army's doctors (see Chapter I). The vilified hospital orderlies were increasingly drawn from the veterans' battalions.

In addition to the general hospitals at home and abroad, there were facilities which shared many of the features of the general hospitals but which had more specific functions. These included convalescent, receiving and passing hospitals. Convalescents were divided into classes depending on their degree of recovery from wounds and sickness. The convalescent hospital was usually established outside the walls of a town. Every week, men were moved from the convalescent wards of the general hospital to the convalescent hospital. No man was discharged from here until he was fit to carry out the soldier's normal duties. When he was fully recovered he then went to the depot, which was under the charge of the military commandant, where he did some duty until his date of discharge when he rejoined his regiment.[51] In theory, the convalescent hospitals were designed to ease the transfer of men back to their regiments from their original placement in the general hospitals. In practice, the policy backfired as certain of the hospitals became a constant source of trouble owing to the indiscipline of the patients and the accumulation of malingerers who had no intention of returning to active duty. The large convalescent hospital at Belem in Lisbon became particularly notorious with its malingerers known as the 'Belem Rangers'. A general order issued in October 1810 noted that the number of men shown as sick in regimental returns was more than double those on the hospital books at Lisbon. Soldiers supposed to be sick had been seen walking around the city entirely well. The order continued, 'Soldiers sent to the convalescent barracks at Belem are not sent for their amusement, but for the benefit of their health.'[52] Often the men placed in charge of these institutions were themselves invalids and were unable to exert the necessary control.

Receiving hospitals were sometimes set up around the edges of towns with larger general hospitals. As the name implies, these were designed initially to receive ill and wounded men and to provide triage, basic hygiene, and any necessary first aid prior to their admission to the general hospital. A large building could be used but on other occasions a smaller house or even tents might suffice.[53] Passing or intermediate hospitals were established along lines of communication and provided the only link between the general and regimental hospitals. They provided care for either the casualties of sick convoys in transit for the general hospitals, or for sick men discharged from other hospitals and returning to the front. Both the receiving and passing hospitals were sensible innovations, plugging gaps in the army's field organisation, and both types were increasingly used in the latter years of the Peninsular War. In general there were not different hospitals for different arms of the service, although in 1811 a hospital for the exclusive use of artillery and engineer units was opened in Lisbon. Its existence reflected the fact that the Ordnance had its own, albeit small, medical establishment. At home there were separate Ordnance hospitals at Woolwich, Plymouth and Chatham.[54]

Outside the fixed general hospitals, the major provision for inpatient treatment were the regimental hospitals, which, it is worth reiterating, were widely used in earlier conflicts. The basic principle was the creation of numerous small hospitals which were under regimental control and close to the line of fighting. By treating the less sick and less severely wounded in their own regimental hospitals, the strain on the general hospitals could be reduced. Particularly there was less overcrowding and a lower demand for medical staff. In Pringle's words the general hospitals needed to 'receive only as the regimental hospitals cannot accommodate and the sick that cannot be moved with the army'.[55]

McGrigor was a powerful supporter of the regimental hospital system in the Peninsula. In his *Sketch of the Medical History of the British Armies in the Peninsula of Spain and Portugal* he describes the normal regimental hospital procedures and the advantages that accrued.

> The divisions of the army composed of from eight to fifteen or sixteen regiments, under the command of a lieutenant-general, were each of them under the medical superintendence of an inspectatorial officer, to whom the regiment reported, and who regulated all the medical concerns of the division. It was his duty to see that, however short a time a battalion or a corps rested in one place, a regimental hospital was established; indeed as they carried with them medicines, bedding, stores, and all the materials of a hospital, a regiment might be said to have its hospital constantly established even on the march. It was frequently established in the face of an enemy, and nearly within the reach of his guns. When a regiment halted, after getting the men under cover in some building, and constructing chimneys, the first object was to make bedsteads, getting at the same time additional mattresses of straw, rushes &c. It was really surprising to see with what rapidity this was done; so much were regiments in the habit of it, that latterly, I found the hospitals complete in every thing, and the

men most comfortably lodged in a few days after a regiment had halted. In short, by making every corps constantly keep up an establishment for itself, we could prevent the general hospitals being crowded: much severe and acute disease was treated in its early and only curative stage, and no slight wounds or ailments were ever sent off from the regiments: by which means the effective force of the army was kept up, or perhaps increased by several thousand men.[56]

The equipment for an average regimental hospital consisted of twenty-four stretchers, twelve sets of bedding, and cooking, feeding and ward utensils. It was normally carried on a bullock cart. The hospitals could treat sixty men with the twelve sets of bedding reserved for the more seriously ill, the others being expected to improvise bedding from straw or rushes. Regimental hospitals were under the immediate supervision of the regimental surgeons who were in turn accountable to the Inspector General of Army Hospitals or other senior members of the medical staff in the vicinity. The surgeons were directed to visit the hospital at least twice a day. Their responsibilities included the routine medical care of the patients, the management of the hospital expenditure, and the maintenance of accurate records of admissions and discharges, and diseases and treatment. They would also be expected to keep the hospital well ventilated and fumigated. Where a regimental hospital lost its own surgeons for whatever reason, and there was no military surgeon available, local civilian practitioners were necessarily employed.

The doctors were helped in their duties by a sergeant, a nurse and an orderly. The sergeant was selected by the surgeon and was expected to take charge of the hospital stores, oversee the nurse and the orderly, and ensure cleanliness and discipline. According to regulations drawn up in 1803 he had to impose a routine in the hospital. He had to make sure that:

> . . . every patient has his face and hands washed, and his hair combed and tied, before the surgeon visits the hospital; and those men who are able to sit up are regularly to fold up their bedding, and to sweep under their beds every morning by six o'clock in summer and eight in winter: they are likewise to separate their bedding and to air it two hours every day in fine weather. As quietness and rest are absolutely required in the hospital, great care is to be taken that every duty be performed with least possible noise, and that at night the house be perfectly quiet. Every man must be in his bed by eight o'clock in winter, and nine in summer; and no conversation should be permitted after that time.

The nurse attended the sick, administered medicine and comforts, and helped to keep the wards clean. She was to wash the bedding, but curiously, the regulations stipulate that the 'personal washing' of the sick was to be done by 'some woman out of the hospitals' who was paid up to 4d. per man per week in the infantry and 6d. in the cavalry. On campaign, female nurses were often unavailable and their duties were performed by male orderlies.[57] During the Flanders campaign, the regimental hospitals proved less of a disaster than the general hospitals, although their role was restricted by the lack of suitable transport to move the sick and by the tactical nature of the fighting. They absorbed some of the work from the general hospitals and there is evidence that the wide dispersal of sick in the barns and outhouses used as regimental hospitals reduced cross-infection and the number of deaths from typhus and other contagious diseases. It is, of course, difficult to work out how much the higher death rates in the general hospitals were attributable to the admission of more severe cases, and how much to the subsequent spread of disease due to overcrowding.

In the Peninsula, regimental hospitals were variably used throughout the war. In the early years their use was limited because of a lack of transport to carry the hospital equipment. This arose mainly out of Wellington's unwillingness to allow the necessary bullock carts to interfere with the movements of the army. At this time up to 90% of admissions were to the general hospitals. There were more soldiers treated at regimental level in 1810 and 1811, but it was McGrigor's arrival in 1812 which raised the profile of the regimental hospitals. He forcefully argued the case for a further increase in their use with Wellington but for some considerable time was frustrated by his chief's reluctance to release the vital transport. Some commanding officers did risk censure by allowing the use of wagons for this purpose. Wellington finally relented in December 1812 and McGrigor was suddenly given a free hand to institute his plans. He was fulsome in his praise of the burgeoning regimental facilities.

> Everywhere was to be seen a comfortable hospital for the sick, surgeons and commanding officers vying with each other who would construct the best and most comfortable hospitals for his corps . . . In a short time, the march of the sick from the regimental to the established hospitals to the rear was stopped: and it was high time, for the number that died on the way was very great.[58]

When McGrigor toured the regimental hospitals in the summer of the following year, he was again impressed with what he found. He attributed to them the reduction in fevers and hospital gangrene and noted that Wellington now fully supported the system, not least because the effective strength of the army had been increased. The soldiers themselves much preferred their own regimental hospitals where they could be treated amongst their friends and avoid the feared general hospitals. Over the course of the whole Peninsular War, death rates were approximately four times greater in the general hospitals than in the regimental facilities. However, again it is difficult to sort out cause and effect. The regimental hospitals may have been superior, or equally it may be that the most seriously ill men ended up in the larger fixed hospitals.

McGrigor invested much effort in the regimental hospital system and in his writings, which are the best single source of information, he understandably does not dwell on the disadvantages. Even more than the general hospitals the regimental institutions were vulnerable to the incompetence of individual medical officers. Private James Gunn of the Black Watch recounts just such a case after the retreat from Burgos. Wellington had previously requested that his general officers make inspections of hospitals when they happened to be in the area. Presumably as a result of this Lord Packenham arrived to inspect the regimental hospital.

As we were beginning to be pretty well rested a fever broke out among us. Nor either did I escape. Our hospital was but a very indifferent one but even although, it was the cause of making the character of a good man appear forcibly, this was our good and kind General Lord Packenham to whose good offices we were indebted for regaining our health to perform our duties again in the next campaign. And it happened in this way. He came one morning early to our village and called at the hospital. The sergeant appearing, he asked for the doctor. He was told none of them was come yet. 'What,' says his Lordship, 'do you mean to say that one of them does not attend here all night? Send for your head doctor immediately.'

The doctors made their appearance and so did the Colonel. The General, addressing the Colonel, said, 'I am surprised you do not command your doctors to attend to their duty and have one here all night.' The head doctor said he left instructions with the hospital sergeant what medicine to give, but if a change of medicine was required he was to send for us. 'Oh, and it is very likely you would come. But I tell you, if I find it so on my next visit, I will find you a passage home and there is plenty there able and willing to come here.' So saying he asked the doctor if those were all his patients. He answered, 'No, our worst cases we put up here', pointing to an outside stair with a tiled roof. His Lordship made a move to go up. The doctor said, 'Please, My Lord, up there is the worst cases we have.' 'Aye,' said His Lordship, 'I see you do not go up there, but walk before me.' So on entering, two poor fellows were laying there on a pallet of straw unconscious, and some snow on the floor. His Lordship enquired of the Colonel if he had not some masons or bricklayers in the regiment, if so to send for them immediately. And on their coming he told them to build a fireplace there. They said they had no lime. 'But,' said he, 'are there not plenty of mud on the street? Take it for mortar.' And so they did. Taking his leave he did come again and left instructions that as soon as any of the patients could be removed they were to be shifted from place to place for the benefit of change of air, which manoeuvre proved very efficacious for when the order came to advance, although not very strong, we were ready for the march and recruited our strength daily [so] that [on] our second days march we were surprised at ourselves.[59]

The army's senior medical officers vigorously debated the relative roles of the regimental and general hospitals. From a modern perspective, it seems clear that both types of hospital were necessary, and to a great degree interdependent. The number of men in each at any given time was bound to be largely determined by the nature of the campaign and the proportion of seriously sick and wounded. William Fergusson, who served in Flanders, the Peninsula and the West Indies, methodically rehearses the arguments in a general order to the Portuguese army medical department.

> The regimental hospital is the cardinal hinge on which the health of an army depends, the first resource of the sick soldier, and best security for maintaining the effective strength of the forces . . . in actual war, and during the rapid movement of troops, the sick must be left behind, and then general hospitals are necessary . . . it is essential that general hospitals should exist, and that too upon a scale commensurate with the greatness and humanity of this Christian country.

However, Fergusson was well aware of the drawbacks of the general hospitals.

> These hospitals will always prove a great, though a necessary evil, destructive of the effective strength of armies . . . A soldier sent to a general hospital is rarely restored to his corps during the campaign. The average duration of sickness in regimental hospitals is always less, and mortality smaller, not from superior medical treatment in the last, but from the unavoidable loss of time, and interruption of the means of cure, in transferring him to the first at the beginning of his distemper, the pains and danger of a journey under such circumstances, the despondency induced by the presence of many sick, the spectres of death about him, and the less tender attendance which he is apprehensive of meeting, and too often does actually meet, at the hands of hospital servants, who are unknown to [him] and therefore feel little interest in him.[60]

117

Fergusson's stance, favouritism for the regimental hospitals with a grudging acceptance of the absolute need for general hospitals, was common among army doctors. Undoubtedly there were divergent views and the hospital system was a cause of much trouble and jealousy. In this 'battle of the hospitals', James McGrigor was supported in his partiality for regimental hospitals by other senior figures such as the Inspector General, Francis Knight, Robert Jackson, Thomas Young and James Borland.[61] Jackson succinctly expressed their case; 'Good soldiers are generally unwilling to go to general hospitals and good surgeons are unwilling to separate good soldiers from their comrades.'[62]

Against them, arguing the case for the general hospitals, were equally respected figures of the time, including the Physician-General Lucas Pepys, the Surgeon-General Thomas Keate, and Physician Nathaniel Bancroft. They claimed, not without some justification, that mortality rates were higher and expenses greater in the general hospitals simply because the patients were more ill. Their insistence that the larger hospitals provided better care because of the higher professional qualifications of the physicians and staff surgeons, and also better food and wine, was a particular cause of resentment. The caustic nature of the debate is obvious from the following extract from a pamphlet written by McGrigor in reply to Bancroft's assertion that only physicians, and not regimental surgeons, were capable of supervising hospitals.

> Away with such dark and assassin-like insinuations. Speak out like a man – I am full prepared to meet you. I challenge you to state any one circumstance, which can occasion me the least pain on recollection. And to compel you, if possible, to accept this challenge, I thus publicly declare, that, unless you do speak out, I shall regard you in no better light than that of a malignant and dastardly assassin.[63]

A review of hospital admissions in the Peninsula during 1811–14 reveals the essential roles that both types of hospital played in the campaign. During this period the total number of hospital treatments, around 350,000, were divided almost equally between regimental and general hospitals. Of these admissions, around 230,000 men, approximately two thirds, were discharged back to duty. Unfortunately, for the earlier years there are no comprehensive returns available. Although the regimental hospitals may not have been used so extensively at this time, it appears that even in 1810 and early 1811, before McGrigor's arrival, they were always treating an average of 1,000 patients.

Whatever the relative merits of different types of hospital, it is evident that the system had its faults. Perhaps the two most important deficiencies were the lack of adequate medical care between the regimental and general facilities, and the absence of a proper trained hospital corps. From the earliest days of the army medical department there had been 'flying' or 'marching' hospitals. They were highly mobile, following the army on campaign and removing wounded from the field, transferring the most serious cases to the general hospitals behind the lines. Flying hospitals made a brief appearance in the Flanders campaign during 1794, but the lessons of earlier conflicts had been largely forgotten and they were little used later in the wars. The 'passing' or 'intermediate' hospitals were essentially rest stations and they crucially lacked the mobility of the flying hospitals. The latter could have provided vital additional medical care and much eased the transfer of men between the general and regimental hospitals. Apparently McGrigor did once raise the possibility of a flying hospital in the Peninsula, but again Wellington was concerned that a medical initiative might restrict the army's movements.

The second major drawback, the lack of a trained corps of men to staff the hospitals, was well known at the time but no decisive action was taken. As early as the Flanders campaign, when a third of the army were in the hospitals, a senior military officer, Major General Harcourt, proposed the formation of a separate medical corps. He appreciated that the use of convalescents to do nursing duties made proper management of the wards impossible. What was needed, said Harcourt, was a permanent hospital corps composed of men who showed, '. . . sobriety, honesty, and assiduous attention to the sick, with implicit and punctual obedience to the medical officers'.[64] A year later in the West Indies, a rare effort was made to form just such an organisation, The Royal Hospital Corps. However, the experiment lasted only a year. William Fergusson, in the West Indies at this time, suggested that the project failed mainly because the selection of men was left in the hands of the regiments.

> Had they a man amongst them whom they were tired of flogging, and could neither be induced to die or desert, he was the elect for the hospital corps, or at best he might be a simpleton, not fit to stand sentry in a position of trust, or so awkward in the ranks that he could not be trusted with a ball-cartridge. In short, such a collection of incorrigible and incapable villains I believe never was brought together, and it was a true relief to the army when their drunkenness and the yellow fever killed them off.[65]

He is supported in his views by Assistant Inspector of Hospitals Hector McLean, who says the men were, 'fitter for Botany Bay than employment requiring humanity or action'.[66] Despite this disaster, Fergusson strongly supported the creation of a hospital corps, and differed from many others in proposing the increased employment of women as nurses as, 'the worst women will generally make a better one, as being more handy and compassionate than an awkward clumsy man'.[67] Although the idea of a

119

hospital corps evidently had some support from military and medical officers, no further serious attempt to form one was made in the Napoleonic period and sick soldiers continued to be nursed by the regiment's outcasts.

It is important to remember that for the great majority of sick and wounded officers, the normal hospital accommodation was not even an option. Officers could not be treated with the men and they were almost invariably housed in private dwellings or hotels. Thus they avoided the worst of the hospitals and the high risk of contagious disease. However, their alternative accommodation was often of low quality. To prevent undue inconvenience to the local inhabitants, general orders were issued limiting the sick officer's claim to a bare room, the size dependent on rank. In Portuguese towns like Coimbra, Abrantes and Celerico, where the sick depots had been long established, the locals had become hardened by the army's constant demands and these orders were taken literally. The sick and exhausted officers arrived and found nothing but the floor to lie on. Furthermore, they relied on comrades or servants to seek out medical help, and any food or comforts had to be paid for.

The calamities which could befall an ill officer are well illustrated by the account of Captain George Wood who developed a debilitating fever after the Battle of Salamanca. Following a harrowing journey he reached a house in the nearby city.

> In this state of wretchedness we arrived at the wished-for town, and billets were procured for us; but on being conducted to mine, the inhabitants were gone out. This circumstance obliged me to lie on the steps of the door till they returned, which was in a few hours. On the arrival of the hostess, who was an old widow woman, she had me directly taken in, and a bed prepared for me, as well as she, being very poor, was able. The bed was on the floor in one corner of the room; however, it was such as generally fell to our subordinate lot. Having, with the assistance of this good woman, got into bed, my servant went in search of a doctor, but he could not procure one at that late hour. Here I lay in a most miserable condition, till my man, Standfast, came in the morning to know what I would take for breakfast, 'Take! my good fellow,' said I; 'what can be got?' He replied that there was a little tea left, after dividing our small stock with my brother sub on parting. 'But then, sir,' added he, 'there is no sugar, milk, bread, butter, or any thing besides.' Here was a state for a sick man to be in! Not a farthing of money had I seen since I left Lisbon; therefore, I desired him to take one of my shirts, and with what sum he could get for it, to buy some sugar, milk, butter and bread; he went, and soon brought me these necessary articles . . . This day a doctor came to me, he told me I was very ill, and sent me some medicine, and desired I

1. Sir James McGrigor
McGrigor headed the medical
department during the latter
years of the Peninsular War.
He was held in high esteem
by Wellington.
(The Army Medical Services
Museum)

2. George Guthrie
The greatest British surgeon of the
Napoleonic Wars.
(The Army Medical Services Museum)

3. The Battle of Corunna 1809
In the foreground the artist has portrayed a French surgeon tending to the wounded.
(Hulton Getty)

4. The Battle of Fuentes de Oñoro 1811
In the right foreground two British regimental surgeons dress the wounded whilst two
soldiers, probably bandsmen (note the discarded drum), carry an improvised stretcher.
The artist, Thomas Staunton St. Clare, served as an infantry officer in the Peninsula and
his paintings are regarded as among the most accurate views of the wars.
(National Army Museum, London)

5. The field of Waterloo
In the space of about six square miles, 50,000 men lay dead or wounded.
(National Army Museum, London)

6. Wounded are removed from the field of Waterloo in wagons
The dead are stripped and buried. The building in the background is the farm of La
Haye Sainte. (National Army Museum, London)

7. British wounded arriving in Brussels after the Battle of Waterloo
The locals gave valuable help which in part compensated for the inadequate hospitals.
(The Trustees of the National Museums of Scotland)

8. "Private, Hospital Corps"
The frontispiece from
The Army Medical Officer's
Manual Upon Active Service
by Regimental Surgeon J. G.
Van Millingen published in
1819. Unfortunately,
Van Millingen's plans for
a hospital corps were not
realised and care of the
wounded on the battlefield
remained haphazard.

9. A wounded officer being evacuated to the rear in the Peninsula
Illustration by Thomas Rowlandson published in David Roberts, *The Military Adventures of Johny Newcome*, 1816. Rowlandson has accurately portrayed the local bullock cart.

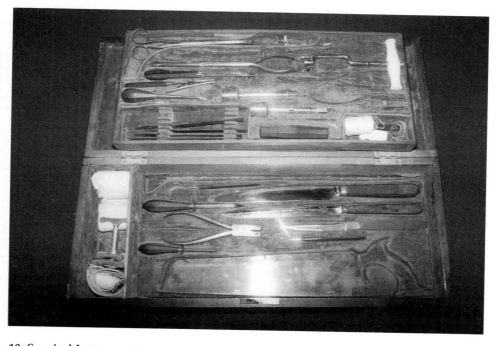

10. Surgical Instruments
This chest belonged to Assistant Surgeon Richard Spencer of the 21st Dragoons.
(The Army Medical Services Museum)

Plates 11–14. Sir Charles Bell's watercolours of the Waterloo wounded
Each is accompanied by Bell's description of the patient.
(The Army Medical Services Museum)

11. A Sabre Wound – a portion of the skull at the vertex completely detached by the sabre cut. The soldier belonged to the 1st Dragoons. He could not speak and stooped languidly with a vacant and indifferent expression of countenance. He was relieved of his symptoms the day after his operation but still could give no account of himself.

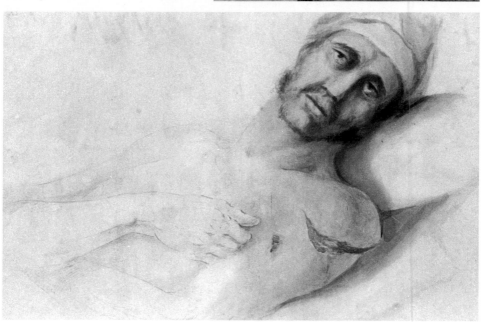

12. Head of left humerus shattered by gunshot. Head of the bone excised by transverse incision. He was James Ellard, Private, 18th Hussars, aged 32 years. Three weeks after the operation he was walking about and his countenance was good.

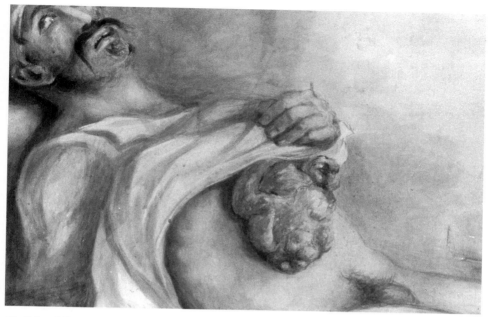

13. Sabre Wound. Colon protruded and completely divided, its ends retracted from each other. Mass was gangrenous when brought to hospital third day after battle. Recovery took place after a long period.

14. Arm carried off by cannon shot close to shoulder joint. Patient is Sergeant Anthony Tuittmeyer 2nd Line Battalion King's German Legion. He rode 15 miles into Brussels after being wounded and presented himself at the hospital where he fainted and remained unconscious for 30 minutes. Later he recovered well.

15. A Sick Officer in the Peninsula
Illustration by Thomas Rowlandson published in David Roberts, *The Military Adventures of Johny Newcome*, 1816. Sick officers were not usually admitted to the general hospitals. Their accommodation in private houses was often of poor quality.

16. Winding up of the Medical Report of the Walcheren Expedition
Illustration by Thomas Rowlandson, March 1810. The two victims in the pillory are Physician-General Lucas Pepys and Surgeon-General Thomas Keate. "A Jack-Son" is Dr Robert Jackson, a severe critic of the army medical board. The barrels are inscribed "TK" as Thomas Keate was accused of misappropriating luxuries, and the case of "oak bark" is an allusion to the shortage of real bark on Walcheren. The public house "A Goose Cured Here" is presumably a hospital ("agues cured here"). (British Museum)

would get some chocolate, some lemons to make lemonade, and other necessaries; I therefore told my trusty servant, Thomas, to take another shirt, which reduced my stock to two; and with this supply he procured me what was requisite. He also brought me an account of one of our officers lying dead in the town, and that my poor comrade was not likely to live the night out. This news affected me very much; but from my weak state of health and depressed condition of mind, I resigned myself to the thoughts of soon experiencing their fate.[68]

Wood only survived because of some good fortune. An old doctor friend, a surgeon in the 85th Regiment, sent him more medicine and gave him money for food. Also, although his surroundings were poverty-stricken, his landlady was kind and tried to give him some assistance. Undoubtedly, many officers in similar circumstances must have had a distressing and lonely death.

These arrangements were also inconvenient for the medical department. Doctors were often called away from general hospitals, where they were presumably tending hundreds of sick soldiers, to attend sick officers in billets. Typical is the account of Captain William Hay who entered the operating room in a general hospital after Waterloo and removed the busy surgeon to see a fellow officer in a Brussels house.[69] At least in this case the officer was severely wounded. An officer of dragoons recalls an episode in northern Spain in 1813 when another officer, billeted in a nearby town, wrote a note requesting the attention of a doctor. On arrival it was clear that his 'wounds' were limited to a few bruises. In the words of the dragoon, the doctor was, 'pretty considerably incensed with the captain for bringing him on so fruitless an errand, when his hands were full at the hospital'.[70]

A hospital designed specifically for officers would have been a substantial improvement. This obvious step was not seriously considered until 1813 when the voluntary provision of a separate hospital for sick and wounded officers was included in regulations. John Hennen strongly supported the idea, suggesting that certain streets or sections of a town or city should be reserved for the officers' use. He acknowledged that without this arrangement it was virtually impossible to give them proper medical assistance. The memoirs of the wars, which were mostly written by officers, show that in reality they continued to be billeted even when sick.[71] Considerations of military rank thus seriously interfered with the administration of adequate medical care.

NOTES

1. Hall, F, *Peninsular Recollections*, p.1736.
2. Woodward, J, *To Do The Sick No Harm*, pp.36–44, 100–1.
3. Anon, *An accurate and impartial narrative of the war*, Vol.II, pp.108–10.
4. Dickson, J, *James Dickson M.A. 1769–1795 Army Surgeon*, pp.91–2.
5. Cantlie, N, *A History of the Army Medical Department*, Vol.I, p.226.
6. Fergusson, W, *Notes and Recollections of a Professional Life*, p.57.
7. Ward, S G P, *Wellington's Headquarters*, p.96.
8. Hennen, J, *Principles of Military Surgery*, p.69.
9. Cooper, J, *Rough Notes of Seven Campaigns*, pp.149–50.
10. Costello, E, *Edward Costello. The Peninsular and Waterloo Campaigns*, p.22.
11. Green, W, *Where My Duty Calls Me*, p.24.
12. Schaumann, A, *On the Road with Wellington*, p.193.
13. Burgoyne, J F, *Life and Correspondence*, Vol.II, p.229.
14. Jordan, A, *Biographical Memoirs of Andrew Jordan*, p.14.
15. Rothenberg, G E, *The Art of Warfare in the Age of Napoleon*, pp.237–8.
16. Blond, G, *La Grande Armée*, p.206.
17. ibid, p.206.
18. Hall, p.1737.
19. Cooke, J, *A True Soldier Gentleman*, p.94.
20. Cantlie, p.327.
21. Napier, G T, *The Early Military Life of General Sir George T Napier*, p.166.
22. *Regulations for the management of the general hospitals in Great Britain*.
23. Hennen, pp.61–70.
24. Lawrence, W, *A Dorset Soldier*, pp.71–2.
25. McGrigor, J, *Sketch of the Medical History of the British Armies*, p.473.
26. Larpent, F S, *The Private Journal of F Seymour Larpent*, p.162.
27. Hale, J, *The Journal of James Hale*, pp.119–20.
28. Wheeler, W, *The Letters of Private Wheeler*, p.153.
29. Green, J, *The Vicissitudes of a Soldier's Life*, p.198.
30. ibid., pp.194–5.
31. Wheeler, p.153.
32. *Selections from the dispatches and general orders*, pp.788–9.
33. McGrigor, J, *Autobiography and Services of Sir James McGrigor*, p.326.
34. Howard, M R, *British Medical Services at the Battle of Waterloo*.
35. Thomson, J, *Report of Observations in the British Military Hospitals*, p.23.
36. Hennen, p.198.
37. Simpson, J, *Paris after Waterloo*, pp.4–7.
38. Costello, p.155.
39. Cantlie, p.249.
40. Fergusson, pp. 67–8.
41. Howard, M R, *Walcheren 1809. A Medical Catastrophe*.
42. Codrington, E, *Memoirs of Admiral Sir Edward Codrington*, Vol.I, p.154.
43. Brett-James, A, *The Walcheren Failure*, p.65.
44. Dunlop, W, *Tiger Dunlop's Upper Canada*, pp.35–6.
45. Gillet, M C, *The Army Medical Department 1775–1818*, pp.196–7.
46. Kempthorne, G A, *The Walcheren Expedition*, p.137.
47. Harris, Rifleman, *Recollections of Riflemen Harris*, pp.177–8.
48. Brett-James, pp.65–6.
49. Anon, *A Soldier of the Seventy-First*, p.45.
50. McGrigor, J, *Observations on the Fever*, p.23; Cantlie N, p.307.
51. McGrigor, *Sketch*, p.475.

52. *Selections from the dispatches*, pp.393–4.
53. Hennen J, p.64.
54. Cantlie, pp.205–8.
55. Blanco, R L, *Wellington's Surgeon General*, p.55.
56. McGrigor, *Sketch*, pp.475–6.
57. *Instructions to Regimental Surgeons*.
58. McGrigor, *Autobiography*, pp.322–3.
59. Gunn, J, *The Memoirs of Private James Gunn*, p.107.
60. Fergusson W, pp.59–60.
61. Chaplin, A, *Medicine in England during the Reign of George III*, pp.81–2.
62. Cantlie, p.194.
63. Haythornthwaite, P, *The Armies of Wellington*, p.133.
64. Cantlie, p.227.
65. Fergusson, pp.62–3.
66. McLean, H, *An enquiry into the nature and causes of the great mortality*, p.235.
67. Fergusson, p.63.
68. Wood, G, *The Subaltern Officer*, pp.130–2.
69. Hay, W, *Reminiscences 1809–1815 under Wellington*, p.208.
70. Anon, *The British Cavalry on the Peninsula*, pp.84–5.
71. Hennen, p.69.

CHAPTER V
Surgery

*On termination of the war in 1814, I expressed at first my regret
that we had not another battle in the South of France to enable me
to decide two or three points in surgery which were doubtful.*

George Guthrie[1]

It would be hard to overstate the differences between surgery as it is today
and the army surgery of the early nineteenth century. We now have the
benefits of accurate diagnosis, well timed intervention, operating theatre
sterility, and an anaesthetic, all provided by highly trained staff. The
soldier of the Napoleonic Wars all too often had an innapropriate
operation performed at the wrong time by a poorly educated surgeon in
dirty conditions with nothing more than the most rudimentary pain relief.
It is predictable that soldiers viewed surgery with dread and that the
complications and mortality were significant. It is more surprising that
much surgery was apparently borne with considerable fortitude and little
complaint, and that the better surgeons attempted difficult technical
procedures under appalling conditions with creditable results. Indeed the
Napoleonic Wars, like other major conflicts, were a catalyst for change in
medical treatment and in the order of the medical profession.

In civilian life, the performance of surgical operations was limited by
ignorance and the pain caused to the patient. It is not clear exactly how
many procedures were carried out as hospitals did not routinely
document the information. The available records suggest that surgery was
a relatively rare event. For instance, in Glasgow in 1800, only forty of 800
patients admitted to the Royal Infirmary came under the knife.[2] The most
common operations were amputations, repairs of fistulae, removal of
cancers, and tapping. Amputations in civil life were most commonly
performed for accidental injury, tuberculosis, or some other bony
deformity. Mortality rates were very variable. In 1800 perhaps 40–50% of
patients undergoing surgery died, but this figure probably fell significantly in the first half of the century.

In war the obvious difficulties of surgery were magnified. Most
operations were carried out in makeshift operating areas in houses, farm
buildings and tents. The operating table was often improvised from a door

or a few planks. The surgeons had no control of their workload and they had to undertake all forms of surgery as there was no specialisation. The overwhelming task facing the medical officers during and after a major battle has already been referred to. Staff and regimental surgeons operated up to eighteen hours a day for days on end. Hospital Mate William Horner had sole responsibility for 173 sick and wounded men after the Battle of Lundy's Lane in 1814. Horner records that, 'My fingers became so sore, from incessant dabbling in water and in pus, that I could sense nothing without pain, and was constantly liable to let articles fall, from the sudden twinge of agony in touching them.'[3]

On occasion civilian doctors entered the fray and were equally exhausted. The famed surgeon and anatomist Charles Bell tended the wounded in Brussels after Waterloo. Bell entered Brussels without a passport, instead showing the officials his surgical instruments. He later recalled in a letter to a friend:

> At six o'clock [in the morning] I took the knife in my hand, and continued incessantly at work till seven in the evening; and so the second and third day. All the decencies of performing surgical operations were soon neglected; while I amputated one man's thigh there lay at one time thirteen, all beseeching to be taken next; one full of entreaty, one calling upon me to remember my promise to take him, another execrating. It was a strange thing to feel my clothes stiff with blood, and my arms powerless with the exertion of using the knife.[4]

To perform these Herculean tasks the surgeons used equipment which was basic and often unsatisfactory. Many eyewitnesses comment on the bluntness of the instruments following continuous use. The well equipped surgeon would have access to knives, saws, scalpels, tourniquets, forceps and needles. Other commonly used items included lint, bandages, sponges, splints, linen, various ligatures, and a few medicines and 'comforts' such as opiates, wines and spirits. The surgery necessary was determined by the destructive nature of the weaponry. Wounds are caused by the transfer of kinetic energy from projectiles to tissues of the body – the greater the transfer of energy the larger the wound. Roundshot fired from cannon often caused fatal injuries but, where limited to the limbs, they caused extensive damage to bones and soft tissues and amputation of the remnant of arm or leg was usually needed. The awesome destructive power of cannon balls is well illustrated by the case of a soldier of the 27th Regiment at Salamanca who deliberately stopped an apparently harmless rolling ricochet ball with his foot. The bones of the foot were completely smashed and amputation was required. The nature of musket ball injuries depended largely on the range of firing. At short range, for instance less than fifty yards, the ball could break large limb bones and destroy joints. At medium range, the ball tended to flatten and disintegrate on impact causing a large, conical-shaped wound. This was because the missile transferred most of its energy in the first four inches of its track. At ranges exceeding two hundred yards, the ball slowed and might only cause a minor injury or even be deflected by pieces of equipment or objects in pockets.

The 'cold steel' of the bayonet may have had a psychological effect but actual bayonet wounds were rare. In a French study of the casualties of a hand-to-hand mêlée between French and Austrian troops, the musket ball wounds outnumbered the bayonet wounds by more than twenty to one.[5] Even at the Battle of Maida in 1806, often quoted as an example of a 'bayonet fight', the majority of wounds were from musket balls. An army surgeon noted that, 'A great delusion is cherished in Great Britain on the subject of the bayonet – a sort of monomania very gratifying to the national vanity, but not quite in accordance with the matter of fact.'[6] The type of sword injury was dependent on the weight and shape of the sword and whether it was used in a thrusting or slashing fashion. Thrusting predictably led to penetrating injuries, often to the chest and abdomen, whereas slashing with a sabre caused lacerations, often to the head and arms. The broadsword carried by heavy dragoons was capable of breaking bones and severing limbs. Crushing injuries could be sustained from falling horses or masonry.

When John Green of the Durham Light Infantry was wounded in the chest by a musket ball in northern Spain in 1813 he was admitted to the general hospital at Passages. Green was an unusually observant witness and he has left a detailed record of the range of wounds and surgical treatments of his fellow patients.

> Among the fifteen wounded men in our ward, there were three that had received wounds in the body, beside myself; ten that were wounded either in the legs or arms; and one that had a fracture occasioned by a fall. One of these, a man of our regiment, had received a ball through his breast bone: whenever the surgeon took off the dressing, the blood and water gushed out of the wound as if it had been pumped out with considerable force ... Another had received a wound in his left arm, so near the shoulder that it could not be amputated. When the surgeons examined him they found that the flies had not only struck his wound, but other parts of his body, and his arm presented a most horrid spectacle, it was literally alive.The surgeons did all in their power to save the poor man, but in vain.
>
> ... A third, who belonged to the guards, lay in the next bed to mine. He had received a severe wound in the shin-bone which seemed to be doing well and we were often reckoning of enjoying ourselves at Chelsea: but how vain was his hope! His wound turned

so bad, that he was obliged to undergo amputation. Three days after, one of the arteries getting loose, the surgeon was sent for. His thigh was opened to take up the artery, but the surgeon could not get the thigh bone covered again. It was more than an inch longer than it should have been. The consequence was that the man had to undergo a second operation. He was very cheerful during the painful process but died the same night. A fourth man had received a ball through his right breast. It passed out at his shoulder-blade. When he drew breath the dressing seemed as though it would have gone into his body. He lingered a few days and then died, apparently without pain.

. . . The fifth case is that of a man whose name was Church. He had received a ball through his groin but was in a very hopeful way . . . However he was taken worse and began to moan most bitterly. He died having been delirious for two whole days. The mortality in our ward was very great. Of four men who had received body wounds, three were already dead and I remained only in a precarious state for the ball could not be extracted.[7]

Although the accounts of ordinary soldiers such as Green give evocative insights into the surgery of the wars, inevitably they are at best anecdotal and at worst unreliable. Greater and more objective detail of the surgical procedures performed is contained in several contemporary textbooks of military surgery. Undoubtedly the greatest British military surgeon and author of the period was George Guthrie. In the Peninsula, he performed his first amputation for gunshot wounds at Roliça in 1808 and his last at Toulouse six years later. He also tended the wounded after Waterloo. Guthrie is described as being robust with keen energetic features and piercing dark eyes. He was highly intelligent, outspoken and self-opinionated, although, as is often said of great men, behind his brusqueness was real kind-heartedness. His most notable work was his *A Treatise on Gunshot Wounds of the Extremities*, first published in 1815. His later *Commentaries on the Surgery of the War* also contains much valuable information.

John Hennen, an Irishman, was Guthrie's only serious competitor in the claim for most influential British army surgeon. Hennen joined the 40th Regiment as an assistant surgeon and served throughout the Peninsular War. He is best remembered for his highly regarded textbook *Principles of Military Surgery*, first published in 1818. The text is a rich source of information on contemporary surgical practice, its attributes well summarised by a German commentator: 'Rare understanding, unusual clarity of conception, enormous knowledge, and wide experience – all the most English of qualities – are united in this book – I cannot recommend the book too highly, and believe sincerely that no surgeon should enter upon a campaign without having read it.'[8]

Also worthy of mention is John Thomson, Professor of Military Surgery at Edinburgh, who visited the hospitals in Brussels after Waterloo. His subsequent book, *Report of Observations made in the British Military Hospitals in Belgium after the Battle of Waterloo with remarks concerning amputation*, is a useful source. However, despite his impressive title, Thomson had relatively little practical experience of military surgery and his work is not quite in the same category as Guthrie's and Hennen's. Although we are mainly considering the surgery of the wars from a British perspective, it would not be possible adequately to describe the surgery of the period without reference to the writings of Dominique Jean Larrey, Surgeon-in-Chief to the armies of Napoleon. Larrey's preeminence was such that Guthrie was praised by being referred to as the 'English Larrey'. The Frenchman was undoubtedly a genius within his profession and his memoirs, *Mémoires de Chirurgie Militaire*, and the later *Relation Médicale de Campagnes et Voyages* are as near to a definitive account of the military surgery of the era as is available. Larrey details a wide range of emergency and elective surgical procedures performed during his campaigning throughout Europe and in Egypt, Syria and Russia. He makes some interesting comparisons between French and English surgery.

The archetypal military surgical operation of the Napoleonic Wars was amputation. Very nearly all serious wounds of the limbs would become infected to some degree. Musket balls often led to compound fractures where the wound was open to the exterior. This type of injury was particularly feared as it was often followed by a prolonged period of infection. Associated damage to blood vessels and nerves from the fractured bones led to a high incidence of haemorrhage and neurological complications. The soldier fortunate enough to survive all this might then succumb to even more aggressive infections such as hospital gangrene and tetanus. The enormous number of possible complications of limb wounds largely explains the attraction of amputation to contemporary surgeons. The operation had the evident advantage of replacing a complicated and infected wound arising from weaponry with a much simpler wound caused by the surgical instruments. Although infection would probably still supervene, at least this would involve the healthy tissue at the amputation site and could be more easily managed.

Some aspects of amputation were agreed among surgeons, but there still remained controversy as to the indications for the procedure, the precise technique and, above all, the optimal timing. The popular view is that arms and legs were chopped off indiscriminately. However, the best surgeons were not enthusiastic operators. Larrey, sometimes regarded as an overzealous surgeon, expressed the following views:

> If it should be said that the amputation of a limb is a cruel and dangerous operation, and one always fraught with grave

consequences for the patient who is left in a mutilated condition, and that for these reasons there is more honour to be gained by preserving the limb than by amputating it, however skilfully and successfully done, the reply which admits of no denial is that amputation is an operation which offers a chance of recovery to an unfortunate individual, whose death appears certain by any other method of treatment.[9]

By the end of the wars surgeons felt confident to state the situations in which amputation was necessary. Hennen lists the indications as follows:

First – When an arm or leg is carried completely off by roundshot. Second – Extensive injuries of the joints. I would still [however] lay it down, as a law of military surgery that no lacerated joint, particularly the knee, ankle or elbow, should ever leave the field unamputated, where the patient is not obviously sinking, and consequently where certain death would follow the operation.

Thirdly – Under the same law are included, by the best and most experienced army surgeons, all compound fractures close to the joints, especially if conjoined with lacerated vessels or nerves, or much comminution of the bone, particularly if the femur is the injured bone. Fourth – Extensive loss of substance or disorganisation of the soft parts by round-shot leaving no hope of the circulation being carried on in consequence of torn arteries or nerves.

Fifthly – Cases where the bones have been fractured, or dislocated without rupture of the skin or great loss of parts, but with great injury or disorganisation of the ligaments and injuries of the vessels, followed by extensive internal effusions of blood among the soft parts.[10]

In practice such guidelines could only be approximate and every case had to be judged on its merits. The location of the wound was also a major factor in the decision to amputate. Arm wounds generally had a better prognosis than wounds of the leg. Whereas a gunshot wound of the thigh was very likely to need immediate amputation, and it was viewed as dangerous to much delay amputation in any serious wound of the leg, a wound of the arm was often managed more conservatively. Where amputation was performed, the emphasis was on speed to minimise pain. A tourniquet was usually applied above the wound to limit blood loss. A surgical knife was selected to cut through the skin, subcutaneous tissues and muscles thus exposing the bone. Often several sweeps of the knife were required. A saw was then taken to cut through the bone. The length of the procedure depended on the complexity of the wound and the skill of the surgeon. Typically it lasted between a few minutes and half an hour. The pressure on the surgeon to finish quickly meant that some rough and ready techniques were used. After Badajoz, Surgeon John Maling of the 52nd Foot was seen with his knife held between his teeth as he used both hands to tie up the arteries.[11]

There are numerous contemporary accounts of amputation. The most graphic recollections are by patients rather than operators. Sergeant Thomas Jackson of the Coldstream Guards needed amputation of a gangrenous leg at Bergen-op-Zoom in 1813.

> They had got me fixed upon the end of a large barrack-room table, sitting upright, with my legs hanging down. A basin was brought for me to drink out of it. I said, 'Sir, let me have a good draught.' He poured out nearly a pint (of rum) which I eagerly drank off. In an instant it raised up my spirits to an invincible courage ... The sergeant was preparing to blindfold me. 'Oh no,' I said, 'I shall sit still and see as well as the rest.' One of the surgeons sat on a stool, to hold the leg steady; the second ripped up my trousers and took down the stocking low enough, then he waited on the head surgeon ... the tourniquet being placed painfully tight above the knee, he put his hand under the calf of the leg and setting the edge of the knife on the shin bone, at one heavy, quick stroke, drew it round till it met the shin bone again ... The blood, quickly following the knife, spread around and formed like a beautiful red fan, downwards ... Next the surgeon with his hand, forced up the flesh towards the knee, to make way for the saw. When the saw was applied, I found it extremely painful; it was worn out ... it stuck as a bad saw would when sawing a green stick. I said, 'Oh sir, have you not a better saw?' He said he was sorry he had not, as they were all worn out. The bone got through, the next thing to be done was still more painful – that of tying up the ligatures. Then followed the drawing down of the flesh to cover the end of the bone, and tightly strapped there with strips of sticking plaster; after this strongly bandaged. And thus ended the operation, which lasted about half an hour.[12]

Jackson was discharged with a wooden leg and a pension of a shilling a day. When George Napier, one of the famous Napier family, had his arm amputated after Ciudad Rodrigo in 1812, the surgeon was George Guthrie. However, according to Napier, even the army's most respected surgeon found it a difficult undertaking, '. . . for want of light and from the number of amputations he had already performed, and other circumstances, his instruments were blunted, it was a long time before the thing was finished, at least twenty minutes, and the pain was great'. To

131

Guthrie's amusement, Napier apparently swore at him 'like a trooper' throughout the surgery.[13]

Although there was general agreement among English and French surgeons as to the procedure for removing the wounded limb, there was controversy surrounding the best way of managing the resulting wound. The usual English practice, as described by Jackson, was to ligate the arteries with silk or waxed linen and then to close the edges of the wound with sutures or tape. Larrey criticised this method of uniting the amputation wound by 'first intention' as he believed it led to haemorrhage and inflammation, complications which only resolved when the wound was again set free. According to Larrey, 'This aspect of English surgery lacks the perfection one would expect from such well informed practitioners.'[14] The Frenchman's own method entailed simple application of linen and lint dressings held loosely in place by bandages.

Pioneering surgeons on both sides, notably Guthrie and Larrey, used the unprecedented surgical opportunities of the wars to perfect new forms of amputation. One of the most ambitious of these novel procedures was amputation at the hip. This had long been regarded as a formidable undertaking and the traditional teaching was that it could not be justified. However, a few army surgeons were prepared to try it in patients in whom the surgery provided the only chance of survival, for instance where the limb was already practically disarticulated by shell or cannonball. Larrey attempted the procedure seven times. He was normally not able to follow up his patients but it seems likely that he was successful on at least one occasion. Similarly, Guthrie's British colleague Staff Surgeon David Brownrigg attempted the operation four or five times in Spain and apparently also had a solitary success although no details are available.[15] In contrast, Guthrie's amputation at the hip in a French soldier after Waterloo is well described in his rather laconic and anecdotal style.

François de Gay, private in the 45th Regiment of French infantry, was wounded at the Battle of Waterloo by a musket ball, which entered behind, fractured the neck of the femur, and made its exit anteriorly, about four inches below the groin. He was admitted into the Elizabeth Hospital on the 5th of July [seventeen days after the battle], much exhausted, not having had until that period any regular attendance. In addition to his wounds which had put on a sloughing appearance, he suffered from an extensive sore on the sacrum, which was caused by lying on the wet ground for five days. The wounds being cleaned and the thigh placed in proper position, he remained until the seventh when the operation of amputation at the hip-joint was considered advisable. The operation was performed by Mr Guthrie at two o'clock on the 7th; nineteen days after the injury. His pulse was 120; and a considerable deviation was observed by Dr

Hennen and Mr Collier between the pulse at the wrist and at the groin, at the termination of the operation; his spirits good; he lost about twenty-four ounces of blood; was immediately put to bed, and had an anodyne draft. In the evening his pulse was only 108; had lemonade for common drink.

Guthrie describes the French soldier's slow recovery in some detail. He was visited by Larrey. After being transferred to the York Hospital in Chelsea, he was finally moved to the Hôtel des Invalides in Paris where, according to Guthrie,

> He is capable of walking as much as three miles at a time, the wooden leg which he has attached to his body being thrown forwards by an exertion of the muscles of the trunk. He is in very good health, not quite so fat as when in England, talks of getting married, and is not, as the French express it, 'sage'.[16]

Guthrie also supported amputation at the shoulder as a feasible and worthwhile procedure. But not all surgeons in England were immediately convinced by Guthrie's claims. The great man was provoked and declared in the Preface to the second edition of his *A Treatise on Gunshot Wounds of the Extremities* that when the army's medical officers returned from Spain in 1814,

> . . . it was not a little amusing to them to hear teachers of surgery gravely informing their students, that amputation at the shoulder-joint was a most formidable operation, on account of the impossibility of effectively preventing the flow of blood through the arteries; and when they did notice amputation of the hip-joint it was only to declare it a murderous operation.

In addition to his groundbreaking surgery at major joints, Guthrie advocated a number of other innovations in operating technique. He condemned the widespread use of the tourniquet, decrying the surgeon in the field of battle who was often, 'groaning under the weight and inconvenience of a sack full of tourniquets, not one of which he would in all probability have a proper opportunity of applying'.[17] Even more surprising to his contemporaries was his aversion to tourniquets in amputation, where he preferred to staunch blood flow from vessels by holding them between the finger and thumb and ligating them. He was the first to demonstrate that both ends of a divided artery must be tied and that secondary haemorrhage under this regimen was very rare. He insisted that in fractures of the femur the leg should be aligned in a straight line rather than in external rotation, the position at the time of injury, as had previously been the case. He also made valuable observations in the treatment of gangrene, nerve injuries and a form of skin infection termed erysipelas.

After this catalogue of Guthrie's innovations in the local management of wounds, it is a measure of his greatness that his major contribution to the surgery of the wars has yet to be discussed. Undoubtedly, it was his forthright advocacy of early rather than delayed amputation following battlefield injury that was to save the greatest number of lives and most establish his subsequent reputation. The optimal timing of amputation had long been contentious. In 1745 the Paris Academy offered a prize for the best dissertation on the subject. That the winner, Faure, a French military surgeon, wrote in favour of delayed amputation indicates that at this time many prominent authorities supported this view.[18] However, the practical experience of the Napoleonic Wars suggested otherwise. Larrey became gradually convinced that in most circumstances amputation should be performed within four hours of the injury, so-called 'primary amputation'. Amongst the factors making early amputation advisable, he quoted the difficulty of transporting wounded men from the battlefield, the dangers inherent in a long stay in hospital such as infection, and the frequent eventuality of having to abandon the wounded soon after a battle.

The simple medical case for early intervention was that it gave the wounded soldier the best chance of avoiding the numerous complications, 'fever, inflammation, suppuration, and gangrene'. Quick amputation removed a dirty traumatised limb which was an ideal breeding ground for infection and left the patient with a relatively simple wound. Furthermore, although the conditions in a dressing station, field ambulance or field hospital were likely to be crude, they were more favourable for avoiding sepsis than the infected wards of the general hospital. Early amputation may have led to some unnecessary procedures, but its advantages were to become increasingly apparent as the fighting continued.

Guthrie was in agreement with Larrey, as indeed were the great majority of military surgeons who learned their surgery in the field of battle. Guthrie's particular contribution was his methodical presentation of a striking collection of statistics from the Peninsular War and Waterloo, which showed unequivocally the better outcome of primary compared with secondary amputation. The following is taken from his treatise on gunshot wounds and his 'commentaries'. There are some discrepancies in the figures given in the two works, for instance in the detailed results of amputation after the Battle of Toulouse, but the messages that emerge are clear.

In his treatise on gunshot wounds, Guthrie quotes the outcomes of amputations over a six-month period in northern Spain in 1813 to support his case for primary amputation. From the advance of the British Army from Portugal up to its establishment in winter quarters in front of Bayonne, a period including the Battle of Vitoria and the hard fought engagements of the Pyrenees, a total of 842 amputations were documented, 459 of the arm (excluding the shoulder) and 383 of the leg. The larger number of operations were delayed or secondary. Thus 551 procedures were performed in the general hospitals, usually several weeks after the injury, the remaining 291 procedures being conducted without undue delay on or around the battlefield with recovery in the smaller regimental and divisional hospitals. After the secondary procedures, nearly half of the patients died. This compared with only one in twelve dying following primary amputation on the field of battle. The difference was equally marked for both amputations of the arm (secondary amputation 40% deaths vs primary 3%) and for the leg (60% vs 15%). Even allowing the likelihood that some of the most difficult cases were deliberately delayed, only one conclusion could be drawn. In Guthrie's own words, 'This difference is certainly very remarkable and it is so well known to all surgeons of the British Army, as a constant occurrence, that there is no longer among them any doubt on the subject'. He then quotes figures for the Battle of Toulouse which he regarded as 'even more satisfactory' as the surgical arrangements were 'more immediately under my observation and control'. On the battlefield, forty-eight primary amputations were performed with only ten deaths. This compared with twenty-one deaths from fifty-two secondary operations in the general hospital.[19]

He was confident in asserting that the increased death rate from delayed surgery was mainly caused by an increased incidence of ulceration, infection and gangrene of the amputation stump with the subsequent demise of the patient from 'internal suppurations', or what we would now term septicaemia. The army's later experiences at Waterloo simply confirmed Guthrie's opinions. Those unfortunate enough to have their limb amputations delayed until they reached the general hospitals in Brussels, ten miles from the field, had almost twice the mortality as those having earlier procedures. Charles Bell quotes the figures as 146 primary amputations with forty deaths (27%) and 225 secondary amputations with 106 deaths, a mortality of 47%.[20] Guthrie was self-critical and acknowledged that the retrospective information he had collected was not ideal. The best test of the optimum timing of surgery would have been to prospectively randomise wounded soldiers between early and late amputation. However, after the Battles of Roliça and Vimeiro, he was already convinced that early intervention was superior. In his treatise on gunshot wounds he explains, 'I did not feel myself authorised to commit murder for the sake of experiment.'[21]

Although Larrey and Guthrie strongly supported early amputation, they both acknowledged that immediate surgery was not always feasible. Larrey pointed out that the patient should be allowed to recover from the first shock of the wound before an operation was undertaken, and that the time needed for the recovery depended on the type of wound and the constitution of the patient. However, once this recovery had occurred, primary amputation should then be done as quickly as possible. Similarly, Guthrie states, 'If a soldier at the end of two, four, or six hours after the injury has recovered from the general constitutional alarm occasioned by the blow, his pulse becomes regular and good, his stomach easy, he is less agitated, his countenance revives, and he begins to feel pain, stiffness, and uneasiness in the part, he will now undergo the operation with greatest advantage . . .' In most cases he believed a delay of one to three hours to be sufficient.[22] Larrey accepted that in certain cases a much greater delay was justified. For example, where there was traumatic gangrene, tetanus, gross infection or other symptoms of significant illness such as diarrhoea.[23]

Amputation has been discussed in detail as it encapsulates many of the surgical dilemmas and controversies of the time. However, it is worth re-emphasising that it was not performed wholesale. Experienced surgeons appeared to become more conservative in the last years of the wars. Guthrie's increasing reluctance to ampututate is illustrated by a nice anecdote. When Sir Vivian Hussey, commanding the cavalry at Toulouse, had his left arm broken by a musket ball, he was advised by the surgeons present to have it amputated. He refused, wishing to see a more senior surgeon first. Guthrie reviewed him and declared that the limb should not be removed. Many years afterwards, when Lord Vivian presented the doctor to his second wife, he did it with the compliment, 'I introduce you to Mr Guthrie, to whom you and I are both indebted for the arm on which you are now leaning.'[24]

In the months after Toulouse, over 1,200 wounded soldiers were treated in the general hospital, but only approximately 100 of these had amputations performed. It is obvious that the overwhelming number of surgical procedures did not end with the loss of a limb. The most common surgery was a non-amputation procedure on the leg or arm – these made up approximately two thirds of the Toulouse cases. They would have included treatment of many types of more minor wound with practices including bandaging, splinting of fractures, extraction of musket balls, and probing for other foreign bodies. The less intensive nature of most of these interventions compared with amputation is illustrated by the much lower chance of death – only one in a hundred men undergoing non-amputation surgery to the arm in the general hospital at Toulouse died.[25]

One of the most frequently performed operations was probing for and then extracting a musket ball. The decision as to whether to actually remove the ball or leave it in the wound depended on its location. Guthrie apparently cut out many balls which were within an inch of the surface without particular complications. However, he was more reluctant when the ball was three or four inches deep and could not be distinctly felt.[26] Probing and extraction was usually done with the fingers or with specially designed forceps. If extraction was feasible, it was much easier to do soon after the injury, before inflammation set in. If probing for the ball was much delayed, its extraction was likely to be difficult and prolonged. Harry Smith, then a subaltern in the Light Division, was wounded by a musket ball in the achilles tendon during fighting on the Coa river. He was moved to the convalescent depot at Belem in Lisbon but rejoined with a stiff ankle and did five months' duty. After the siege of Ciudad Rodrigo, he returned to Lisbon to be reviewed by an eminent medical board including the staff surgeons William Morell, Summers Higgins and David Brownrigg, the latter mistakenly referred to by Smith as 'Brownlow'.

> They examined my leg. I was all for the operation. Morell and Higgins recommended me to remain with a stiff leg as better than a wooden one, for the wounds in Lisbon had sloughed so of late and they were dubious of the result. Brownlow said, 'If it were my leg, out should come the ball.' On which I roared out, 'Hurrah, Brownlow, you are the doctor for me.' So Morell says, 'Very well if you are desirous we will do it directly.' My pluck was somewhat cooled but I cocked up my leg and said, 'There it is – slash away!' It was five minutes, most painful indeed, before it was extracted. The ball was jagged and the tendinous fibres had grown into it. It was half dissected and half torn out, with the most excruciating torture for a moment, the forceps breaking which had hold of the ball.

Smith was left with a wound four to five inches long but made a good recovery.[27]

It was not unusual for foreign bodies other than musket balls to be extracted from wounds. These included buttons, other fragments of uniform, coins, parts of watches, and other people's bones and teeth. Soldiers were inclined to believe that some of the more bizarre incidents had special significance. A good example is that of a Hanoverian soldier at Waterloo who was struck by grape shot on the outside of the thigh. He was subsequently operated on by John Hennen who felt the case worthy of inclusion in his surgical textbook.

> On the second day he was brought into the hospital and the usual dressings were applied. On the fifth day a long narrow passage was discovered by the probe, seeming to run nearly the length of the vastus externus muscle. On cutting into this, three pieces of coin were extracted from the parts. The poor fellow, a raw recruit, had no

money whatever about him, nor even a pocket to contain it, and fervently protested against his right to this forced loan. He accounted for it by supposing that the money was carried from the pocket of his comrade, who stood before him in the ranks, and who was killed by the same shot which wounded him. The coins, consisting of two five-franc pieces and a Dutch stiver, were obviously first struck by the shot, and carried along by it; for nearly one half of their flat surfaces, the silver pieces adhered closely together; on the other, where the ball had struck their edges, the metal was flattened out, and somewhat hollowed. In this hollow lay the copper coin, in some degree adapted to the shape of the depression of the large pieces.

Hennen continues in a vein which reveals him as a keen observer of human behaviour as well as an expert surgeon:

I cannot omit noticing here a trait strongly illustrative of the mobility of mind which characterises soldiers, and their proneness to superstition and believing in omens, which a surgeon acquainted with their character can often turn to their benefit. The part of these two coins which had been flattened out happened to be that on which Napoleon's head was impressed. From one it was nearly effaced; and on observing this circumstance to the patient and his comrades, a universal burst of joy echoed through the ward. The young Hanoverian exulted in the share he conceived he had personally had of contributing to the downfall of the French Emperor; his health rapidly improved, and I have no doubt that this simple circumstance produced a good effect upon every man who witnessed it.[28]

Often, probing for musket balls or other foreign bodies was performed with the wounded man standing in the same position as when he was hit. This supposedly simplified the operation. There were even stories of cavalrymen being remounted to have their wounds explored although these may well have been apocryphal.

Incised wounds were either managed with adhesive plasters or by stitching and bandaging. Any obvious abscess would be drained and slough cleared away, but formal debridement of the wound as we know it today, thorough cleansing and removal of dead tissue, was not routinely performed. The practice of dilating the wound, in order to allow 'poisons' out, had mostly fallen out of favour with the British but was still carried out by some French surgeons. There was little consistency in the choice of dressings for wounds. Larrey reverted to 'stimulating' dressing materials, such as had been used in the middle ages. He covered wounds with compresses soaked in wine of camphor, red wine or salt water, and then bandaged the entire limb. The British favoured more simple dressings and salves, notably dry lint and cold water. Hennen wrote that dressings could be moistened with cold water alone, or mixed with a little spirits, vinegar or wine.[29]

In reality, clean good quality dressings were often unavailable and either the army's doctors had to improvise or wounds were left untended. Shortage of surgical supplies was a particular problem for much of the Peninsular War. Cornet William Tomkinson received treatment for a wound in Oporto in June 1809.

> I still continued to complain much of the pain occasioned from the wound in my left arm. It was so painful, I could not move it, nor allow the blood on the hand, which had clotted on it (from never being washed), to be removed. The dressings began to be very scarce, no ship having arrived with medical supplies, and what few the army could spare, with those found in the town, were nearly expended. I had once or twice been dressed with something like tallow or hog's-lard, and my wounds kept bound up for want of dressings, so that they began to smell before they dared again to open them, fearing they should soon be quite without any dressing.

Tomkinson's condition further worsened until a vessel laden with supplies arrived in the Douro river and he was properly dressed with lint, 'a greater comfort could not be conceived'.[30]

Wound dressings were usually left in place for at least three days. Once the initial field dressing was removed, a poultice might be applied. In Hennen's words, '. . . a soft and moderately warm poultice of bread, meal, bran, pumpkin, carrot, and any other emollient substance, carefully applied, and removed at least twice a day, until the slough begins to loosen from the edges and a purulent oozing is seen . . .'[31] Once this stage was reached, Hennen recommended removal of the poultice. This might be followed by the application of cloth doused in cold water. 'With cold water,' commented the British surgeon, 'one is never at a loss.' Soldiers generally approved of the use of poultices. When John Douglas of the 1st Royal Scots was struck by grape-shot in the leg at San Sebastian his wound soon became infected:

> The wound I received mortified in common with many others . . . I shall quote the remedy applied. This was a poultice compounded of brown sugar, lees of wine and linseed meal. For my part I actually thought the limb was being dragged off me, but in the morning, on the removal of the poultice, the limb had the appearance of being dipped in tar, the mortified flesh falling off in black streams.

The doctors advised that Douglas's leg be amputated, but he refused and eventually recovered with the limb intact.[32]

For fractures, whalebone splints were commonly used. Patients with fractures of the leg bones were traditionally treated lying on their side to relax the muscles. As has been referred to, Guthrie advocated the splinting of the leg in a straight position as opposed to the previous practice of immobilising it in a bent position which frequently left the patient with a deformed limb. Guthrie first used a long straight splint in Lisbon in 1813. This was applied with the patient lying on his back and apparently gave a good chance of full recovery from a fractured femur. For fractures below the knee, there were various methods of splinting, with the leg either straight or bent and the patient either lying on his side or back. Hennen supported the use of splints but he also noted that, 'I have seen numerous cases where they have been omitted and the patient has done perfectly well, the parts being merely covered with compresses moistened with cold water.'[33]

As would be expected, Larrey fully appreciated the importance of immobilising a fractured limb and developed his own innovative methods. His 'appareil inamovible' was fashioned of simple materials such as straw, bandages and bags of chaff.[34] This appliance surrounded and supported the limb whilst allowing the patient some mobility on crutches – echoes of the now ubiquitous plaster method for treating fractures. Although the above treatments gave an excellent chance of recovery from an uncomplicated fracture, the chances of survival from more complicated compound fractures, where there was much associated tissue damage, was considerably less. Even at Toulouse, where the British surgery in the general hospital appears to have been of a very high quality, over a third of patients with compound fractures died from their wounds.

Having reviewed the various characteristics of limb injuries, we can now turn to the managements of wounds to other parts of the body. The nature of Napoleonic warfare was such that head injuries from either musket balls or sword were common. Lacerations such as sabre cuts were easily managed with stitching and a supporting bandage. Where the skull was fractured, the choice of treatment became more difficult. Considerable controversy surrounded the indications for trephining (also called trepanning), the removal of sections of bone from the skull. This had previously been very extensively performed in head injuries but experienced surgeons, including Larrey, advocated caution, limiting its use to cases where fractured skull had been driven inwards damaging the brain, where a foreign body was lodged between pieces of broken skull, or where it was believed that the brain was being compressed by a collection of blood. Following removal of bone, the wound was where possible covered with a scalp soft tissue flap. Hennen supported the use of both local cold applications and poultices in head injuries. Occasionally, projectiles could be removed from the brain following detection with a sound, but where the missile was deep in the organ, it was acknowledged that an operation would do more harm than good.

All surgery to the head must have been particularly unpleasant for the patient, but often the aftermath was even worse. The initial injury and surgery were commonly followed by a grim catalogue of complications including haemorrhage, nerve injury, cerebral abscess, air embolism (air drawn in to neck veins) and meningitis. Charles Bell documented several cases of head injury and subsequent complications in his watercolours of the wounded after Waterloo. Some sequelae of head wounds were mysterious. One of Hennen's more intriguing cases is entiled 'Affection of the genital organs from wound of the occiput'. Fortunate to survive his experiences in the Battle of Waterloo was William Verner of the 7th Hussars who received a musket ball wound to the side of his head. This was simply managed on the field by the application of sticking plaster, but by the time he reached Brussels, he had developed a violent fever and was delirious. He was bled, had his head shaved and blistered, and leeches applied to his temples. He eventually recovered, although he attributed this more to the inspiring effect of a visit by the Duke of Wellington and plenty of 'Guiness's porter' than to his medical management.[35] Of those head injuries serious enough to need treatment in the British general hospitals of the Peninsula about a fifth died. However, it was believed that around a half of all head injuries perished on the field before any assistance could be given.[36]

Serious injuries to the chest from musket balls and swords were also associated with numerous complications and were regarded as very likely to result in death. Wounds to the upper part of the lungs were believed to be particularly dangerous. British figures for the general hospital at Toulouse show that slightly more than a third of soldiers with chest wounds died. However, it must be presumed that these included a number of more minor injuries as it is recorded that in the Crimean War there were 120 deaths in 147 cases of penetrating gun-shot wounds to the chest. Certainly, soldiers often made a spontaneous recovery from non-penetrating chest wounds. Guthrie quotes an example in his inimitable fashion.

> A soldier was struck, on the hill of Talavera, on the breast plate by a ball which, as he believed, had gone through his body. He was as white as a sheet and desperately frightened. On opening his coat, I found the ball had indented his breast plate, and made a round red mark on the skin without going deeper. I did not see him again for several days, until after crossing the bridge of Arzobispo, on the retreat to Truxillo. He was then engaged in disembowelling a fine fat wild hog, amongst a herd of which we had, unluckily for them, just fallen. He recognised me at once; said that, as I told him, he had been more frightened than hurt; that he had been bled largely and well physicked, and after two or three days he had thought no more of it.

I am bound to add, that, in gratitude, he offered me a leg of the pig, which, having nothing to eat, I could not but accept. It supplied a dinner for three others who are now no more.[37]

Wellington suffered a similar wound during the same action, a spent ball striking him on the clavicle (collar bone).

Patients with more significant chest injuries were nursed lying on the wounded side. Previously, penetrating chest wounds had been kept open by the insertion of tubes, but Guthrie recommended early closure by suture and Larrey also supported this approach. It was felt that this was the best way of minimising the incidence of potentially fatal complications such as pneumothorax (entry of air into the chest cavity), haemorrhage and infection. Where pus did accumulate in the thorax (empyema), this could be drained by the introduction of a tube. The only reason for delaying closure of a stabbing wound was to remove a foreign body with forceps. In his memoirs, Larrey describes two cases where he extracted foreign bodies from the lungs, one by sawing through the ribs. However, it is unlikely that the ordinary army surgeon would have attempted such a major procedure. More complicated wounds of the thorax including multiple rib fractures and spinal injury would have been almost invariably fatal and beyond surgical intervention.

Abdominal wounds posed equally daunting problems for the army's surgeons. Guthrie roughly divided them into those only affecting the abdominal wall, those extending into the abdominal cavity, and those actually damaging the contents including the bowel.[38] Most patients with serious abdominal injuries died, but a few survived, giving encouragement for the future. Most wounds were caused by musket balls or penetrating sword thrusts and where the bowel was damaged, there was the possibility of fistula formation (a track connecting different organs) or peritonitis. Superficial injuries were more amenable to treatment. Guthrie recommended that an accessible ball in the abdominal wall should be removed, but that if more deeply placed it was best left alone. Simple incised wounds were closed with sutures or tape.

Injured bowel was usually stitched to the skin at the site of the wound to prevent it falling back into the abdominal cavity and spilling its contents into the peritoneum with resulting life-threatening infection. Some surgeons, however, did advocate suturing the divided parts of the bowel together. It was Larrey's opinion that wounds to the intestine from cold steel caused more inflammation than wounds from musket balls and that the former therefore had a worse prognosis. Thomson in his account of the Waterloo wounded gives a number of examples of fistula formation arising from gunshot wounds.[39] Most memorable, if not typical, was a soldier who received a musket wound to the abdominal wall and eventually passed the ball through the rectum. Some survivals were truly remarkable. Charles Bell describes a Waterloo soldier wounded in the abdomen by a sabre whose colon was completely divided and gangrenous, but whose recovery took place after a 'long period'.

In describing the military surgery of the era, it is inevitable that the bulk of information is derived from the accounts of great surgeons such as Larrey, Guthrie and Hennen. However, it has to be acknowledged that these were exceptional men and that in reality many of the army's surgeons would not have attempted some of the procedures described. Indeed, there were surgeons who performed the simplest operation incompetently. John Hunter, the great military surgeon of the eighteenth century, asserted at the start of the wars that it was hardly necessary for a man to be a surgeon to practise in the army. Many of the surgical anecdotes of the wars reflect the wide range of experience and competence of the surgeons. Some learning on the job was inevitable, as remains the case today. After the Battle of Fuentes de Oñoro, William Grattan of the Connaught Rangers witnessed a junior doctor in action.

> . . . an assistant surgeon was taking off the leg of an old German sergeant of the 60th. The doctor was evidently a young practitioner, and Bell, our staff-surgeon, took much trouble in instructing him . . . The young doctor seemed much pleased when he had the sergeant fairly out of his hands, and it would be difficult to decide whether he or his patient was most happy; but, from everything I could observe, I was of the opinion that the doctor made his debut on the old German's stump. I offered up a few words – prayers they could not be called – that, if ever it fell to my lot to lose any of my members, the young fellow who essayed on the sergeant should not be the person to operate on me.[40]

There were sometimes disagreements between surgeons as to the correct course of action. A good example is that of Robert Blakeney, who was severely wounded in the leg during the Battle of the Nivelle in November 1813. Both lower bones of the leg, the tibia and fibula, were smashed by a musket ball. Complicated open (or compound) fractures of the sort suffered by Blakeney were regarded as a good reason for amputation. Initially it was agreed that the leg would be amputated, but this was delayed as the limb was very inflamed and swollen. Instead the fracture was set and the staff surgeon, after discussion with Blakeney, decided to undertake a trial of observation alone, hoping the limb might be saved. The doctor did point out to his patient 'the immediate danger attending the experiment'. Blakeney survived, although he suffered from an open wound for many years. When he returned home and attended a board of senior medical officers, the staff surgeon was severely criticised for his conservative treatment, '. . . for there were ninety-nine chances to one against my life'.[41]

The reluctance of both the surgeon and patient to perform and undergo an operation must have been influenced by the unpleasantness of surgery. To the contemporary mind the full implications of such an extensive range of surgical procedures without the benefit of an anaesthetic are difficult to grasp. The wines, spirits and opiates were essentially designed to relax the patient and had limited analgesic effect. The Napoleonic soldier was expected to bear the agonising pain of surgery with stoicism. Most surviving eyewitness accounts of surgery suggest that he did, although we must assume that in at least some cases the writer exaggerated the heroism shown and a number of these anecdotes now have an apocryphal air to them. Take for example one of the most famous of all operations, that of Lord Uxbridge, Wellington's cavalry commander at Waterloo. Uxbridge had his leg amputated after the battle. The scene is described by Captain Thomas Wildman of the 7th Hussars who was an aide-de-camp to Uxbridge:

> He told me immediately he must lose his leg and then began conversing about the action and seemed to forget his wound in the exultation for the Victory; when the surgeons examined it, they all agreed that it would be at the imminent danger of his life to attempt to save the limb. He only said, 'Well, Gentlemen, I thought so myself and if amputation is to take place, the sooner it is done the better.' He wrote a short note to Lady Uxbridge, saying that if he had been a young single man he would probably have run the risk, but that he would preserve his life for her and the children if possible. During the operation he never moved or complained, no one even held his hands. He once said quite calmly that he thought the instrument was not very sharp – when it was over, his nerves did not appear the least shaken and the surgeon observed his pulse was not altered – He said smiling, 'I have had a pretty long run, I have been a Beau these 47 years and it would not be fair to cut the young men out any longer', and then asked if we did not admire his vanity.[42]

We have no reason to doubt Lord Uxbridge's bravery or eloquence, but the whole episode is more reminiscent of a Victorian melodrama than an emergency operation on the edge of a battlefield. It seems inconceivable that even one of the most admired officers in the British Army could have a limb amputated without any change in pulse. Another variation in this genre of 'heroic amputation' is the favourable comparison of the conduct of British soldiers with that of the enemy (or vice versa, depending on the nationality of the author). Edward Costello of the 95th Rifles remained in Brussels after Waterloo where he had the opportunity to witness surgery. Costello begrudgingly admits that the French could be brave in battle but they were apparently not able to face surgery with the 'cool unflinching spirit' of the British. He proceeds to illustrate this:

An incident which here came under my notice may in some measure show the difference of the two nations. An English soldier, evidently an old weather-beaten warfarer, while undergoing the amputation of an arm below the elbow, held the injured limb with his other hand without betraying the slightest emotion, save occasionally helping out his pain by spirting forth the proceeds of a large plug of tobacco, which he chewed most unmercifully while under the operation. Near to him was a Frenchman, bellowing lustily, while a surgeon was probing for a ball near the shoulder. This seemed to annoy the Englishman more than anything else, and so much so, that as soon as his arm was amputated, he struck the Frenchman a smart blow across the breech with the severed limb, holding it at the wrist, saying, 'Here take that, and stuff it down your throat, and stop your damned bellowing!'[43]

The surgeons presumably regarded the pain of surgery as a grim inevitability and therefore rarely acknowledge it in their writings. There seems to have been little consistency in the use of any particular spirit or opiate. William Horner operated on the wounded following the Battle of Lundy's Lane in 1814 and did express some opinions on the pain suffered by his patients. He was later to become a Professor of Anatomy so his views are noteworthy. He acknowledges that soldiers were encouraged to repress the expression of pain, considering it unmanly. However, he criticised this, judging that it was better for the soldier to breath deeply and groan, rather than holding his breath in an effort to remain quiet. He also dissaproved of the practice of chewing a bullet during surgery. Horner noted that the amount of pain experienced by different individuals appeared to vary widely. Some soldiers did tolerate surgery with remarkable fortitude. At one operation at which he assisted the man 'smoked tranquilly' during the amputation of his leg.[44]

The possibility of surgery may have been viewed with horror, but the average soldier understood that it might be the only alternative to certain death. Once he had survived the immediate trauma and shock of the surgery, his greatest enemy was infection. There was little understanding of the importance of antisepsis until the observations of Lister in the late nineteenth century. The prompt administration of antibiotics and immunisation against tetanus is a vital part of the modern management of complicated and contaminated wounds. In the Napoleonic era, surgery was routinely performed in dirty conditions and operating instruments used repeatedly with only a rough wipe to remove blood between procedures. Under the circumstances, infection of amputation stumps and other surgical wounds was almost inevitable, and the appearance of the signs of infection was regarded as a normal stage of healing (hence the phrase 'laudable pus'). Surgeons did also appreciate the potential dangers

145

of what we would now recognise as bacterial infection. Hennen considered inflammation of the vessels and metastatic abscess formation in joints, organs and body cavities to be the principal cause of death after amputation.[45]

The most feared form of post-surgical infection acquired the name 'hospital gangrene'. In modern terms this was a bacterial infection carried between cases on the hands of medical and nursing staff, and on instruments and dressings. It was different from what we now most commonly refer to as 'gangrene', the death of previously healthy tissue due to the loss of a normal blood supply. It was also different from the 'gas gangrene' of the First World War which was caused by a different microbe. The incidence of hospital gangrene varied greatly throughout the wars, but once it made an appearance in a hospital the effects could be devastating. 'It is like a plague,' despaired one surgeon, 'no operation dare be performed, every cure stands still, every wound becomes a sore, and every sore is apt to run into gangrene.'

Although there was no insight into the microbial nature of the disease, the doctors of the period did understand the contagious nature of hospital gangrene. The author of an 1813 text on 'inflammation' noted that it might be communicated to persons at a distance by sponges, bandages or clothing, and that it could affect slight wounds of medical staff dressing infected patients. He observed that initially only one person was affected but that the problem could then spread rapidly through the ward.[46] These theories of contagion were, however, couched in the terminology of the age. William Fergusson attributed its presence in crowded hospitals to an 'accumulated exhalation from human bodies causing an impure and vitiated atmosphere'. The disease often commenced with vague symptoms such as headache, insomnia and fever. Then the open wound became painful and dry, taking on a shiny appearance. Within twenty-four hours a circular black area appeared around the wound and the whole limb became swollen. The patient continued to deteriorate rapidly with short periods of bleeding from the wound, and vomiting and diarrhoea, most often terminating in death. Even a previously well, wounded soldier could die of the affliction within forty-eight hours.

For most of the Peninsular War, the British Army was spared the worst ravages of hospital gangrene, but in 1813 a severe outbreak occurred in the general hospital at Bilbao where John Hennen had responsibility for the wounded. He attributed the appearance of the disease to the poor conditions in the hospital, where large numbers of sick and wounded were forced to lie on straw on the floor. Proper supplies were unavailable, one man describing his wounds being wrapped in brown paper. Hennen had a good understanding of the precautions which could prevent these outbreaks. Previously, at the hospital at Elvas in 1812 and at Vitoria earlier in 1813, he had enforced cleanliness and good ventilation and divided the patients into different wards. However, at Bilbao he had arrived too late to institute these measures and nearly 500 men succumbed to the epidemic.[47]

There are few surviving descriptions of hospital gangrene by the sufferers. Probably the best account is that of Private William Wheeler, who was wounded in the leg at the Nivelle, and developed the sinister complication several months later. The contemporary view of the prognosis is reflected by his admission to the 'incurable ward' in the hospital at Fuenterrabia in northern Spain. Wheeler undoubtedly understood the infectious and dangerous nature of his affliction. He informed his family of his disease and remarkable recovery in a letter dated 14 June 1814.

> Banish your fears about my safety, I am fast recovering. It was in the afternoon of the 3rd May that I felt a beating in my wound as if any one was tapping the place with their finger, in the night the beating increased attended with pain, the next morning when the doctor opened it, it was declared to be sluffed. I was then moved upstairs to what we call the incurable ward, none of the other patients in the hospital are allowed to enter this ward as the sluff is infectious, so that it is a kind of senetar. My wound continued to get worse, I had every attendance that could possibly be given and all the remedies applied to prevent mortification, at length my leg and thigh was reduced so small that I could span it with my hand, but the wounded part and foot were swollen to an enormous size, and the wound was as large over as a tea saucer.
>
> It was at length agreed to amputate my leg, this I joyfully agreed to being heartily tired of such a frightful troublesome member. Twice were I removed to the surgery to undergo the operation, but each time the little Spanish doctor, who had charge of me, overruled it and I was taken back to my bed. I understood my Doctor wished to try something else, then if that failed the leg was to come off. He brought from his home a small bottle filled with some thing like pepper and salt mixed, with this he covered the wound on which he put lint, bandaged it up, crossed himself, muttered something to himself and left me.
>
> Several times that day he visited me and my answers to his questions seemed to perplex him much. The next morning my answers seemed to please him, he took off the bandage in good spirits – when all the sluff excepting two spots, one about the size of a sixpence, the other smaller, came off with the lint. My wound now was changed from a nasty sickly whitebrown colour to a bright red. He capered about like a mad fellow, called the other doctors who all seemed surprised, he put some more stuff out of the bottle on the

spots and the next morning I was removed down stairs. This was on the 9th inst. Since then my wound improves surprisingly.[48]

Hospital gangrene had a high death rate – hence the general surprise at Wheeler's recovery. It may have been the Spanish doctor's prayers that were most helpful, as there was no proven treatment. The French, including Larrey, believed the local application of a hot iron to the infected wound (cautery) to be helpful, but this view was not shared by the British. Instead they variably tried local applications and poultices of Fowler's solution, turpentine, camphor in oil, opium and dilute nitric or citric acid. Ulcerating wounds were exposed to the fumes of nitrous acid gas. Patients were also bled and given internal treatments such as enemas, purgatives and bark, but Hennen believed all these measures to be almost useless.[49] A French surgeon pointedly remarked, 'The surgeon stands by as a pure observer, and at most can prognose the melancholy course of a disease which he can not ward off, heal, or limit.'[50]

Probably the most fatal of all diseases complicating surgery was tetanus. This feared disorder is caused by a bacterium which enters wounds through the soil. The main symptom is severe spasm of the muscles (including the jaw – hence the term 'lockjaw'). Sufferers can then develop breathing difficulties leading to death. Even today there is no specific cure and we largely rely on prevention by immunisation. In Napoleonic times, tetanus was recognised but its cause poorly understood. Some attributed it to nerve injuries, others to the chilling of the wound. Most surgeons agreed that all treatment was futile and that the outcome was almost invariably fatal. When intervention was attempted, it included amputation, cautery, deep incision of the wound, blister formation and administration of opium and camphor. Hennen recommended a combination of opiates, purgatives and warm bathing but admitted to never having cured an acute case.[51] McGrigor comments that in the Peninsula tetanus was 'frequent and fatal'. He was also pessimistic of the chances of finding an effective remedy but felt venesection and digitalis (extracted from foxglove) to be worth a trial.[52] There are anecdotal reports of successful treatments and surviving patients, but these are mostly unconvincing. After the Battle of Toulouse, thirteen cases of tetanus were recorded, roughly one percent of the surgical cases in the general hospital, and all died.

In order to try and rescue patients from the distressing complications of surgery, particularly infection, surgeons resorted to various measures which are usually collectively referred to as 'antiphlogistic' remedies. These medical treatments of the surgical patient included bleeding (also termed venesection or phlebotomy), and the prescription of drugs such as emetics and purgatives. The rationale was to remove impurities contained in the blood and thus relieve inflammation and fever. It is one of the paradoxes of the medicine of the wars that the same doctors who heroically pioneered new surgical techniques also supported practices that belonged more to the world of Galen than modern surgery. Most of the respected surgeons of the era, including Guthrie and Hennen, strongly supported the use of antiphlogistic measures. Hennen believed that soldiers especially benefited from purging and bleeding. He argued that army life gave them such vigour that they could tolerate the loss of blood better than civilians:

> The recruit just taken from the plough with all the appearance of health, which a ruddy countenance and a corpulent person can convey, will not bear the lancet nearly so well as the same individual in a few months after having been accustomed to the fare and mode of living of a soldier.[53]

Larrey was a less enthusiastic exponent of bleeding than the British but he also used it. Although the drug-induced vomiting and diarrhoea can hardly have helped the recovery of the wounded or post-operative soldier, it was the removal of blood which, in retrospect, must have caused the most damage. Many of the wounds and surgical procedures described will have inevitably caused considerable spontaneous blood loss. For instance, an uncomplicated fracture of the femur is associated with haemorrhage of up to two and a half litres. Once blood loss exceeds a critical level, the patient becomes shocked with pallor, a fall in blood pressure and urine output, and a thready rapid pulse. The modern intervention is blood transfusion. Although Napoleonic surgeons commented on these symptoms and signs of shock in wounded soldiers, the underlying processes at work were not understood and their response was unfortunately designed to worsen the outcome.

Many soldiers must have died after venesection who otherwise would have lived. Guthrie recommended the removal of up to twenty ounces of blood (approximately 500 millilitres) every day for three days where there was any inflammation after gunshot wounds. It has been argued that he was encouraged in his use of bleeding by seeing benefit in soldiers with lung complaints when he was a regimental surgeon early in the war. It may be that some of these patients had incipient heart failure associated with pneumonia, and bleeding could well have relieved this. In truth, Guthrie would probably have supported its use anyway. Bloodletting was almost universal and the amounts involved were often considerable. When Sir Andrew Barnard received a musket ball in the chest at the Nivelle, blood gushed from his mouth. Guthrie says that this only stopped after 'he was completely exhausted by bleeding from the arm to the amount of two quarts'. He was bled again the same evening and the following morning. Despite discharging pieces of cloth from the wound and suffering from breathing difficulties, he resumed command eight weeks later.[54]

Surgeon Walter Henry records the case of a soldier wounded in the lung who 'had been most judiciously and tenderly treated, and his life saved, hitherto, by enormous bleeding, to the extent of three hundred ounces in two days'.[55] Bleeding was approved of by wounded soldiers. Typical were the views of Lieutenant Colonel Frederick Ponsonby of the 12th Light Dragoons, injured at Waterloo, 'I had received several wounds; a surgeon slept in my room and I was saved by excessive bleeding.'[56] Rifleman George Simmons was also wounded at Waterloo, and he too had great faith in the antiphlogistic treatment of his case. His wound was a severe one, a musket ball had broken two ribs and caused damage to the liver before lodging in the sternum (breastbone). He developed a fever, pain over the liver, and then there was a subsequent soaking of his bedclothes with 'matter'. His sudden recovery suggests that a subphrenic abscess, a collection of pus between the liver and the lung, had complicated his liver injury and ultimately resolved by discharging through the skin. Before entering the Rifles as a second-lieutenant Simmons had served as an assistant surgeon in the Royal South Lincolnshire Militia. Perhaps because of his medical background, he wrote a detailed account of his antiphlogistic treatment regimen. To us it appears as a series of indignities simply calculated to make him feel more wretched and unlikely to survive.

A good surgeon, a friend of mine, instantly came to examine my wound. My breast was dreadfully swelled. He made a deep cut under the right pap, and dislodged from the breast-bone a musket-ball. I was suffocating with the injury my lungs had sustained. He took a quart of blood from my arm . . . [Simmons was then moved to a house in Brussels] . . . I had everything possible got for me, a surgeon sent for, a quart of blood taken from me, wrapped up in poultices, and a most excellent nurse. In four days I had six quarts of blood taken from me, the inflammation ran so high in my lungs. At present everything is going on well. I am so weak, if I lift my head from the pillow I faint . . . On the 3rd [July] I was attacked with convulsions, and at night with vomiting. Afterwards I lay in a state of insensibility until the morning when a violent inflammation had taken place in my body. I was bled three times, which gave me temporary ease. In this way I went on for seven days, bled regularly two or three times a day. I felt better, but continued in a stupor for four days, when the inflammation recommenced with far more violence than ever. The lancet was the only thing to save me, so I was bled again very largely. My liver now was much swollen, and consequently my body was a good deal enlarged. I had always an intolerable burning pain in the liver. I never slept – often in dread of suffocation. Bleeding was the only remedy for it.

In this way I went on for seven days more, when one evening, the pain being very violent, I sent for my surgeon to bleed me. He took two large basins from my arm. The pain abated much. I requested a little more might be taken, but I suddenly fainted. It was about half an hour before I could be brought to life. This alarmed my friend so much that he did not like to try bleeding again. He went and brought an eminent physician to see me, who recommended leeches. I had thirty immediately provided and applied to my sides. The next day, I had twenty-five more on the same spot, and the day after, twenty-five more. The last application of them was horrible. My side was inflamed and nearly raw from the biting of the others. I got fresh leeches every time; they bit directly. I was in the greatest state of debility when the last were put on the raw part; all taking hold at once made me entirely mad with anguish. I kicked, roared, and swore, and tried to drag them off, but my hands were held. Such torture I never experienced. As soon as they came off I ordered my servant to kill them, as well as about fifty more I had in the house ... I suddenly found my body very wet, and called my nurse, who was astonished to find me speak. The bed-clothes being turned down, there I was deluged in matter. The plaster was taken off the wound, when the matter flowed forth as from a fountain. I was immediately rational and my body began to decrease. I knew in a moment my life was saved. My surgeon came and jumped for joy at my good fortune.[57]

Simmons' recovery was no doubt enhanced by his surgeon's decision to stop bleeding with the lancet after his loss of consciousness. Not all were so fortunate. Sir William Howe De Lancey, quartermaster-general at Waterloo, was wounded by a spent cannon-ball which knocked him from his horse. He had multiple rib fracture which must have caused significant haemorrhage. During his subsequent management by several eminent doctors including John Hume, Wellington's personal physician, he was bled 'constantly' and had leeches applied. His gradual deterioration and death in a peasant's cottage nine days after the battle were poignantly documented by his young wife.[58]

Any overview of the war's surgery must acknowledge the stark contrasts. On the one hand, there were considerable advances in the quality of surgical technique. The surgeons of Wellington's army benefited from the opportunity to perform numbers of operations unprecedented in civil life. In Guthrie's words, at the end of the wars, 'Great experience and reflection had at this time created among us a body of operators such as never were excelled, if ever before equalled in the British Army.' There were real innovations. British surgeons, notably

Guthrie, made significant refinements to existing procedures and pioneered new operations. However, on the other hand, surgery remained a brutal, risky and haphazard business. The wounded soldier still needed considerable luck to survive. Misguided practices, such as venesection, persisted. Anaesthesia would have to wait another thirty years and routine antisepsis another sixty years.

It can be argued that the most significant change was not in the actual process of surgery but in the status of the army surgeon. As has been discussed in the first chapter, the army doctor had a lowly reputation, and the regimental surgeon particularly so. It would be wrong to suggest that this had dramatically changed by the time of Waterloo. It would take many years more before the army's surgeons achieved full recognition of their services. However, both in England and France, the wars did highlight the unique value of the surgeon as a practical man who could make an immediate contribution to the care of sick and wounded men. The medical heroes of the wars were the surgeons. The physicians, in contrast, all too often appeared to be overly intellectual, aristocratic and ultimately ineffectual.

We will close this chapter by briefly reviewing the later careers of a few of the major characters. Dominique Jean Larrey survived capture by the Prussians at Waterloo and returned to his former duties of Inspector General of the army medical services, and at the Guards Hospital in Paris. His experiences in the years 1815–40, including his visits to Britain and Ireland, are detailed in the fifth volume of his memoirs, *Campaigns and Travels*. George Guthrie's experiences in the Peninsula and following Waterloo provided the platform for a highly successful career in civil life. He became an acknowledged master of ophthalmic surgery in addition to general surgery. His subsequent appointments and honours included Surgeon at the Westminster Hospital, Fellow of the Royal Society, Professor of Anatomy at the Royal College of Surgeons, and President of the Royal College of Surgeons. He refused a knighthood in 1826 on the grounds that he was too poor. Guthrie died in 1856. In contrast to Larrey, he has not, to date, been the subject of a full length biography and details of his life have to be culled from his own surgical writings and a handful of biographical sketches. John Hennen was less fortunate than his more famous colleagues. At the end of the war, he was promoted to Deputy Inspector of Hospitals but he died in 1828 of yellow fever whilst fighting an epidemic of the disease in Gibraltar. The monument to his memory in the King's Chapel is one of the few reminders of this great army surgeon.

NOTES

1. Guthrie, G J, *Commentaries on the Surgery of the War*, p.v.
2. Woodward, J, *To Do The Sick No Harm*, p.76.

3. Horner, W E, *A military hospital at Buffalo*, p.767.
4. Bell, C, *Letters of Sir Charles Bell*, pp.241–3.
5. Chandler, D, *The Campaigns of Napoleon*, pp. 343–4.
6. Guthrie, pp.15–16.
7. Green, J, *The Vicissitudes of a Soldier's Life*, pp.195–7.
8. Billroth, T, *Historical Studies on the Nature and Treatment of Gunshot Wounds*, p.67.
9. Dible, H, *Napoleon's Surgeon*, p.120.
10. Hennen, J, *Principles of Military Surgery*, pp.52–4.
11. Dobbs, J, *Recollections of an old 52nd Man*, p.38.
12. Brereton, J M, *The British Soldier. A social history*, pp.54–5.
13. Napier, G T, *The Early Military Life of General Sir George T Napier*, p.184.
14. Dible, p.303.
15. Cooper, S, *A Dictionary of Practical Surgery*, Vol.I, p.77.
16. Guthrie, G J, *A Treatise on Gunshot Wounds*, pp.342–51.
17. Watts, J C, *George James Guthrie, Peninsular Surgeon*, p.767.
18. Trohler, U, *To Improve the Evidence of Medicine*, p.96.
19. Guthrie, *Treatise*, pp.42–4; *Commentaries*, pp.154–6.
20. Cantlie, N, *A History of the Army Medical Department*,Vol. I, p.391.
21. Guthrie, *Treatise*, p.39; Trohler, pp.100–3.
22. Guthrie, *Treatise*, p.226.
23. Dible, p.123.
24. Anon, *Biographical Sketch of G J Guthrie*, p.730.
25. Guthrie, *Commentaries*, p.154.
26. Guthrie, *Treatise*, pp.94–5.
27. Smith, H, *The Autobiography of Sir Harry Smith*, pp.39–40.
28. Hennen, p.86.
29. ibid., p.71.
30. Tomkinson, W, *The Diary of a Cavalry Officer*, pp.13–14.
31. Hennen, p.71.
32. Douglas, J, *Douglas's Tale of the Peninsula and Waterloo*, p.87.
33. Hennen, p.108.
34. Dible, p.136.
35. Verner, W, *Reminiscences of William Verner*, p.51.
36. Hennen, p.227.
37. Guthrie, *Commentaries*, pp.391–2.
38. ibid., p.535.
39. Crumplin, M K H, *Surgery at Waterloo*, p.40.
40. Grattan, W, *Adventures in the Connaught Rangers*, p.77.
41. Blakeney, R, *A Boy in the Peninsular War*, pp.326–7.
42. Anglesey, Marquess of, *One Leg. The Life and Letters of Henry William Paget*, p.150.
43. Costello, E, *Edward Costello. The Peninsular and Waterloo Campaigns*, p.156.
44. Horner, p.7.
45. Hennen, pp.220–3.
46. Thomson, J, *Lectures on Inflammation*, pp.484–5.
47. Hennen, pp.178–201.
48. Wheeler, W, *The Letters of Private Wheeler*, pp.152–3.
49. Hennen, p.200.
50. Billroth, p.73.
51. Hennen, pp.204–8.
52. McGrigor, J, *Sketch of the Medical History of the British Armies*, p.459.
53. Hennen, p.73.

54. Guthrie, *Commentaries*, p.468.
55. Henry, W, *Surgeon Henry's Trifles*, p.82.
56. Cotton, E, *A Voice from Waterloo*, p.266.
57. Simmons, G, *A British Rifleman*, pp.367–371.
58. De Lancey, Lady, *A Week at Waterloo in 1815*.

CHAPTER VI
Disease

We are an army of convalescents.
The Duke of Wellington, Spain, 1811

The greatest enemy of the Napoleonic soldier was not war itself but the disease that followed it. In all theatres of war between 1793 and 1815, total British losses were in the region of 240,000 men with probably fewer than 30,000 of these deaths being caused by wounds.[1] The rest were swept away in a tide of malignant and little understood contagious disease. In the Tropics they died of malaria and yellow fever, in the Middle East of plague, and in the Peninsula and northern Europe cold and deprivation brought the misery of typhus and dysentery.

Of course, life-threatening disease was not limited to army life. In the lower reaches of society a combination of bad habits, poor sanitation and chronic undernutrition made illness routine. The rapid and unregulated growth of towns and cities and a rising population favoured the spread of diseases of filth such as typhoid and urban diseases like tuberculosis.[2] In 1801 the most common cause of death in London was tuberculosis ('consumption') followed by 'convulsions' and then a wide variety of fevers, smallpox, and, only then, old age. Not far short of half the deaths were of children under 5 years of age. A survey of the labouring poor in Sheffield between 1798 and 1820 lists the common diseases as, 'Rheumatism, scrophula [tuberculosis], ulcers, hernia, gastrodynia, amenorrhoea, paralysis, abscess, cephalea, caries, febris, lumbago, pleurodynia, and vitia cutis.' Notwithstanding the obscure terminology, this was evidently a depressing catalogue of disease arising out of deprivation. The author of the report noted that many, 'were in a state of great feebleness, left by the sequelae of various acute diseases, and by difficult parturition, and old age ... A great many of the patients suffered, apparently under dyspepsia, brought on by irregular and poor living, and by a constant habit of smoking tobacco and drinking spiritous liquers'.[3]

Alcohol was widely available and undoubtedly the cause of much ill health. Most popular was cheap gin, which, according to one London magistrate, was the 'principal sustenance' of more than 10,000 people in the metropolis. Some individuals consumed prodigious amounts. For

155

instance, a London merchant was calculated to have drunk in excess of 35,000 bottles of port during twenty years of attendance at the Bull Inn in addition to his constant drinking at home.[4] Another survey of health in the 1790s declared resoundingly that British people were, 'as long lived as the people of any nation in the world', but later the author was forced to add, more pessimistically, 'on the other hand, by reason of intemperance, and of an unhappy excess that has obtained in spiritous liquors, there is no part of the world wherein people are more subject to die suddenly'.[5]

Wellington was in no doubt why men from the bottom of society, the 'scum of the earth', volunteered for the army: 'People talk of their enlisting from their fine military feeling – all stuff – no such thing. Some of our men enlist from having got bastard children – some for minor offences – many more for drink.'[6] Whatever their motives for becoming soldiers, the men who fought in the ranks on the road to Waterloo were almost entirely drawn from the unhealthy 'labouring classes'. There is ample evidence to prove this. Among the rank and file of the 23rd Regiment at Waterloo, previous occupations were listed as follows: labourers 332, textile workers 100, metalworkers 39, shoemakers 38, clothing-makers 32 and wood-workers 19.[7] When a Dr Woolcombe collected detailed social and medical information from 52 men in militia regiments in southern England in 1811, he also listed their old occupations: 18 labourers, 13 weavers, 5 shoemakers, 3 tailors, 2 gardeners, 1 flax-dresser, 1 clothier, 1 hatter, 1 needle-pointer, 1 butcher, 1 nailor, 1 blacksmith, 1 schoolmaster and 2 unknown.[8] Their medical conditions were a predictable collection of the ailments of the day, with the exception of one man whose hospital admission arose 'from playing on wind-instruments'.

We also have some knowledge of the age and physique of Wellington's soldiers. Young recruits were always preferred, but there were usually a number of middle-aged men in the regiment. The following range of ages for the Gordon Highlanders at Waterloo is probably typical.

```
50 years and upwards     3
45          „             7
40          „            26
35          „            59
30          „            95
25          „           105
20          „           110
18          „            48
under 18 years           4
```
The heights of the men were as follows:
```
6 feet 2 inches and upwards   0
6 feet      „                11
5 feet 11   „                11
```

5 feet 10	„	30
5 feet 9	„	71
5 feet 8	„	70
5 feet 7	„	77
5 feet 6	„	110
5 feet 5	„	77
under 5 feet 5 inches		94.[9]

The large number of men at the lower heights in all likelihood reflects a significant incidence of malnutrition. Efforts were made to apply a minimum height limit of 5 feet 4 inches for service, but this was often difficult to enforce. Men played tricks to increase or reduce their apparent height dependent on their motivation to either enrol into or avoid the army. Henry Marshall, a deputy inspector of hospitals, believed the only way of getting an accurate measurement was to lay the man on his back.

In addition to measurement of height, new recruits were also subject to a medical examination in order to weed out the poorest specimens. Regulations for regimental surgeons in 1803 recommend that the new soldier should have 'perfect use of his eyes and ears, and the full motion of every joint and limb'. He was to be regarded as unfit if he had a rupture (hernia), diseased enlargement of bones or joints, or if he was consumptive or subject to fits.[10] It is likely that this examination was rudimentary although the soldier was expected to strip off all his clothes. Around a third of applicants were considered unfit. For example, in a survey of the 107th Regiment in 1795, 182 men out of 539 were judged unfit to serve. The major problems were damaged limbs, 'rheumatics' and ruptures. Ages ranged from 16 to 80 years.[11]

Once he had successfully enlisted, the British soldier substantially increased his chance of developing serious disease. Much depended on where he was posted as the prevailing diseases were largely determined by geography and climate. In the early years of the Napoleonic Wars, the vast majority of disease deaths afflicted the army's forces campaigning in the West Indies. Mortality statistics are both impressive and frightening. During the period 1793–1815, approximately 97,000 British troops and mercenaries in British pay served in the region. There were 352,000 'casualties', that is to say, documented episodes of sickness, wounding, reported missing, or death. Approximately 70,000 troops died with fewer than 10% of these deaths caused by wounding.[12] This number of deaths may be an underestimate as it does not include sailors and soldiers who died whilst serving on board transports and warships, nor the later deaths of soldiers invalided back to England. Among the black soldiers of the West India Regiments, sick rates were appreciably lower but there were still 5,000 deaths.

If this scale of destruction is difficult to comprehend, then the figures for individual regiments and garrisons are more immediate and, in a sense, more chilling. For instance, the 66th Regiment, the Durham Light Infantry, had 2,330 men serving in the West Indies between 1801 and 1806, and suffered 1,588 fatalities. The overwhelming number of these deaths were from disease. During one particularly bad period on St Lucia, over 500 men died within six months. In the Leeward and Windward Islands between 1796 and 1805, 25,000 troops died, effectively destroying the garrison twice over. In the worst years, over a third of the men perished. Military families could be horribly affected. The death of Sir William Myers on the Leeward Islands meant that fourteen members of his family had died on the islands during the wars.[13]

When the York Hussars disembarked on St Domingo in July 1796, the regiment lost a quarter of its strength in less than two weeks. This was just the start. By a year later, disease had reduced the regiment from an initial strength of 640 to only 230 men of all ranks. Lieutenant Thomas Phipps Howard describes the first arrival of fever.

> In about three or four days after our arrival, the Troops barracked below began to feel in the most horrid manner the Plague, for I can call it by no other name. They had got it from onboard the transport ships. Carts were constantly employed in conducting the unfortunate victims to the different temporary hospitals allotted for them, for until now no regular Hospital had been constructed, Government not dreaming of the Mortality that was to take place; so that any Stable or Barn that would contain a quantity of Beds was obliged to be converted into a Sick House, out of which, from want of those necessaries requisite to be had & the inveteracy of the Disorder; very few ever came out except to their Graves. It is impossible for words to express the horror that presented itself at this time to those who were still able to crawl about. 30 Negroes were constantly employed in digging Graves & burying the unhappy wretches that perished; & scarcely could they, working the whole of the Day, tho' three, four & five were tumbled into the same Grave together. The Dead Carts were constantly employed, & scarcely was one empty, tho' they held from 8 to 12 each, but another was full. Men were taken ill at dinner, who had been in the most apparent Health during the Morn; & were carried to their long Homes at Night. In short, the putridity of the Disorder at last arose to such an height that hundreds, almost, were absolutely drowned in their own Blood, bursting from them at every Pore. Some died raving Mad, others forming plans for attacking, the others desponding; in fact Death presented itself under every form an unlimited Imagination could invent.[14]

According to Howard, 'Some Regiments seeing the mortality around them gave themselves totally up for lost, & instead of attempting to stop the progress of the disease, did everything in their Power to promote it to be the sooner out of their Misery.' The demoralising effects of such an epidemic of disease were not limited to the British Army. Moreau de Jonnes, a staff officer and later a renowned statistician, has left a record of the impact of disease on the French army in Martinique in 1802. De Jonnes says that the 'scourge' or 'malignant fever' spread rapidly through the troops and 'terror was rampant'. Men abandoned their posts. Whole regiments left their barracks to bivouac in the open, and malicious rumours circulated as to the cause of the disease which included deliberate poisoning of the soldiers' water supply. Discipline broke down almost entirely and de Jonnes protected his men by concealing their disobedience from senior officers.[15]

Inevitably, the news of the wholesale destruction of European armies in the West Indies reached home. Troops bound for the region were soon fearing disease far more than the enemy. George Pinchard, a physician who accompanied Sir Ralph Abercromby's expedition in 1796, describes the increasing panic in England.

> A degree of horror seems to have overspread the nation from the late destructive effects of yellow-fever, or what the multitude denominates, the West India plague; insomuch that a sense of terror attaches to the very name of the West Indies – many, even, considering it synonymous with the grave; and, perhaps, it were not too much to say, that all, who have friends in the expedition apprehend more from disease than the sword. Such discouraging sentiments I am sorry to find have not been concealed from the troops. The fearful farewell of desponding friends is every day, and hour, either heedlessly, or artfully sounded in their ears. People walking about the camp, attending a review, or a parade, or merely upon seeing parties of soldiers in the streets, are heard to exclaim, – 'ah, poor fellows! You are going to your last home! What a pity such brave men should go to that West India grave! – to that hateful climate to be killed by the plague! Poor fellow, good bye, farewell! We shall never see you back again!' With such like accents are the ears of soldiers incessantly saluted; and the hopeless predictions are loudly echoed, for the worst of purposes, by the designing, whose turbulent spirits would feast in exciting discontentment among the troops.[16]

What were the diseases which terrorised and destroyed the army? Although there are many references to 'plague' in the writing of the time, bubonic plague was one of the few infectious diseases not to make an appearance in the West Indies. Most deaths were attributable to some form of feverish illness. The medical terminology of the period is confusing, and the general term 'fever' was used to encompass a wide range of what we would now recognise as infectious diseases. An eminent eighteenth-century physician described fever as a combination of rapid pulse, shivering and heat.[17] The army's doctors recognised that this feared disease could be subdivided dependent on the symptoms and clinical signs. Most simply, it was divisible into four basic types: typhus, intermittent fever, simple continued fever, and remittent fever. Typhus is the disease we know today. Intermittent fever was malaria, and simple continued and remittent fevers were probably a mixture of infectious diseases including malaria, typhoid, relapsing fever and dysentery. In the West Indies, there were other diseases present and the classification was necessarily extended. A notable addition was yellow fever. This disease had acquired a number of other names including yellow jack, black vomit, Havana fever, Guinea fever, and Bolam fever. Little wonder that the medical officers were confused.

There is evidence that garrisons in the West Indies suffered from a wide range of ills; dysentery, diarrhoea, pulmonary ailments, rheumatism, leg ulcers and venereal disease were all prevalent. However, we can say with confidence that just two diseases, yellow fever and malaria, accounted for the overwhelming number of deaths. Yellow fever is a disease with such characteristic symptoms that it is easily identified from the eyewitness accounts of soldiers and doctors. It is caused by a virus which is carried from person to person by a mosquito. The yellow fever virus attacks the liver, causing a deep jaundice which gives the disease its modern name. Because of liver failure, there is a bleeding tendency and the vomiting of dark blood (usually described as 'coffee grounds') accounts for the contemporary term 'black vomit'. The unfortunate victim can bleed everywhere – from the nose, mouth, rectum, and any open skin lesions – and is usually delirious and distressed.[18] When Lieutenant Howard says that his men 'drowned in their own blood' and 'died raving mad', he is describing the symptoms of advanced yellow fever. Where death occurs, it classically happens after six or seven days of illness, but it seems that one of the chief features of the yellow fever of the Napoleonic Wars was the very rapid, and almost casual, way it took life. William Fergusson, at this time surgeon of the 67th Regiment, gives some examples.

> Lieutenant Wright, one of my earliest patients at Port au Prince, St. Domingo, on the fourth day of the fever rose from his bed in perfect possession of his senses, dressed himself correctly, and went into the market-place accompanied by myself, where he spent some time purchasing fruits and other things, returned to his barrack-room, where he shortly expired in a torrent of black vomit. Lieutenant Mackay, of the quartermaster-general's department, Cape St. Nicholas Mole, on the day of his death, was up and dressed on the

sofa, with books and papers before him at ten in the morning, passing jokes of comparison between his own dingy complexion, made so by the disease, and that of his mulatto nurse; at two he expired in the same way as Lieutenant Wright.[19]

Modern estimates of mortality from yellow fever, which can vary markedly in severity, are around 10%, that is one death for every ten ill patients. But for epidemics in the eighteenth and nineteenth centuries, the figure was much higher, probably around 70%. Although we have no precise statistics for individual diseases affecting the British Army in the West Indies, the latter figure is probably close to the truth. It was widely held at the time that not all the troops and attending civilians were equally vulnerable to the disease. De Jonnes believed that in the French forces yellow fever first attacked 'sailors and soldiers given to excess and frequenters of places of ill fame' and then next attacked the youngest and officers with onerous duties.[20] A British naval surgeon gave the following order in which the disease attacked Europeans; first sailors, 'especially the robust and young', then soldiers and other white males lately arrived in the region, then 'all other white males', and finally, women.[21]

The second great killer, malaria, was more widespread at the time of the Napoleonic wars than it is today. It afflicted British troops in the Iberian Peninsula and even in the Low Countries. The type of malaria prevalent in the West Indies was more virulent than these European forms. Like yellow fever, malaria is a mosquito-borne disease, but there are four different species of the micro-organisms (called plasmodia) which cause it. Three of the four are debilitating, but it is the other type, falciparum malaria, which is the major cause of death. One of the classic symptoms of the disease is an intermittent high fever with associated rigors and exhaustion on the first and third day, hence it was sometimes referred to as 'malignant tertian fever'.[22] Most British army doctors simply called the disease intermittent or remittent fever, and affected soldiers complained of the 'ague'. Although the cause of malaria was completely unknown to the medical officers, it was common knowledge that it was most prevalent in low-lying coastal areas, particularly around swamps and marshes, and that the worst time of the year in the West Indies was after the rainy season between the months of October and January.

Infection was not the only cause of ill health among the troops. According to one authority on the British army in the West Indies, more soldiers may have died from the effects of chronic alcohol abuse than from infectious diseases.[23] This was certainly the opinion of experienced soldiers and doctors. Major-General Hugh Carmichael, commander in chief of Jamaica in 1808, believed the principal cause of disease to be the 'corrosive and insidious effect of rum'. William Fergusson witnessed the damage inflicted by alcohol on a freshly drafted regiment.

When the 67th Regiment, then newly arrived and in garrison at St. Domingo was ordered upon an expedition up the country, the troops, previously to making off, were supplied with a full ration of spirits. It was, as might have been foreseen, speedily consumed, and the men marching under a burning sun, through a dry rocky country that furnished no water, fell down at almost every step. Nineteen actually died upon the road, and those who arrived at the end of the march – a distance of about twelve miles – were in a state of exhaustion and distress that cannot be described. No one, even amongst the officers, who ventured so much as to taste their undiluted spirit, escaped with impunity.[24]

Some of the adverse effects of drink may have been caused by constituents other than alcohol. The 'new rum' of the West Indies was often contaminated with high levels of lead. Diseases such as 'colic' and 'dry bellyache' were quite possibly lead poisoning caused by rum.[25]

The medical treatments adopted in response to the appalling diseases of the West Indies were typical of the time and appear incredible today. It may be thought that the following account of the treatment of fever cases in the West Indies in 1801, written by a hospital mate, is exaggerated, but other sources suggest its reliability.

The men on admission were conducted to a wash house containing warm and cold baths. They were instantly bled to the quantity from 16 to 20 ounces. They were, on revival from fainting, which generally occurred, plunged into a warm bath in numbers of four to six together and confined in by blankets fastened over the machine till about suffocated. From hence they were dashed into cold baths and confined until apparently lifeless. Immediately after, a strong emetic was administered, they were carried to bed, and a dose of 8 grains of calomel and 6 grains of James's powder given as a purge, which occasioned a train of distressing symptoms for the relief of which they were bled again and blistered from head to foot. They were bled a fourth and fifth time in the space of thirty hours, and usually lost 60 to 70 ounces of blood.[26]

It seems that the sick soldiers were subjected to a series of indignities which can only have made them more miserable and less likely to survive. The combination of bleeding by lancet or other methods, drenching in cold water, and the administration of drugs such as purgatives (designed to induce diarrhoea), emetics (inducing nausea and vomiting), and agents producing profound sweating and salivation, formed the mainstay of treatment of disease. We have already encountered the 'antiphlogistic' regimen in the context of wound management. Contemporary views on the causation of disease will be discussed in more detail later, but in simple terms, the rationale of antiphlogistic type treatment was to remove 'impurities' which were presumed to be inhabiting the blood. Different diseases were treated with different drugs and other methods, but this basic philosophy remained constant.

Although many elements of treatment are disconcerting to the modern observer, perhaps the practice which now appears most perverse was the removal of large volumes of blood from men already debilitated by the effects of infectious disease. Just as in surgery, where venesection was supported by leading army surgeons including Guthrie and Hennen, in medicine it was practised by respected army physicians such as Robert Jackson, William Fergusson and James McGrigor. In his acclaimed work, *A Sketch of the History and Cure of Febrile Diseases*, first published in 1817, Jackson notes that bleeding 'presents itself as the first remedy in point of time, as it is the most important in point of power for the cure of febrile diseases of any which we have knowledge'.[27] Fergusson supported venesection but was also wary of its overuse, as the following rather threatening passage from his autobiography illustrates.

> Fever is everywhere our most dangerous disease, and whoever, through prejudice, refuses the aid of the lancet under any circumstances, will have the sin of omission branded on his soul when called to his account for the lives committed to his charge; but his case will be far worse who, as a matter of system, indiscriminately uses it upon all who are brought before him. He will then have offered sacrifice in vindication of a creed that was baseless, and the sin of commission will be deeper and more indelible.[28]

McGrigor performed venesection selectively, advocating it in pneumonia, where he believed that the amount of blood removed was to be judged by the relief of symptoms. Even after a large bleeding, if the patient was no better, the procedure was to be repeated again a few hours later, and if necessary, several more times. In a comment similar to Hennen's proposal that soldiers tolerate bleeding unusually well, McGrigor says that the military doctor 'must not judge by what he has seen in private [civilian] practice where the sudden abstraction of a large quantity of blood would perhaps be improper'.[29] McGrigor cannot have been altogether convinced of the benefit of venesection as he sanctioned a trial of its use in the midst of the Peninsular War. This experiment, far in advance of its time in concept and methodology, is described in the 1816 doctoral thesis of Alexander Hamilton, formerly an assistant surgeon in the 42nd Foot. Three regimental surgeons managed a total of 366 sick soldiers indiscriminately except that two did not employ the lancet and one did. In the two thirds not venesected, only seven died, whereas in the one third who were bled, thirty-five died. This indictment of venesection was probably little known outside Edinburgh and a small circle of army doctors.[30]

There is much written about the theory of bleeding, but we have to dig a little deeper into contemporary medical texts to understand exactly what the fever-stricken soldier was subjected to.[31] Blood could be removed from a convenient vein with a sharp instrument called a lancet; this was known as 'general' blood-letting and was the commonest method used in fevers. Alternatively, 'topical' blood-letting could be undertaken using an instrument called a scarificator, and a cupping glass, or using leeches. General blood-letting was intended to reduce the whole volume of circulating blood, whilst topical letting might be employed in a particular diseased part of the body. For general blood-letting using the lancet, veins in the arm, at the ankle or in the neck were most easily accessed. On occasion, the temporal artery over the forehead was opened. When an arm vein was selected, the doctor improvised a tourniquet from a piece of bandage or linen tied around the arm above the vein, and then incised the vein carefully with the lancet. The blood was then allowed to flow into a basin until a sufficient quantity was collected. Bleeding was stopped by releasing the tourniquet and by applying thumb pressure and then a bandage to the wound. In topical blood-letting, the scarificator was a fearsome looking instrument comprising a large number of lancets and a spring device designed to make a series of punctures in the skin. The flow of blood from the wounds was encouraged by placing a heated cupping glass over the area to create a vacuum. The procedure was sometimes referred to as 'cupping'. Leeches were normally applied to the skin by hand. They were liable to 'bite better' if they were removed from water at least an hour before use. Once attached they became engorged with blood within ten to fifteen minutes and then dropped off.[32]

Immersion in cold water was also commonly resorted to in fever cases. There are numerous accounts, many by the sufferers, of feverish soldiers being either placed in cold baths or having cold water poured over them. An officer of the 43rd Regiment recalls,

> The assistant surgeon felt my pulse and asked, 'Whether I would permit him to throw some water on my head?' I readily assented to this, entreating him to do anything to make me well. Lifted out of bed, and divested of my linen garment, I was placed in a chair; the doctor standing on a table, emptied two pitchers of spring water on my crown, which produced a most painful sensation.[33]

In his discussion of 'fever as an army disease' William Fergusson lauds cold water as the 'treatment I have found most successful in various countries and climates'.[34] At least the liberal use of cold water, sometimes called the 'cold affusion', probably did less harm than excessive bleeding. Joseph Gilpin, Inspector of Army Hospitals at Gibraltar, makes some interesting comparisons between bleeding and cold water treatment with respect to the management of fever cases in the garrison in 1813. He concedes that the supporters of bleeding are 'no doubt very respectable' but makes a case for the cold affusion of water, arguing that it similarly checked the 'congestion and topical inflammation' of fever whilst it 'possessed one great advantage over that of the lancet; . . . it certainly does not diminish the patient's strength, but leaves him in a state that may enable him to bear the operation of any other energetic remedy that may be thought necessary'.[35]

The other energetic remedies referred to by Gilpin constituted the remainder of the antiphlogistic regimen. A bewildering number of therapies were tried, most apparently only unified by their unpleasantness and inefficacy. In a relentless effort to rid the body of invisible substances presumed to be causing fever or other systemic disease, many drugs were administered. The major classes of drugs were given names describing their primary action; thus there were purgatives, emetics, cathartics, tonics, stimulants, astringents and sudorifics. Their precise mode of action and indications for use are couched in the medical language of the time and do not merit detailed consideration here. They were often administered in combination and a single drug might be included in several classes. Most of the drugs are alien to modern medicine – commonly used agents included calomel (mercurous chloride), acetate of lead, antimony, camphor, arsenic and ammonia. A handful of drugs have survived. Ipecacuanha is still used as an emetic, senna is widely prescribed as a laxative, and derivatives of opium are important for their sedative and analgesic effects. Perhaps the drug of greatest potential benefit was Peruvian bark, the cinchona from which quinine was later to be extracted. Quinine remains an important drug in the management of malaria. Its efficacy in the Napoleonic era depended on the exact type of bark used and the amount ingested. Unsurprisingly, bark was found to be ineffective in non-malarial fevers. Where the patient did benefit from treatment it was difficult to know which, if any, of the drugs had been effective. Several potions became popular as panaceas. The best known was Dr James's Powder, a mixture of antimony and potash of lime, the 'aspirin of the eighteenth century'. Where all oral medications were seen to fail, and this was often the case, the army doctor might try other approaches, such as a variety of enemas, or the application of irritant substances to the skin to raise blisters.

It would be unfair to imply that all antiphlogistic treatments were unpleasant. Warm baths must have been soothing, and comfortable clothes such as flannels were advocated. Sick soldiers were given specially prepared food as the correct diet was believed to be crucial to the outcome.

When feverish they might be limited to bread, milk and tea. As the disease subsided, the diet was enriched with other items like meat, potatoes, rice and wine. Other harmless measures would now be regarded as mere eccentricities. For instance, bathing in warm milk, and the ingestion of rhubarb and spider's web.

With this background information, it is possible to understand better the treatment regimens used for the fevers of the West Indies. Soldiers with yellow fever were initially bled and then vomiting was induced with tartar emetic and purgation undertaken with calomel and salts. Further bleeding and blisterings could be accompanied by James's Powder and stimulants such as brandy, wine and camphor. Deterioration required drastic measures. One strategy employed a large glass of gin containing hartshorn, bark, snakeroot and opium, all repeated every two hours. Most treatment was to no avail. Jackson estimated that two thirds of soldiers expired from the disease. Malaria was mainly treated with bark and this may well have resolved some symptoms and even given a cure. The quality varied and 'red bark' was preferred to 'yellow bark'. Other less helpful interventions included purging, blistering and dousing with cold water. Bleeding was probably used less than in yellow fever because of concern at the debility it could cause.

In view of the nastiness of many of the treatments prescribed by the medical staff, it is hardly surprising that some soldiers devised their own 'cures' or sought advice elsewhere. Thomas Henry Browne contracted malaria in Martinique in 1808 and was helped by a native American whom he had befriended in an earlier campaign.

> I had a very bad attack of ague about this time, caught I believe on the lakes where I was constantly at work, with my old friend Whisker Tom, whose attachment seemed to increase for me daily ... He recommended me all sorts of remedies for my ague, but it obstinately resisted them all, and from Tertian became Quotidian until I was reduced to an absolute skeleton. It yielded at length to the constant attacks I made upon it with bark, Cayenne pepper, and Madeira, but my strength was sadly exhausted, and my spirits completely subdued.[36]

Alcohol featured prominently in attempts at self-medication. Rifleman Jonathan Leach tried to cure his debilitating fever by drinking a jug of boiling Madeira wine. It seemed to work, although by his own admission it was 'a kill or cure business and worthy only of a wild youth'.[37] Lest we be overly contemptuous of the more extreme treatments tried by army doctors and soldiers in the West Indies, it is worth remembering that yellow fever and malaria remain major health problems today. Yellow fever is controlled to some degree by elimination of the mosquito vector and vaccination, but there is still no specific treatment for established disease. For malaria, hopes of elimination have receded and, although there are effective treatments, emerging resistance to drugs is a real problem. The disease affects over one hundred countries and causes between one and two million deaths each year.

During the Peninsular War, the British Army continued to be undermined by a plethora of different infectious diseases. The effect of these diseases on the army's capability is not much acknowledged in military histories of the period. Between the years 1808 and 1814 in Spain and Portugal, it has been estimated that nearly three times as many British soldiers died from disease as from wounds. Hospital records for the last three years of the war show that wounds accounted for only 15% of deaths.[38] The sick rate averaged around 20% but it was not unusual for 30% of the whole army to be sick and in the winter of 1812 this approached 40%.[39] The first major challenge for the army's doctors followed Sir John Moore's Corunna campaign. During the notorious retreat from Sahagun to Corunna, a combination of appalling weather, inadequate supplies and low morale took an increasing toll of the men. Corunna was finally reached in January 1809 and a defeat inflicted on Soult's pursuing army. Approximately 28,000 filthy, exhausted, disease-ridden British soldiers disembarked on the south coast of England to the consternation of the local populus. Probably around 6,000 men, 20% of the returning force, were sick enough to require immediate medical attention.[40]

James McGrigor has left a detailed account of the management of the sick at Portsmouth, and Richard Hooper, a surgeon, made a comparable record of events at Plymouth.[41] The two most common causes of illness and death were typhus and dysentery, both diseases that thrive in conditions of cold, deprivation and overcrowding. It has been said that 'the history of typhus is the history of human misery'. Epidemics of the disease have long been associated with war. In 1812 typhus was a significant cause of death during Napoleon's retreat from Moscow. The disease is caused by rickettsia, micro-organisms somewhere between bacteria and viruses. Typhus can be transferred to man by a variety of insects but epidemic typhus, the type seen in the Peninsula, is passed from person to person by the human body louse.[42] Although McGrigor comments that typhus is 'a term in by far too general use', there is little doubt that the disease was the cause of the 'Spanish fever' affecting the troops under his care. Characteristic symptoms and signs of typhus described by McGrigor include malaise, rigors, headache, the appearance of small haemorrhages in the skin (petechiae) and gangrene of the extremities. Fatal cases developed increasing drowsiness and coma, death occurring between the fifth and fourteenth days. The mortality from fever in the Portsmouth area, presumably nearly all typhus, was 13%. Treatments followed normal antiphlogistic patterns with plenty of purgatives, emetics, cordials, stimulants, dousing with cold water, warm baths and venesection. Dr Clarke, the physician in charge of the general hospital at Portsmouth, himself developed the fever and attributed his recovery to being bled nine times, a total of 127 ounces (approximately 3.5 litres). Many other drugs were tried, individual practitioners almost invariably claiming success for their own particular approach.

Hooper confirms much of McGrigor's account of typhus and also gives a lengthy account of the dysentery he encountered. This depressing affliction is caused by a variety of bacteria and is associated with the passage of bloody diarrhoea. In severe cases there is increasing weakness and dehydration. Hooper describes all the typical symptoms in the Corunna soldiers. Treatment was predictably complicated with greater resort to enemas and opium than was the case for other disorders. In desperation, large quantities of wine and even cobweb were administered. The latter was supposed to have 'extraordinary qualities' in chronic dysentery. The mortality from dysentery was usually great, not least because the disorder had a tendency to intervene in the advanced stages of other diseases. After Corunna, the death rate from the disease was 26%, double that from typhus. Compared with the massive impact of typhus and dysentery, wounds were not a major cause of mortality. Of the 241 deaths at Plymouth, only twenty-five were from wounds and most of these also had disease.

The incidence and severity of disease gradually diminished through the spring of 1809. However, for most of the regiments who had fought in the campaign it would take a considerable time to recover. John Harris remembered the decimation of his battalion of the 95th Rifles, one of the army's elite units.

> After the disastrous retreat to Corunna, the Rifles were reduced to a sickly skeleton, if I may so term it. Out of perhaps nine hundred as of active and fine fellows as ever held a weapon in an enemy's country, was paraded some three hundred weak and crestfallen invalids. I myself stood the third man in my own company, which was reduced from near a hundred men to but three. Indeed I think we had scarce a company on parade stronger than ten or twelve men at the first parade. After a few parades, however, our companies gradually were augmented (by those of the sick who recovered) but many of those who did not sink in hospital were never more of much service as soldiers.[43]

Disease spread to soldiers who had not campaigned in Spain and also to civilians. In a laudable initiative, the War Office ordered soldiers' clothes to be burnt, the men receiving money to replace their belongings. Where such measures were taken, spread was often reduced and, even where there were recurrences, symptoms were milder. Just how extensively the diseases affected the civilian population is less easy to establish. It is likely that they did to a significant extent at Portsmouth and Plymouth where the locals showed generous hospitality to the returning army. A contemporary London doctor recalled:

> Within a few yards of where I now write, the greater part of a family fell sacrifice to the effects of fomites that lurked in a blanket purchased from one of the soldiers after their return from Corunna.[44]

The best sources for the medicine of the remainder of the Peninsular War are McGrigor's autobiography and his *Sketch of the Medical History of the British Armies in the Peninsula of Spain and Portugal during the late campaigns*. The latter article, published in the journal *Transactions of the Medico-Chirurgical Society* in 1815, includes details of all the diseases affecting the army and the preferred treatments. Typhus continued to be a scourge, flaring up whenever the troops were most debilitated and demoralised. It was prevalent after the retreat from Burgos in the winter of 1812, when the army suffered deprivations equal to and perhaps even greater than those experienced during the earlier retreat to Corunna. The devastation that could be wreaked by typhus is well illustrated by the fate of another of the army's elite regiments, the 1st Battalion of the 1st Regiment of Foot Guards. When these troops entered Spain in the autumn of 1812, they were regarded as among the finest in the army, 'exciting the admiration of every officer who saw them'. By the time they had completed several long marches in severe weather over the mountains of Galicia, they were, in the words of the battalion's assistant surgeon, John Bacot, 'in a state of miserable deprivation, dirty in their persons, worn down with fatigue, wasted most strikingly in flesh, and depressed in spirits'.[45] The men were quartered in the town of Vizeu, often three or four sharing a house. Owing to incessant rain there were few parades or inspections to promote cleanliness. An outbreak of typhus was inevitable. The Guards entered Vizeu in January 1813 with nearly 1,100 men. Twelve weeks later, only 358 marched out. Some companies were particularly singled out. In one, out of the 119 men only twelve escaped the disease – seven of the twelve were officers' batmen and two were regimental tailors.

McGrigor dedicated a considerable part of his 'sketch' to dysentery.[46] This was easy to justify as it caused more deaths during the Peninsular War than any other single disease. As was the case after Corunna, this was in part because it often proved fatal to patients with other diseases and wounds. McGrigor attempted to subdivide dysentery into several types, which may have correlated with different causative organisms. As the disease occurred in similar circumstances to typhus, it is unsurprising that it also reached its peak in the winter of 1812–13.

Treatments for both typhus and dysentery throughout the course of the war did not differ substantially from those tried after Corunna. According to McGrigor's figures, for all hospitals in the final years of the Peninsular War, 1812–14, there were 2,300 deaths from typhus and 4,700 from dysentery. During the same period, 2,700 hospital deaths were attributed to wounds.

During these years, the other most common cause of death, second only to dysentery, was 'continued fever'. McGrigor commonly divided the fevers of the Peninsula into 'continued' (sometimes quaintly referred to as the 'synochus of Cullen'), intermittent, remittent and typhus. 'Simple continued fever' was the commonest reason for admission to regimental hospitals and it probably included more trivial illnesses such as the common cold. However, the large number of deaths arising from continued fever implies that at least some had more serious disorders. One possibility is typhoid, an infectious disease caused by a bacterium spread by a combination of poor hygiene, flies and contaminated water supplies.[47] The two great killers of the West Indies were both present in the Peninsular army. Only malaria, usually referred to as intermittent fever or ague, was widespread. This disease was endemic in the native population; 'so common is ague in many parts of Spain and Portugal that the inhabitants do not term it a disease'.[48] The malaria season lasted from June to September. Although there were some 'malignant tertian fevers', presumably the dreaded falciparum type, many cases were more benign with a protracted course marked by frequent relapses. Deaths from intermittent fever during 1812–14 were fewer than 300, only a fraction of those caused by dysentery, typhoid and typhus. Treatment was similar to that described in the Tropics with bark apparently curing many soldiers. It was recommended that an ounce or an ounce and a half be given in the six hours before the expected paroxysm of fever with smaller quantities in the intervals between attacks. Where bark failed, it was probably either of poor quality or given in insufficient amounts.

Perhaps because malaria was often a debilitating rather than a fatal disease, it makes frequent appearances in the memoirs of the Peninsula. Many soldiers describe their ague and its peculiar treatments and surprising cures. Typical is the account of Ensign George Bell who was plagued by symptoms of the disease for several months during 1813.

> Since we finished off the retreat from Burgos and Madrid there was great mortality amongst the troops, fever and ague prevailing. I caught both and suffered severely. There was no cure. All the charms the doctors got from the medical department at home was some rotten old bark intended to be mixed with some country wine, to dose the soldiers. Some fusty sawdust would have had the same effect! . . . The cold shivering fit first came on, nothing would warm me, then

after a few hours the hot or burning fever fit succeeded, with a
splitting headache that nearly drove me crazy. The next day I was
quite well and fit for anything . . . The 7th of July was one of my very
worst ague days, but turned out afterwards a day of rejoicing. I was
lying under an apple tree in the beautiful valley, hors-de-combat, in a
hot fit, my head splitting open, as I thought, with pain. The day was
extremely hot, which only aggravated the malady, and increased my
sufferings . . . I lay under a cold damp fog all night; the ague took
flight and never returned during the war! Some fellows said that it
was frightened out of me! Maybe so. I wish it had been frightened out
of me sooner.[49]

When Assistant Surgeon Walter Henry developed malaria in the region of
the Guadiana river in central Spain in 1812, he was subjected to a
particularly aggressive antiphlogistic treatment regimen under the
supervision of a fellow doctor.

From a desire to save the vital fluid and economise strength, he
would not bleed me from the arm or temporal artery, as I wished; but
when the symptoms of determination to the head became urgent, he
sheered and shaved my curly locks one hot afternoon, and attached
three dozen of leeches to my poor caput [head]. A few hours after,
they carried me into the yard, placed me erect, and poured four or
five-and-twenty buckets of cold well-water over me from a third floor
window. After this terrible shower-bath, I was rubbed dry and put to
bed. For the first two hours I was not quite sure whether my head had
not been carried away in the flood, for I felt as if there was no living
part, and all was numb and cold above my shoulders but there was
violent reaction during the night, and I became delirious the next
morning. However I was not destined to leave my bones in Badajoz –
there were but too many British bones there already.

Henry's disease relapsed and did not respond to all the usual treatments.
He then adopted the rather eccentric plan of 'outrunning' his fever.
Having drunk a draught of hot spiced wine, he mounted his horse and as
the 'ague-fiend's cold fingers' gripped him he galloped across the plain,
'and at length, by dint of perseverance and good management, I fairly
distanced my villainous pursuer'. The young surgeon was not further
troubled by malaria.[50]

Napoleonic soldiers frequently developed chest problems, notably
simple pneumonia and tuberculosis. Both these diseases were less
common in the Peninsula than in some other theatres of war, and
tuberculosis was much rarer than in the towns and cities of Britain where
its devastating effects peaked around 1800. McGrigor records that fewer

than 300 men died in hospital from tuberculosis in the latter years of the war. This was in marked contrast to home where in some regiments up to half the mortality was caused by this single disease.[51] Such a difference was predictable as it had long been known that patients with tuberculosis much benefited by travelling to a warmer southern European climate, especially Portugal. It is probable that the majority of affected soldiers in the Peninsula contracted the disease before leaving England, and that the deaths were mainly among men who arrived on campaign with the disease already in an advanced stage.

After the commoner fevers, dysentery, diarrhoea and wounds, the next most frequent causes of admission to the regimental hospitals were 'ulcera' and 'rheumatism'. Ulceration of the legs had been commonplace in previous campaigns due to rubbing by gaiters, but it persisted even after trousers were introduced. The risk was increased by inadequate foot wear and insect bites and the ulcers could obstinately refuse to heal and become chronic. The term rheumatism was used to describe a wide range of musculoskeletal disorders arising out of exposure to the elements and overexertion. 'Rheumatism of the feet' was very common after the retreat from Burgos, particularly in the 5th Division, and was treated with opium and immersion in warm water.[52] Venereal disease afflicted Wellington's Peninsular army as much as any other army of the times, although its presence is rarely acknowledged in contemporary memoirs or historical accounts. Both prostitution and promiscuity were routine. According to William Fergusson men regularly had 'intercourse with the common women of the country'[53], and John Hennen comments that, 'soldiers are gregarious in their habits and we have frequently several men at the same time in hospital infected by the same woman with whom they have had connexion in very rapid succession'.[54] The major diseases were syphilis and gonorrhoea, referred to by the French as the 'gross lot' (big prize) and 'petit lot'. A number of medical accounts suggest that when British soldiers contracted syphilis they developed more symptoms than the locals. The standard treatment of the time explains the oft quoted aphorism, 'a night with Venus and a lifetime with Mercury'. Side effects of mercury were frequently worse than the disease, and British army doctors gradually realised that they were doing more harm than good. Fergusson admitted that he was shaken by the superior results obtained by Portuguese doctors and the realisation that 'the wisest amongst us should have been destroying instead of saving their patients by murderous and unnecessary courses of mercury'.[55] Venereal diseases have always been under-reported, but the best figures we have for the Peninsular War are the regimental hospital returns for 1811–14 which include just under 5,000 cases of syphilis out of a total of 175,000 men admitted. Despite the misguided treatment, deaths from venereal disease were unusual, only thirty-five in all types of hospital during the same period.[56]

Surprisingly, the most destructive epidemic of disease attacking the British army in Europe occurred not in the Peninsula but on an island off the Dutch coast. In July 1809 the largest British expeditionary force ever assembled weighed anchor off the Kent coast and sailed for the island of Walcheren in the Scheldt Estuary. The ultimate failure of the venture was ensured by ponderous preparations and the appointment of inappropriate senior army and naval staff. But, whatever the military bungling, an account of the Walcheren expedition is essentially a medical history. Within a few weeks, in an apparently innocuous area of the Netherlands, an army of 40,000 men was almost entirely destroyed by disease, the nature of which remains open to speculation.[57]

The contemporary descriptions of Walcheren seem to describe two different countries. When the troops first landed they saw 'a flat fen turned into a garden'. However, a British expedition to the region in 1747 had been decimated by an illness well described by John Pringle. John Webbe, an inspector of hospitals, perceived this darker side of the island in a letter of September 1809.

> The bottom of every canal that has direct communication with the sea is thickly covered with an ooze which, when the tide is out, emits a most offensive effluvia. Each ditch is filled with water which is loaded with animal and vegetable substances in a state of putrefaction, and the whole island is so flat and near the sea, that a large proportion of it is little better than a swamp, and there is scarcely a place where water of tolerably good quality can be procured. The effects of all these causes of disease is strongly marked in the inhabitants, the greater part of whom are pale and listless.[58]

The progress of 'Walcheren fever' or 'Flushing sickness' was relentless. In early August there were fewer than 700 men sick, but by September over 8,000 were in hospital. In late October the 9,000 troops sick on Walcheren easily outnumbered those fit for duty. By the time the expedition ended in February 1810, the fever had caused the death of sixty officers and 3,900 soldiers. Over 40% of the force had been struck down by disease, and six months later around 11,000 men were still registered sick. This compared with only 100 killed in the sporadic fighting of what had become an irrelevant military adventure. Many of those who survived the disease were left permanently debilitated. In the Peninsula, the Walcheren regiments were always the first to fall ill.

What was Walcheren fever? We have the memoirs of soldiers, regimental doctors, and also more specialised accounts of the disease by senior army doctors which include details of post-mortems. William Keep gives a typical soldier's view of an attack of Walcheren fever.

The disease usually comes on with a cold shivering, so great that the patient feels no benefit from the clothes piled upon him in bed, but continues to shiver still, as if enclosed in ice, the teeth chattering and cheeks blanched. This lasts some time, and is followed by the opposite extremes of heat, so that the pulse often rises to 100 in a short space. The face is then flushed and eyes dilated, but with little thirst. It subsides, and then is succeeded by another paroxysm, or cold fit, and so on until the patient's strength is quite reduced, and he sinks into the arms of death.[59]

An increase in the size of the spleen (splenomegaly) was a common finding. John Harris's spleen was so enlarged that he carried an 'extra paunch' for many years.[60] Another key characteristic of the disease was its propensity to relapse. General William Dyott was well when he returned from Walcheren to England, but then he had an attack of fever lasting fourteen days. Of 130 members of a light infantry company of the Scots Guards which left England only forty marched back into London, and all except two subsequently developed fever.[61]

These soldiers' accounts are of a relapsing fever associated with an enlarged spleen occurring in swamps known to be infested by mosquitoes. Some historians have understandably attributed Walcheren fever to malaria alone. However, there are problems with this hypothesis. The high death rate in such a short period is not compatible with the types of malaria known to have affected the Netherlands at this time. Only the virulent falciparum type could have caused such destruction and this was restricted to more southern climes. There is enough evidence to implicate malaria as a major component of Walcheren fever, but a more thorough review of all sources, including the primary medical accounts, suggests that other diseases were present. There are frequent references to dysentery in both military and medical memoirs. English authorities on the fever, including a number of senior physicians, all state that the intermittent fever often terminated in dysentery and diarrhoea. The post-mortem findings were predominantly of fluid retention (oedema), enlargement of the liver and spleen, and ulcerated and inflamed intestines. The valuable first-hand account of Walcheren by Assistant Surgeon George Hargrove implies the presence of further infectious diseases. He describes both a type of fever and the presence of signs, including petechiae, which are compatible with typhoid and typhus. Notably, Hargrove says that these syndromes mainly affected the troops living in crowded and dirty conditions.[62]

Another 'statistical' account of the fever states that the remittent fever often transformed to a continued or 'typhoid' form with severe headache, coated tongue, loss of appetite and delirium.[63] French sources also support the presence of multiple infections. The clinician Jean-

Baptiste Tresal concluded that whereas strangers to the islands were mainly affected by malaria, the inhabitants contracted other diseases.[64] That some soldiers had immunity to disease, presumably malaria, is implied in a report by three British army doctors, who noticed that men who had been recruited from 'dry mountainous districts' were more likely to fall victim than those from 'flat and fenny countries'.[65] Taken as a whole, the available sources suggest that Walcheren fever was not a newly discovered killer disease but a lethal combination of familiar diseases – malaria, typhus, typhoid and dysentery – acting together in a group of men made vulnerable by previous campaigning (some had been in the retreat to Corunna), and a life of poverty in the lower reaches of society.

In Egypt in 1801 the routine occurrence of dysentery was accompanied by outbreaks of plague and a potentially blinding eye disorder called 'ophthalmia'. Bubonic plague was understandably feared as it was the same disease as the 'black death' of the early middle ages which had a death toll of catastrophic proportions. It disappeared from Europe in 1720 but persisted in Egypt until the mid nineteenth century. Plague is caused by a bacterium which infects fleas which in turn feed on rats. When sick rats die, the fleas then bite their new human hosts passing on the infection.[66] Of course, at the time, there was no understanding of this chain of events. By the end of 1801 plague had spread along the Nile and a quarter of the British army was struck down. Treatment was predictably dramatic but unhelpful – for instance, a mixture of calomel, opium and nitric acid with mercurial ointment and regular nitric baths. According to a surgeon in the Royal Artillery, the best prophylactic against plague was 'external friction with warm oil'. James McGrigor, in charge of medical arrangements for David Baird's army, suspected the contagious nature of the disease and introduced strict quarantine provisions and measures ensuring better sanitation. Under his leadership, the numbers of deaths from plague fell sharply. This was unfortunately not before four of thirteen heroic regimental surgeons who had volunteered to tend plague victims had caught the disease and died.[67]

Ophthalmia might be regarded as the second plague of Egypt. One regimental surgeon described it as 'one of the most dreadful diseases that has ever visited mankind'. During the campaign of 1801, it was the cause of partial or total blindness in thousands of British and French troops. In modern terminology, the disorder was a form of purulent conjunctivitis which in the worst cases led to severe damage to the eyeball. The infection was spread by personal contact, towels or by the swarms of flies. Attempts at cure included normal antiphlogistic treatments with copious blood-letting, local applications, and also various surgical procedures on the eyes. The French were generally more conservative than the English, eschewing surgical intervention and applications of powerful drugs.[68] For

175

those afflicted it was a nightmarish experience. Andrew Pearson of the 61st Regiment was only 18 years old when he developed ophthalmia.

> That malady soon became a greater terror to all of us than anything we had yet seen or heard, because the army was more or less affected with the disease, and every man was afraid that he would lose his eye-sight. In the course of a few weeks the hospital was besieged with men and officers, whose eyes bore unmistakable symptoms of ophthalmia. Our hospital consisted of a temporary shed, erected on the sand, and covered in with wooden boards. To my horror I soon discovered my eye-sight failing me; and in little more than a month from the date at which we encamped at Rosetta, I found myself, in company with upwards of 2,000 men, totally blind, lying in this shed waiting orders. We were taken out daily for inspection by the medical officers, and the method adopted to lead us from place to place was certainly ingenious, and must have given no little amusement, to those who could witness it. We were told off in squads of thirty and the man who could discern objects was constituted leader. Being in single file, the man on the right of the leader took hold of the tail of his coat, and each man of the squad followed the same example, till the whole were in marching order. When all was ready, we received orders to move, when we sallied forth – a most amusing, yet mournful band.[69]

Pearson was told that the disease was incurable but he did eventually recover his sight following painful surgery and the application of laudanum to his eyes.

The end of the Egyptian campaign did not bring relief from ophthalmia. The disease pursued the British army all over Europe and even to South America. By 1810 there were over 2,000 soldiers on the pension list for blindness. The way in which ophthalmia not only infected men in a single regiment but moved from one force to another, even to distant parts, was mystifying to medical officers of the time and it remains puzzling today. One popular contemporary theory was that a considerable number of the cases were not genuine. It was suspected that soldiers were self-inflicting damage to their eyes in order to obtain a favourable discharge from the army. William Fergusson was a chief proponent of the 'ophthalmia conspiracy', claiming that men simulated ophthalmia by rubbing mercury into their eyes. When this was not available they allegedly used mortar from the walls mixed with their own urine. Fergusson supported his case by pointing out that in the Peninsula, where the morale of the troops was boosted by military success, there was very little ophthalmia. He also recounted the case of the 28th Regiment, where remorseful soldiers confessed their malingering to the colonel. Further circumstantial evidence for malingering was the rarity of the disease in officers and doctors.[70] Not all army medical men agreed with Fergusson. Staff Surgeon Charles Farrell, the author of a treatise on the disease published in 1811, acknowledges the conspiracy theory, but then adds:

> I have now had under my care many thousands of ophthalmia patients and although I have used a vigilance sharpened by a bias towards that opinion, I have not as yet been able to make out clearly a case in which the soldier produced the disease in himself by improper means.[71]

India and Ceylon were other potential graveyards for the British Army. The troops were exposed to mosquito- and leech-infested swamps and extremes of climate. On Ceylon in 1803, the 51st Regiment lost 300 out of a total strength of 400 men within a three-month period. The 19th Regiment died from a virulent fever at a rate of 400 per thousand in 1803, 200 per thousand in 1804, and eighty-three per thousand in 1805. Even the Duke of Wellington, a soldier with a notably robust constitution, fell ill whilst campaigning on the subcontinent. In Bombay in 1801, the young Arthur Wellesley developed what was in his own words, an 'intermittent fever'.[72] The fever, probably a mild bout of malaria, soon resolved, but it had left him weak and he contracted an unpleasant skin disorder, most likely the 'Malabar itch', a form of ringworm infection. He was treated with a course of nitric acid baths, so strong as to burn the towels he dried himself with, and to leave yellow stains on the rice paper of his correspondence. Fortunately for his country, he eventually made a complete recovery.[73]

James McGrigor, apparently omnipresent, had been in Bombay only a year earlier, and listed the main diseases affecting his regiment as 'tetanus, cholera, dysentery, hepatitis, pneumonia, measles, scurvy, ophthalmia, venereal disease, and Guinea worm'.[74] Whilst ill, Wellesley had pined for a colder climate, and undoubtedly the extreme heat of India took a severe toll on the men. Ensign Bayly of the 12th Suffolk Regiment served in Madras during 1796.

> One morning, after a two hours drill on the well-trod glacis of Fort St.George, the sun rose with its usual splendour; the heat was insufferable at 8 o'clock. The movements of the men from fatigue, appearing to the Colonel to proceed from neglect and indifference to duty, he kept us on the ground until 9 o'clock, when we returned to the Fort, tout en eau. As I entered my quarters I fell suddenly on my face, deprived of all sensation. My servants placed me on a couch; the surgeon was called, pronouncing my malady as a coup de soleil [sunstroke]. My nose, on which I had fallen, bled profusely, and this

circumstance, in his opinion, saved my life. The excessive heat and unusual long drill produced this affliction.[75]

Some other health problems were induced by the soldiers themselves. Alcohol was just as much a factor in India and Ceylon as in the West Indies. Popular drinks included arrack and toddy (coarse spirits distilled from grain, rice, coconut or sugar cane), brandy and sangaree (a tumbler of Madeira, sugar and nutmeg diluted with a wineglass of water). Despite punishments to the soldiers and the suppliers of spirits, alcohol continued to be smuggled into garrisons. Many became so accustomed to their drinking habits that they would exchange into the relieving battalion rather than leave India.[76]

British soldiers were equally vulnerable to disease when at sea. This was especially so during longer voyages to destinations such as the West and East Indies and Africa. Scurvy is normally thought of as a disease of the navy. Between 1600 and 1800 it killed more than one million sailors – probably more than the deaths from all other diseases, wounds, and shipwrecks combined. Scurvy also attacked soldiers afloat and during prolonged periods of hardship on land. The French army was afflicted during the siege of Alexandria and the retreat from Moscow.[77] In comparison, the British appear to have largely escaped scurvy during their land campaigns and the best descriptions of the disease are by soldiers at sea. John Shipp, a lieutenant in the 87th Regiment, suffered from scurvy at the end of a hazardous passage to South Africa and gives a graphic account of the symptoms.

> It would be difficult to imagine a set of men more hideously situated than we were, but to add yet more to our misery the scurvy broke out in a most frightful manner. Scarcely one escaped the swollen legs, and rotten, distorted gums, which showed the malignancy of the disease. None but the dying were left to bury the dead ... The skill of our medical attendants was completely baffled. My poor legs were as big as drums, and my gums swollen to an enormous size, and my tongue too big for my mouth. All I could eat was raw potatoes and vinegar ... We were all so reduced by suffering that even strong men could not restrain themselves from weeping, they knew not why. And so the time went by, men dying in dozens, and almost before the breath was out of their bodies being thrown into the sea for the sharks to quarrel over.[78]

A quarter of the Europeans and more than two-thirds of the East Indian sailors died. We now know that scurvy is caused by a deficiency of vitamin C – it is possible that the presence of this vitamin in potatoes saved Shipp's life. The realisation, towards the end of the eighteenth century, that the disease could be prevented by including lemon or lime juice in the diet was one of the great medical advances of the era.

Even with better control of scurvy, disease was as much an enemy at sea as on land. In the twenty-two years of the Revolutionary and Napoleonic Wars, the British Navy lost fewer than 2,000 men killed in battle compared with over 70,000 from disease and accidents.[79] The heavy army losses in the West Indies have already been discussed, but large numbers of soldiers were fated not even to reach the islands. George Pinchard noted that many were in poor health even before they reached Portsmouth. The long confinement in overcrowded and unsanitary transport ships and a poor diet did the rest. By the time Sir Ralph Abercromby's 1796 expedition reached Barbados there were already a thousand men sick. This was not yellow fever or malaria but a disease termed 'shipfever', in all likelihood typhus or typhoid.[80]

Wherever men have waged war, there have been diseases of the mind. The emotional breakdown that affected soldiers in the First World War was initially thought to be caused by concussion of the brain by the close explosion of a shell – hence the term 'shellshock'. In the American Civil War, thirty years after the Napoleonic era, two to three soldiers in every thousand developed a disabling psychiatric condition referred to as 'nostalgia'.[81] This term had been used in Europe as early as the seventeenth century to describe feelings of despair in soldiers. Did Napoleonic soldiers suffer from 'shellshock' or similar mental disorders? The answer is a definite yes, but the incidence is difficult to estimate because of a paucity of records, the use of obscure nomenclature, and probably also a lack of recognition by army doctors. In his unparalleled records of Peninsular War disease, McGrigor makes only a solitary reference to nostalgia as the cause of a death. In contrast, in soldiers' memoirs there are a number of episodes and experiences which are most reasonably interpreted as forms of psychiatric disease. One possible outcome of these psychoneuroses of war was suicide and there are numerous examples of this, particularly in the Peninsula. Joseph Donaldson recalls the sad case of a young comrade who twice reported sick, but because he complained only of weakness, was ordered to rejoin the ranks, '. . . he crawled off the road into a field, and, tired of a world in which he had met with such cruel treatment, loaded his musket, and taking off his stocking, put his toe on the trigger, and blew out his brains.' Other methods of suicide included stabbing and overdosing with opium. Some stopped short of killing themselves but performed self-mutilation. Donaldson relates the case of a soldier who cut off his right hand with an axe.[82]

The term 'insanity' was employed to describe bizarre or inexplicable behaviour. For example, Charles Baldock of the Royal Artillery, who, according to Lieutenant Swabey, was only happy when 'strutting about in the street in my pelisse, and overturning all the apples etc. that he met with in the streets'.[83] Symptoms which we might refer to as 'depression' were often viewed in a spiritual context, the term 'religious melancholy' being commonly used. The most convincing account of severe depression is that of Quartermaster William Surtees who interpreted his turmoil of emotions in Spain during 1812 as a religious experience. Both his mental and physical symptoms, for instance constipation, are commonly seen in depression.

> ... the gloom still seemed to thicken, and a dark cloud seemed impending over me, of which I was fully aware, and wrote home to my friends to that effect. At length my birthday, the 4th of August, arrived, and which must, as my unhappy companions in sin urged on me, be kept with all due jollity. Accordingly, a dozen of strong port-wine was procured, and we boozed away most joyfully, the whole being drank by about four or five of us. This produced constipation in the bowels, and had nigh brought me to my end; but my mind was more affected, if possible, than my body ... I endeavoured to compose myself to sleep. I did sleep for a while, during which I was troubled with some confused and incoherent dreams; but soon after waking, gracious God! what were my feelings then? Despair, black despair, had seized upon me. I rushed out of bed, and rolled upon the floor like one distracted, as indeed I was. Oh! what would I then have given that I had never been born, or that I could cease to exist! Had it been possible, by throwing my body into the flames, to annihilate for ever my consciousness of being, how gladly would I have done it! But now the terrors of the Lord were upon me, and drank up my spirits; and no one who has not been in a similar situation can form the most distant idea of the misery which preyed upon me.[84]

Against the background of life-threatening physical disease there was little formal treatment for mental disorders, and men like Surtees were left to sort themselves out. Psychiatric disease was probably often wrongly assumed by medical and military officers to be malingering. This was, in part, forgivable, as there was a considerable amount of real malingering. The 'ophthalmia conspiracy' has been referred to. Other methods of feigning disease were legion. They included putting rotten cheese up the nostrils to simulate infection, rubbing irritant substances into skin ulcers to exacerbate them, and faking heart disease by inserting tobacco or garlic into the anus. Hennen documents practices such as eating India figs to turn the urine red, throwing vermicelli into the urine to simulate worms, and inflating the scrotum by inserting a quill or straw and blowing air through it. Some soldiers acquired the skill to dislocate bones such as the patella (knee bone) or femur (thigh bone). Others fabricated dysentery by bribing hospital orderlies to supply them with bedpans which had been previously filled by patients in the advanced stage of the disease. One soldier in the hospital at Abrantes stole a treatise on dysentery from the medical officers and concealed it under his bedsheets.[85] Many chronic malingerers congregated at the large convalescent depot in the Belem suburb of Lisbon. Ensign Robert Blakeney's views on the 'Belem Rangers' are representative of most of the army.

> Some were unwillingly kept back from debility of constitution or through wounds, but a large majority were inflicted with a disease which, baffling the skill of learned doctors, loudly called for a remedy far different from that of medical treatment . . . it might truthfully be said that the movement of the whole army was attended with less difficulty than the movement of a single Belemite to the front.[86]

A few malingerers were made examples of. A soldier with chronic leg ulceration had the limb locked in an iron box to prevent him further interfering with the skin. When the ulcer promptly healed, he received 500 lashes.[87] Some malingering was more difficult to prove. Andrew Pearson noted the behaviour of the colonel of the 61st Regiment in Spain:

> Whenever the pickets were heard firing, the surgeon was immediately sent for, and it was always found necessary to remove him to the rear in consequence of severe indisposition. It was very unfortunate for us, that so soon as the engagement was over he recovered.[88]

Army doctors often took a pragmatic approach to suspected malingerers. An American army surgeon recommended blistering, which, he said, was 'a good test, in doubtful cases, whether a man was really sick. Rather than submit to the pain of blistering a second time, unless absolutely diseased, he would prefer going to duty . . . so that, whether a man was actually sick or only feignedly ill, blistering was an excellent remedy.'[89]

For every malingerer there were several other soldiers attempting to disguise their disease in order to stay on active duty. Colonel Ponsonby of the 12th Light Dragoons suffered severely from malaria in Spain in 1813 but gave strict instructions to Captain William Hay to conceal his disease from others.[90]

In the midst of so much real disease there was inevitably a great deal of conjecture as to what the causes were. Both soldiers and doctors had their own views. Captain Moyle Sherer was described by a friend as being not only an able soldier but a 'gentleman, a scholar, and an author'. His reflections on disease in the Peninsula represent the opinions of many military men.

181

The autumnal season, in Estramadura, is proverbially unhealthy, and numbers of the inhabitants die annually of the alarming fever [malaria] which prevails in the dreaded month of September. The unwholesome vapours, which arise from the beds of the many stagnant pools scattered over the surface of these plains, and always dried up by the summer heat, are said to produce this evil.[91]

Most soldiers thus attributed the diseases that afflicted them to an unfortunate combination of country and season or climate. Ensign John Aitchison refers to the same 'Estramadura fever' as Moyle Sherer, and blames it on 'exposure to the dew in the night during the warm season'.[92] Diet and alcohol were also implicated. Captain Rees Howell Gronow thought that the severe outbreak of typhus that attacked the Guards at Vizeu in 1812 was caused by a change in diet and 'the substituting of the horrid wine of the country for the porter they had been accustomed to at home'.[93] Most agreed that alcohol was a factor in disease, but there was considerable confusion as to whether it was the cause or the cure. Some were in no doubt that it was a bad thing. Major William Harness of the 80th Regiment commented of his men in Ceylon, 'Is it to be wondered at, that of between eight and nine hundred soldiers who drink of the vilest spirits, the worst of arrack, ten should be fluxt and six should have inflamed their livers.'[94] A colonel in India regarded the troops as being 'victims of their own imprudence rather than to the noxious vapours or climate'.[95]

These soldiers' opinions of disease causation were simplified versions of the medical theories of the day. The doctors of Wellington's army held views that were little different from those of the physicians who treated the black death over 500 years earlier. Most believed that the majority of diseases were caused by 'miasma' or 'miasmata', invisible poisons in the air which were exuded from rotting animal and vegetable material, the soil and standing water. In the eighteenth century, diseases of soldiers had been explained by their exposure to the 'putrid Steams of dead horses, of the Privies, and of other corrupted Animal and Vegetable substances, after their juices had been exalted by the Heat of Summer'.[96] Similar language, with frequent references to local topography, the season and climate, is used in the medical writings of the Napoleonic Wars. James McGrigor cites the main causes of malaria in the Peninsula as 'the effluvia from marshes or the exhalations raised by a powerful sun acting on a humid or luxuriant soil'. He later notes that relapses of the disease could be induced by exposure to rain, or direct sunlight, intemperance or great fatigue. Similarly, in Egypt, he identifies the effluvia arising from the mud and putrid animal and vegetable matter of the Nile valley. Other factors invoked included the 'extreme filth of the inhabitants', the dry parching wind, the improper diet, and consumption of alcohol.[97] Thus, elements of lifestyle, and particularly diet, alcohol and exposure to hardship, were presumed to also play a role.

The traditional 'miasmatists' had to confront some alternative views on disease. An increasing number of army doctors favoured the 'contagion' theory, in which disease was somehow passed from person to person. When yellow fever struck Gibraltar in 1813, thirteen of the fifteen medical officers in the garrison were staunch 'contagionists'. The Inspector of Hospitals, Joseph Gilpin, elaborated his reasons for supporting the contagion theory.

> I find a difficulty in viewing it as an endemic proceeding from marsh miasmata, or other noxious exhalations, as a considerable number of persons entirely escaped the disease, although strictly confined to only situations where I conceive the effluvia may be supposed to exist, the dock-yard and navy garden. I find, too, a difficulty in attributing it to the prevalent state of the atmosphere, at the period of its appearance; for during the number of years that have elapsed since we have held the rock, surely the state of the atmosphere, and supposed prevalence of marsh miasmata, & c., must frequently have been as they were in 1804, 1810, and 1813 [the years of yellow fever outbreaks]; and I have not heard that a fever of a similar type to that which prevailed during those years is on record . . . I am inclined, therefore, to believe, that this infectious fever was brought into the garrison by a person who died of it.[98]

Although the contagion theory was closer to the truth than the miasmatic theory, the Napoleonic Wars pre-dated by a full century the emergence of the science of microbiology with its insights into the disease-causing organisms found in water and on insects and rodents. The real culprits were overlooked. As assistant surgeon in the Walcheren expedition comments with unconscious irony, 'during the hot weather we were much annoyed by a description of Moschetos who attacked us in immense swarms . . . the buzzing noise they make is more alarming than any harm they inflict.'[99]

The mysterious nature of disease and the futility of most treatments meant that soldiers were always searching for ways to avoid it. Advice given by senior army officers was generally well meaning, and sometimes very sensible.

> The Lieutenant-Colonel earnestly recommends that no gentleman shall lie down to sleep while warm, or with wet feet; but, however fatigued, always to take time to cool gradually, and to put on his dry stockings and shoes. In case of being very wet, it is useful to rub the body and limbs with spirits, warm if possible, taking at the same time

a mouthful, and not more, inwardly, diluted with warm water, if to be had.[100]

The memoirs of the wars are full of anecdotal preventative measures, most of which fall into the category of 'old wives' tales'. Tobacco and alcohol formed the basis of many recommendations. Much of this advice was conflicting and some officers chose to take a phlegmatic view of the dangers. Captain William Bragge of the 3rd Dragoons wrote home from Abrantes in 1811: 'With regard to eating and drinking there is, I believe, not a single thing which some kind advisor has not recommended us to avoid, stating that his own illness was occasioned by it. We have even been warned against the Pernicious Custom of eating Soups and Broth'.[101]

The army's medical officers were even more preoccupied with measures that might stem the tide of disease. Their failure to understand the causes presented a considerable hurdle, but it did not prevent progress. The more able and experienced medical officers began to make real connections between the prevalence of certain diseases and the way the army was managed. These general observations, made over the whole period of the wars, led to much commonsensical advice being issued. This started with the screening of new soldiers and their introduction to campaign life, and extended to all aspects of military protocol including diet, clothing, shelter and discipline. Undoubtedly the army's doctors were influenced by the advances which had already been made in the navy. Under the guidance of enlightened physicians such as James Lind, Thomas Trotter and, above all, Sir Gilbert Blane, scurvy had been largely defeated by the introduction of citrus fruit juice, and there had been other improvements in the diet, living quarters and medical care of seamen. Disease remained a threat to Nelson's sailors, but the losses were much fewer than in earlier years. In 1779 just under one in three sailors could expect to become sick with one in forty-two dying. The equivalent figures for 1813 were one in eleven sick and only one in every 143 dying. Blane pointed out that if sickness had continued at the same level during the Napoleonic Wars as before, the navy would have been shattered. The death toll for the period 1793–1814 would have equated to the navy's entire strength in an average year.[102]

It was clear to all that the recruitment of weak or unhealthy soldiers would lead to a sickly force in the field. McGrigor stressed the importance of inspecting new recruits, and of weeding out those with disease. He had firm opinions on the suitability of different occupations for the army: 'I believe it will be found that caeteris paribus, tradesmen, and manufacturers, particularly those from large towns, are soonest swept away by the fatigues and diseases of an army; and that those who have followed agricultural pursuits are the most healthy.' He supported this statement by quoting alarming mortality figures for new recruits in the 7th Regiment in Portugal during 1810–11. In this notoriously unhealthy infantry unit 60% of recruits from urban manufacturing occupations died compared with a death rate of 40% among those from farming backgrounds.[103] William Fergusson believed that the ideal soldier was aged between 22 and 38 years. He also emphasised the importance of rejecting feeble recruits, but decried the practice of favouring tall men, 'the short strong man is in fact a bundle of thews and sinews'.[104]

Once the soldier had been selected, it was best that he be cautiously introduced to campaign life, especially where his first excursion abroad was to a hot climate. Strategies used, when military priorities permitted, included detaining new troops for some time at the port of embarkation, sending new levies to an initial spell of garrison duty, and having troops disembark at an interim destination to habituate them to the climate and lifestyle. An example of the latter policy was the sending of troops destined for service in the Peninsular War for a period of indoctrination in Gibraltar or Cadiz. Here they could be drilled in the sun to inure them to some of the hardships they would eventually face on active duty. Ideally, the new troops then joined their regiments near the close of the year's campaigning, when the army was about to enter quarters. In the West Indies, a winter arrival was preferred. It was well known that all corps sent most men to hospital during their first year in the Peninsula. In McGrigor's opinion, 300 men who had served five years were more militarily effective than a new regiment of 1,000 men. As always he was able to provide figures from the Peninsula to support his views. In the 7th Regiment between August 1811 and May 1812, 169 out of 353 new recruits died from disease compared with only seventy-seven deaths out of the 1,145 old soldiers.[105] He quotes similar figures for the 40th Regiment, and John Bacot in his account of typhus at Vizeu noted a much higher mortality in the recently arrived militia-men than in the veterans of the Guards Regiment.[106]

In theatres of war such as the West Indies and India, even the most elaborate precautions proved unable to prevent the ravages of disease. A more radical solution was to protect white troops by employing native soldiers. William Fergusson devotes an entire chapter of his autobiography to a discussion of the merits of black troops in the West Indies, a subject which he says was little understood by military men. His views are expressed in terms that would now be considered politically incorrect, but he includes emotive arguments against the further sacrifice of European troops in the region.

> The 50th and 92nd Regiments were, in the Peninsula, the elites of British valour, their character stood as high in the army as did that of the tenth Roman legion in the estimation of Julius Caesar, for they

were as exemplary in ordinary conduct as they were heroic in the field, and their first reward, on the return of peace, was a mission to die in the pestilential swamps and savannahs of Jamaica.[107]

The resistance of local British planters to the recruitment of their native workforce was gradually overcome, and the West India Regiments undoubtedly spared the lives of thousands of British soldiers.

Other practical measures to counter disease were taken with respect to the location and nature of soldiers' accommodation. Despite their ignorance of insect vectors, doctors were well aware that the careless siting of hospitals and camps increased the incidence of fevers. In the West Indies, senior medical officers urged their military commanders to avoid the low marshy areas and sea coasts wherever possible. Cramped soldiers' accommodation in all its guises brought many of the same dangers as overcrowded hospitals. One interesting statistic of the wars is the higher disease mortality among the men compared with their officers. This was clearly the case both for the Walcheren expedition and the Peninsular War, campaigns for which this type of information is accessible. Several possible explanations are feasible. Officers were likely to have entered the army better nourished and with a lower incidence of chronic disease than the less privileged lower ranks. Their ongoing medical and nursing care, diet and clothing were all likely to be of higher quality than in the ranks. It is striking that in the Peninsula, this difference in mortality usually only existed during the winter months.[108] It would appear likely that it was overcrowding in cantonments with the spread of typhus and dysentery that accounted for most of the increased deaths in the men. This argument is further supported by a disappearance of the excess mortality in the last winter of the war when the army remained in the field. The lower sickness and mortality rates among the privates of the cavalry and artillery compared to the infantry were probably also attributable to the less overcrowded conditions in these parts of the service.

Bivouacking in the open air brought its own dangers and McGrigor strongly supported the provision of shelter for the troops which was the case after 1812 in the Peninsula. This was in the form of tents, the construction of small huts, or by quartering in towns. He particularly encouraged the construction of fireplaces to keep the men warm. Inadequate clothing was also regarded by army doctors as a potential cause of disease, especially where the troops were exposed to inclement weather or deprived of shelter. Unfortunately, the military authorities were slow to respond to these concerns and the regulation uniform was often entirely unsuitable. In the heat of the West Indies, men frequently wore woollen clothes originally designed for European winter service. In the Peninsula, not even the simplest steps were taken to protect the men. Joseph Donaldson remembered that,

Many of the officers had oilskin cloaks that completely covered them. Some such thing for the men would have been neither expensive nor heavy to carry and would have been the means of saving many lives. Much more attention ought also to be paid to the quality of the shoes served out to the army, for they are in general of the very worst kind, and it was no uncommon thing for our store shoes to be in tatters before we had worn them a week.[109]

McGrigor advised linen trousers for the warm weather in the Peninsula with a change to cloth pantaloons for the cold and rainy season. He noted that, 'the best clothed were generally among the most healthy regiments'.[110]

A good diet has always been essential to health, and inequalities in disease rates between different divisions of the Peninsular army may have been partly caused by differences in the quality of provisions. Whereas some divisions were well provisioned, others were not so fortunate with poor quality meat, substitution of spirits for wine, and biscuit instead of bread. The superintending medical officers of divisions had to report directly to McGrigor when poor diet threatened to contribute to disease. Even well supplied soldiers had to be educated to eat properly by their military and medical officers. All too often, 'if left to himself, the soldier would broil his modicum of meat and eat it at one meal, drinking his allowance of wine or spirits at a draught'.[111] This meant three days' rations lasting only one day, and it left the soldier dependent on luck for the next two days' food. Wellington encouraged the division of the men into messes under the supervision of their officers where regular meals could be organised. The deleterious effect of excessive alcohol has been elucidated. Enlightened medical officers encouraged the men to drink mostly water, but for much of the wars the soldier's daily ration included either a third of a pint of rum or a pint of wine, and this was often supplemented by plundering.

The importance of discipline in maintaining the health of the army is difficult to overstate. Lord Nelson himself wrote, 'The great thing in all military service is health; and you will agree with me that it is easiest for an officer to keep men healthy, than for a physician to cure them.' McGrigor commented that a good commanding officer usually had an effective and healthy regiment. This arose out of good 'internal economy', with much attention paid to clothing, diet, personal cleanliness, well maintained quarters and regular exercise. Where there was poor leadership, the incidence of malingering increased. In addition to his general recommendations to improve the health of regiments, McGrigor took specific actions to formalise the management of the sick and root out abuses. All ill men and officers in convalescent depots such as Lisbon were regularly reviewed by a medical board, and only those definitely not recovering were sent home. Also, no sick or wounded were sent to the rear unless approved by a medical board or unless there were exceptional circumstances such as immediately after an action or during a retreat. These measures were much approved of by Wellington as they increased the effective strength of the army. Although elite regiments were not immune to disease, it was often the best disciplined units that escaped the worst of the mortality. One remarkable example is that of the 1st Hussars of the King's German Legion, widely acknowledged as the best cavalry regiment in the Peninsula, which lost not a single man or even sent one to hospital, during the horrific retreat from Burgos.[112]

Apart from their support for improvements in the soldier's lifestyle, the army's senior medical officers advocated two more specific medical measures, which with the hindsight of two hundred years, we can applaud as being especially beneficial. The first was quarantine, the forced separation of sick from well men, a public health measure which first emerged in the Middle Ages. The contagious element of disease was well enough appreciated for there to be several good examples of effective quarantines. When plague attacked Baird's army in Egypt, McGrigor's prompt enforcement of emergency quarantine measures helped check the spread of the disease. Dominique Larrey similarly stressed the importance of isolating ill men in his management of British sick during the pursuit of Sir John Moore's army by Napoleon.[113] Such initiatives were not the sole prerogative of the wars' greatest doctors. The medical officers in Moore's retreating army also understood the dangers of intermixing diseased and healthy soldiers. When the British troops entered Astorga in December 1809, they were joined by the typhus-ravaged remnants of a Spanish army. Surgeon Henry Milburne arrived at the town before the main British army and did his best to avert a further epidemic.

> Here I found the hospitals, convents, and many private houses crowded with the sick and wounded of the Spanish army; many labouring under contagious diseases and all badly accommodated and in want of almost every medical necessary ... Under all these circumstances and aware of the danger to which the British troops would be exposed on their arrival at a place where the sick of contagious diseases were indiscriminately lodged in almost every house; I thought it a duty incumbent upon me to wait on General Fraser, then commanding the British troops at Astorga, to represent the danger to him, and tender my service in the removal of such part of the sick as could with propriety be removed, and to mark such houses as I considered improper for the reception of healthy troops.[114]

Fraser wrote to the Junta of Astorga recommending Milburne and advising the separation of the sick Spanish troops from the British army.

The final preventative measure to be considered is the most familiar today, inoculation, or as it was eventually termed, vaccination. Smallpox, or the 'speckled monster', had been virulent in Europe for several hundred years, in bad years causing up to one tenth of all deaths. It had been known since the early eighteenth century that inoculation with a mild dose of the 'virus' conferred subsequent protection against severe smallpox. Some British soldiers in the American War of Independence had been inoculated, and the army suffered less from the disease than the Americans. The real breakthrough was English country doctor Edward Jenner's observation that inoculation with the milder disease cowpox, classically caught by dairy-maids, conferred immunity against smallpox. The word spread rapidly and Sir Ralph Abercromby's army in Egypt in 1801 was the first to be systematically vaccinated.[115] Regulations for regimental surgeons in 1803 stated that cowpox inoculation was to be 'constantly practised' in all men who did not have the scars of previous smallpox.[116] Napoleon, although generally sceptical of medicine, was not a man to miss a real advance and the French army was soon also vaccinated.

We have seen that the surgery of the Napoleonic Wars was associated with numerous innovations and significant progress. Was the same true of the management of disease? It is fair to say that army doctors made no major discoveries in the classification or treatment of disease. They remained confused by ancient theories of disease causation and any effective treatments were fortuitous. Even at the close of the war sick soldiers were still being subjected to antiphlogistic treatment which was unpleasant and likely to worsen their prognosis. The few dissenting army doctors who produced data showing the harm of these regimens were largely ignored.[117] Damaging interventions like venesection were only finally discredited several decades later when civilian physicians subjected them to objective clinical experiments. The scepticism regarding these heroic treatments was particularly strong in France, the Paris hospitals being notorious for their therapeutic nihilism. It was cynically stated at the time that 'the English kill their patients; the French let them die'.

Despite their shortcomings, Wellington's doctors did make real contributions to the health of the Napoleonic soldier and his successor in later wars. The actions taken to prevent disease have been described. Their cumulative effect was to increase the chance of an individual soldier avoiding debilitating or fatal disease and to increase the strength of the army. Undoubtedly, the single greatest step forward was McGrigor's institution of detailed records of the soldiers' health. Prior to his arrival in the Peninsula, the medical board had made little attempt to keep accurate records of the diseases of the army. They appeared far more interested in money, 'The duties of regimental surgeon and assistant surgeon were chiefly those of clerks and accountants to the public for the expenditure on each sick man'. Whilst the most minor discrepancy in expenditure on medical supplies was closely scrutinised, only 'an extraordinary mortality' in any part of the army would be noticed.[118] McGrigor encouraged his colleagues to collect information relating to the diseases of the army not just for military reasons, but for the benefit of medical knowledge. He explained that the army medical officer was in a privileged position to study disease and its treatment as he worked in a very controlled environment, with his patients and the hospital staff all under military supervision.

McGrigor's initiatives did not immediately bear fruit. He continued to sponsor the collection of medical returns from around the empire in his role as Director General of the army medical department in the forty years after Waterloo. By 1836 there were 160 volumes of information. The opportunity to analyse and publish this data came a year later when two army officers with an interest in statistics, Henry Marshall, a retired Inspector of Hospitals, and Lieutenant Alexander Murray Tulloch, were invited to undertake the task. Their resulting work, *The Statistical Report on the Sickness, Mortality, and Invaliding among the Troops in the West Indies*, became a landmark in the health of the army. It traced the medical history of the British forces in the West Indies during the previous twenty years.[119]

The authors were able to undermine many of the traditional miasmatic and climatic theories of disease, and instead made specific proposals for improving the health of the troops. They authoritatively recommended larger and better ventilated barracks built at higher altitudes, improved sanitation, better diet and reduced alcohol intake, shorter periods of service, and increased use of the native West Indian troops. Although much of the advice was not novel, it was now crucially based on real evidence. The eminent medical journal *The Lancet* was approving, concluding that the report would 'inevitably lead to the salvation of thousands of lives'. Scrutiny of mortality figures for the West Indies and the Indian subcontinent in the years immediately after Waterloo and sixty years later show the full impact of improvements in 'military hygiene'. In 1817–21, out of every thousand soldiers campaigning in Jamaica, Bermuda, Ceylon and India, the number of expected deaths were 185, 75, 111 and 87 respectively. By 1876–85, these appalling mortality rates had fallen dramatically to 16, 7, 14 and 16.[120] This enormous saving of lives can be directly traced back to James McGrigor's pioneering collection of medical data during the Peninsular War.

NOTES

1. Edmonds, T R, *On the Mortality and Sickness of Soldiers engaged in War*.
2. Porter, R, *The Greatest Benefit to Mankind*, p.301.

3.   Woodward, J, *To Do The Sick No Harm*, p.58.
4.   Haythornthwaite, P, *The Armies of Wellington*, p.64.
5.   Pope, D, *Life in Nelson's Navy*, p.3.
6.   Longford, E, *Wellington. The Years of the Sword*, p.380.
7.   Haythornthwaite, p.49.
8.   McGrigor, J, *Sketch of the Medical History of the British Armies*, p.447.
9.   Sutherland, J, *Men of Waterloo*, p.57.
10. *Instructions to Regimental Surgeons.*
11. Guy, A J, *The Road to Waterloo*, p.21.
12. Buckley, R W, *The destruction of the British Army in the West Indies*, p.80.
13. Haythornthwaite, pp.214–15.
14. Howard, T P, *The Haitian Journal of Lieutenant Howard*, pp.49–50.
15. De Jonnes, A M, *Adventures in the Wars*, p.270.
16. Pinchard, G, *Notes on the West Indies*, Vol.I, pp.15–16.
17. Trohler, U, *To Improve the Evidence of Medicine*, p.23.
18. Kiple, K F, *Plague, Pox and Pestilence*, pp.86–91.
19. Fergusson, W, *Notes and Recollections of a Professional Life*, p.147.
20. De Jonnes, p.270.
21. Turnbull, W, *The Naval Surgeon.*
22. Kiple, pp.98–103.
23. Buckley, p.84.
24. Fergusson, p.71.
25. Howard, M R, *Red Jackets and Red Noses.*
26. Kempthorne, G A, *The Army Medical Services at Home and Abroad*, pp.228–9.
27. Jackson, R, *A Sketch of the History and Cure of Febrile Diseases*, p.182.
28. Fergusson, p.91.
29. McGrigor, p.438.
30. Trohler, p.49.
31. Cooper, S, *A Dictionary of Practical Surgery*, Vol.I, pp.185–90.
32. ibid., p.188.
33. Cooke, J, *A True Soldier Gentleman*, p.153.
34. Fergusson, p.91.
35. Gilpin, D A, *Remarks on the Fever which Occurred at Gibraltar*, p.314.
36. Browne,T N, *The Napoleonic War Journal of Thomas Henry Browne*, p.116.
37. Leach, J, *Rough Sketches of the Life of an Old Soldier*, p.15.
38. McGrigor, pp.482–8.
39. Cantlie, N, *A History of the Army Medical Department*, Vol.I, pp.504–5.
40. Howard, M R, *Medical Aspects of Sir John Moore's Corunna Campaign*, p.300.
41. McGrigor, J, *Observations on the Fever which appeared in the Army from Spain*; Hooper, R, *Account of Diseases of the Sick landed at Plymouth from Corunna.*
42. Kiple, pp.104–9; Zinsser, H, *Rats, Lice and History*, pp.161–4.
43. Harris, Rifleman, *Recollections of Rifleman Harris*, p.162.
44. Creighton, C, *A History of Epidemics in Britain*, Vol.II, p.166.
45. Bacot, J, *A Sketch of the Medical History of the First Battalion*, p.378.
46. McGrigor, pp.420–37.
47. Kiple, pp.14–19.
48. McGrigor, p.415.
49. Bell, G, *Soldier's Glory*, pp. 64, 80–1.
50. Henry, W, *Surgeon Henry's Trifles*, pp.50, 62.
51. McGrigor, p.440.
52. ibid., pp.448–9.
53. Fergusson, p.123.
54. Hennen, J, *Principles of Military Surgery*, p.411.

55. Fergusson, p.119.
56. McGrigor, pp.479–88.
57. Howard, M R, *Walcheren 1809: A Medical Catastrophe.*
58. Chaplin, A, *Medicine in England during the Reign of George III*, pp.92–3.
59. Keep, W T, *In the Service of the King*, p.60.
60. Harris, p.179.
61. McGuffie, T H, *The Walcheren expedition and the Walcheren fever.*
62. Hargrove, G, *An Account of the Islands of Walcheren and South Beveland.*
63. Feibel, R M, *What happened at Walcheren: the primary medical sources*, p.74.
64. Tresal, J B, *Essai sur la fièvre adynamique qui a regné dans l'île de Walcheren*, p.64.
65. Borland, J, *Report on the prevailing malady among His Majesty's forces*, p.184.
66. Kiple, pp.60–7.
67. McGrigor, J, *Medical Sketches of the Military Expedition to Egypt from India.*
68. Cantlie, pp.273–81.
69. Pearson, A, *The Soldier Who Walked Away*, pp.28–9.
70. Fergusson, pp.110–12.
71. Cantlie, p.275.
72. *Selections from the dispatches and general orders*, p.19.
73. Longford, pp.87–8.
74. Blanco, R L, *Wellington's Surgeon General*, p.68.
75. Bayly, Col., *The Diary of Colonel Bayly*, p.222.
76. Howard, M R, *Red Jackets and Red Noses.*
77. Kiple, pp.68–73.
78. Shipp, J, *The Path of Glory*, p.25.
79. Pope, p.131.
80. Buckley, p.83.
81. Adams, G W, *Doctors in Blue*, p.228.
82. Donaldson, J, *Recollections of the Eventful Life of a Soldier*, pp.220, 256.
83. Haythornthwaite, p.142.
84. Surtees, W, *Twenty Five Years in the Rifle Brigade*, pp.171–2.
85. Hennen, pp.360–74.
86. Blakeney, R, *A Boy in the Peninsular War*, pp.281–2.
87. Haythornthwaite, p.135.
88. Pearson, p.83.
89. Gillet, M C, *The Army Medical Department 1775–1818*, p.192.
90. Hay, W, *Reminiscences 1809–1815 under Wellington*, p.109.
91. Sherer, M, *Recollections of the Peninsula*, pp.71–2.
92. Aitchison, J, *An Ensign in the Peninsular War*, p.153.
93. Gronow, R H, *The Reminiscences and Recollections of Captain Gronow*, Vol.II, p.201.
94. Harness, W, *Trusty and Well-Beloved*, p.114.
95. Bayly, p.226.
96. Monro, D, *Observations on the Means of Preserving the Health of Soldiers*, pp.57–8.
97. Blanco, p.82.
98. Gilpin, pp.315–16.
99. Hargrove, p.77.
100. Haythornthwaite, pp.134–5.
101. Bragge, W, *Peninsular Portrait 1811–1814*, p.18.
102. Hall, C D, *British Strategy in the Napoleonic War*, p.14.
103. McGrigor, pp.467–8.
104. Fergusson, pp.28–9.
105. McGrigor, *Sketch*, p.467.

106. Bacot, p.385.
107. Fergusson, pp.208–9.
108. Edmonds, p.143.
109. Donaldson, pp.96–7.
110. McGrigor, *Sketch*, p.469.
111. ibid., p.470.
112. ibid., p.471.
113. Dible, H, *Napoleon's Surgeon*, p.106.
114. Milburne, H, *A narrative of circumstances attending the retreat*, pp.13–14.
115. Cantlie, pp.281–2.
116. *Instructions to Regimental Surgeons.*
117. Trohler, pp.31–51.
118. McGrigor, J, *Autobiography and Services of Sir James McGrigor*, p.179.
119. Blanco, p.170; Cantlie, pp.439–42.
120. Chaplin, A, *Mortality Rates in the British Army 100 Years Ago*, p.96.

CHAPTER VII
On Campaign

*I am myself a good deal indisposed, and not much the better for
being shut up in a little, noisome, damp cabin, with six other
officers. Four of them are extremely ill and generally raving all
night long . . . it blows so violent a gale accompanied with thick
weather, that I can write no longer. Farewell.*

Physician Adam Neale returning from Corunna, 1809[1]

Just as the ordinary soldier only spent a minority of his time actually in
combat, Wellington's doctors were infrequently employed on the
battlefield or in a busy field hospital. Much of their time was filled with
routine duties such as attendance to trivial illnesses and the supervision of
convalescents. Like their fellow officers, the doctors spared no effort in
making their life on campaign as civilised and pleasant as was possible.
We have much evidence of this in their writings. Many of the regimental
doctors clearly believed that their experiences of foreign travel and
anecdotes of military life would interest the reader more than a detailed
account of their medical duties. A good example of this is the memoir,
actually a collection of letters to a friend, of Samuel Broughton, assistant
surgeon to the 2nd Life Guards, who served in the Peninsula and France
between 1812 and 1814. In Broughton's 400-page book the only clue to his
occupation is a solitary reference to his 'professional duties'. The
Peninsular reminiscences of Charles Boutflower and the lesser known
George Burroughs, assistant surgeon of the Royal Dragoons, are similar.
The lack of medical information is frustrating, but this type of memoir
does provide details of the everyday existence of a medical officer on
campaign in Wellington's army.

The wars were fought on foreign soil and so the opening of any
campaign was a journey by sea. Accommodation on board was usually
rudimentary. Surgeon William Lidderdale of the 15th Dragoons embarked at Cork for Corunna in 1808. The berths provided on the transport
were so bad that he had to sleep instead in a cot slung in the cabin to avoid
the risk of being poisoned by the smell of bilge water.[2] When a staff
surgeon and regimental surgeon sailed for the American War in 1812, the
cabin provided comprised two narrow berths on each side and two dark

holes with doorways marked as state cabins from which came an 'effluvium which was a mixture of the most offensive and sickening compounds'. The voyage across the Atlantic took six weeks.[3]

However filthy the conditions, the chief anxiety was the safety of ships and crew. Assistant Surgeon Samuel Good of the 3rd Guards set sail from Spithead in early 1809 in the transport vessel *Shaw*. The ship's company were of low calibre and when a violent storm blew up, it was the soldiers who had to take control. It was some time before the troops could get the faulty pumps to work to clear the water from the hold.[4] James McGrigor faced equal dangers on a passage from Grenada in 1796. The ship was 'an old crank transport, of the worse description, and, as afterwards appeared, ought never had been taken up for service'. The captain was no better, 'we found him not infrequently lying dead drunk opposite the companion door'. The vessel survived Atlantic storms more by luck than judgement, the troops eventually removing the drunken captain from his post. The officer put in charge, a midshipman in his youth, got the vessel safely home, although he did mistake the mouth of the Mersey for the Channel.[5] At least Good and McGrigor finally reached their destinations. Not all were so fortunate. William Dent survived all the dangers of campaigning in the Peninsula only to be drowned on a return voyage from the West Indies.

For many doctors their arrival at a foreign port was their first experience of life outside Britain. In the Peninsula, Lisbon was the commonest destination. From the harbour the hilltop city with its white buildings and surrounding vineyards appeared idyllic. Closer acquaintance was not so favourable. In Walter Henry's words, 'though all is majestic and magnificent without all is stench and filth within'.[6] Medical officers were disgusted and exasperated by the dirt. Charles Boutflower spoke for many when he concluded that 'I dislike it more than any place I was ever in.'[7] The immediate preoccupation for all soldiers arriving abroad was decent accommodation. In Lisbon, the troops of a fresh battalion were usually housed in barracks or in convents in the suburb of Belem. Officers, including the doctors, were allocated quarters in the house of a local resident, in a public building such as a chapel, or in an inn. Regimental surgeons (as captains) were entitled to two rooms and assistant surgeons (as subalterns) one room. In his general orders Wellington specified what the officer might reasonably expect. He was not allowed to personally select his billet or to exchange it with another officer. The provision of bedding and furniture was to be regarded as a favour given by the owner rather than a right.

In Portugal, the quality of billets varied enormously. An officer might occupy a nobleman's house but a dirty vermin infested hovel was more likely. Samuel Broughton says that in Lisbon houses, 'the dirt is rarely swept from the floors, and to the comforts of a scrubbing brush and soap and water they are total strangers. In order to dissipate the effluvia pretty generally prevailing in this town they are accustomed to burn lavender in all their rooms.'[8] Charles Boutflower's billet in a village near Lisbon was afflicted by a common problem, 'my bed looked tolerably clean, but before the morning I was nearly eat up in it, the irritation I suffered nearly threw me into a fever'. The only means of heating most Portuguese dwellings was a pan of charcoal. This could not be used with the windows shut or the fumes produced 'pernicious headaches'.

Soldiers generally preferred the accommodation in Spain. Here, the locals were mostly more energetic than the Portuguese in repairing and whitewashing their houses, and also in installing improvements such as fireplaces. Boutflower cursed his luck when he was campaigning on the border and happened to end up in a Portuguese village. 'There is an air of cleanliness in the Spanish villages one can never meet with in Portugal, which renders the former so infinitely preferable as a cantonment.'[9] Any predilection for Spain was only relative as even here the accommodation could be very basic. On the retreat from Burgos, George Burroughs slept wrapped in his cloak on straw in a hovel from which all the furniture and even the flooring had been removed. Only the central roof beam had not been stripped for firewood.[10]

For a variety of reasons, the Portuguese and Spanish were more begrudging in their hospitality as the war progressed. As a result it became difficult to find any sort of billet, particularly in the larger towns and cities where the competition for good accommodation was intense. In a letter written in November 1812, Broughton notes the problems he encountered finding a bed in Lisbon. Charles Boutflower discovered the same when he arrived in the city in March 1813 suffering from malaria. He made several attempts to locate a billet but he was 'shocked at the pitiful evasions' he met with at the several houses he visited. Fortunately, George Guthrie was able to provide his sick colleague with a bed in his own billet.

The increasing Portuguese and Spanish reluctance to supply billets was in part due to a minority of officers abusing the normal arrangements. The medical department did not escape official criticism. A general order issued in September 1811 commenced with the following.

> The frequent complaints which the Commander of the Forces receives of the conduct of the officers, principally of the Commissariat and Medical departments, both in the mode of taking their quarters and in the conduct towards their landlords, when employed at a distance from the army, oblige the Commander of the Forces to publish over again the Orders which have been repeatedly given and enforced upon the subject.

Wellington makes it clear that all quarters were a privilege, and that the officers had to be satisfied with what the towns of Portugal and Spain could reasonably provide. He concludes his order with a threat to court-martial any officer who behaved improperly in quarters and to carry out the sentence whatever its severity.[11]

Wellington's order lacks detail of the misdemeanours referred to, but the obvious implication is that some medical and commissariat officers had unrealistic expectations of their accommodation. An anecdote related by Captain Rees Howell Gronow gives support to this notion. The 'gallant officer' referred to was General Sir Warren Peacocke, Governor of Lisbon.

> Some of the complaints made to the gallant officer were frivolous in the extreme. On one occasion an assistant surgeon complained, in no measured terms, of the quarters allotted to him, stating that he was obliged to sleep in a pigsty; upon which Sir Warren inquired of one of his subalterns if he knew anything of the said pigsty. The answer was, that the quarters which the surgeon complained of were very good, in fact, better than the majority of the officers occupied. 'Oh, then, sir,' said Peacocke, turning to the injured medico, 'if you are a prince in disguise, declare yourself; but if you are only what your diploma states you to be, I consider the quarters you have quite good enough.'[12]

Often at the end of a day's march there were no suitable buildings for billets, and men and officers had to bivouac in the open. A camp would ideally be formed near to the edge of a wood, close to a supply of fresh water. Sleeping bags were improvised from blankets and greatcoats, and knapsacks used for pillows. In bad weather, or in poor locations, bivouacking was a miserable experience. A Peninsular veteran reflects that 'In the camp or bivouac, in fine weather all went on merrily, but there came moments of which the mere remembrance even now recalls ancient twinges of rheumatism, which the iron frame of the most hardy could not always resist.'[13] In the rain the priorities were procuring enough wood for a fire and finding a half dry place to sleep. John Gordon Smith, assistant surgeon of the 12th Light Dragoons, spent the notoriously wet night before Waterloo to the rear of the farm of Mont St Jean.

> The adjoining village furnished fuel in abundance. Doors, and window shutters – furniture of every description – carts, ploughs, harrows, clock-cases, casks, tables, &c. &c., were carried or trundled out to the bivouac, and being broken up, made powerful fires, in spite of the rain. Chairs were otherwise disposed of. Officers were paying two francs each for them, and the men seemed, at first, to be very able to keep up the supply. This, at last, failed, and, for one, I was fain to buy a bundle of straw. In front of the field which the horses occupied,

ran a miry cart-road (upon which the officers' fires were kindled) and by the side of this road was a drain, or shallow ditch. Here a party of us deposited our straw, and resolved to establish ourselves for the night, under cover of our cloaks; but such was the clayey nature of its bottom, that the rain did not sink into the earth, but rose like a leak in a ship, among the straw, and we were, in consequence, more drenched from below than from above.[14]

There were plenty of damp bivouacs in the Peninsula. George Burroughs, on the retreat from Burgos, camped in a vineyard where the ground was so wet that 'at every step we sunk deep in the soft mound surrounding the trunks of the vines'.[15] On such nights, sleep had be encouraged by the consumption of lots of grog and cigars. In contrast, a bivouac in fine weather in a fertile region was one of the pleasures of army life, long lingering in the memory. Burroughs again.

We encamped towards the close of the evening in an olive wood, on the banks of the Douro; and began to cook our provisions, and send our baggage animals for forage. The wood soon began to ring with the sturdy strokes of the axe, and the crackling blaze of the fires of the olive leaf illuminated the camp. The lofty clamours of the Portuguese; the nasal murmurs of the Spaniards; mingled with the neighing of horses, the lowing of cows, and the braying of asses, could not fail of reminding one of the medley scenes and discordant sounds of Saint Bartholomew's fair.[16]

Tents were intermittently available to officers in the early years of the Peninsular War and were issued to all British and German infantry units before the campaign of 1813. A general order in March 1813 reminded all officers arriving in Lisbon to obtain a tent from the public stores. The 'medical staff', presumably the surgeons of a regiment, were allowed one among them. Doctors in the Peninsula applauded this move as it both contributed to the health of the army (as discussed in the last chapter) and improved their own comfort. This use of tents by medical officers was not an innovation. The best description of life under canvas is by Assistant Surgeon James Dickson in Flanders almost twenty years earlier.

My tent is always pitched 15 yards in the rear of the Colonel's who pitches in the centre of the line of the Regiment a good way back in the rear. It is a sound one with a pole in the middle. I have nothing in it but my bed and 2 medicine boxes, which serve me one for a chair, the other for a table. My bed consists of some straw laid on the ground – above that a blanket, and then another double one to cover me. My pillow is my portmanteau.[17]

Dickson's narrative provides a good illustration of the contrasting types of accommodation that a medical officer could encounter on campaign. In three months during the spring of 1794 he was in his tent, billeted in cottages and housed in a château. The only decent village homes were usually taken by the commanding officers and he was obliged to sleep fully clothed on an old mattress stuffed with straw and without blankets.

> What I most dread in this country, when I sleep on the floor of a cottage, is the frogs, which are very numerous and often enter at the scudle holes. Their croaking is a most disagreeable noise. The spiders also are very noxious.[18]

In the château belonging to a local noblewoman, the officers were 'exceedingly well lodged'. Each occupied one of the seventy bedrooms. Outside there were extensive gardens and canals where they sailed and fished.

Such interludes of luxury were a welcome respite from the usual hardships of campaigning. James McGrigor enjoyed an idyllic existence when he accompanied the 'Indian army' to Egypt in 1801. Of his establishment at El Hamed near Rosetta on the Nile, he remembers,

> I had upwards of a dozen Indian servants, with their wives, besides my English soldier servant, and for my stock three camels, two horses, twenty-four sheep, three goats, several dozen of fowls, with a good many pigeons, rabbits, etc. My own large Indian marquee was in the centre, and around were the small Arab tents which my Indian servants had raised for themselves. In another quarter were found all my animals and a store tent, in which some of the servants nightly kept watch, and made rounds to see that no marauders made incursions upon us; which, however, they did occasionally, carrying off fowls, sheep, etc. Outside the whole I had a high mound thrown up, made from the vegetation on the bank of the river, having only one large gate to my premises. El Hamed was on the border of the desert and a sandy plain, but my animals were fed with grasses from the bank of the river and the grain which my blacks, with two Arab servants, could collect. I can never forget the astonishment of some officers of the English army, old friends who had visited me, on my showing them the extent of my premises. They told me that I brought to their mind the age of the patriarchs of old, with their herds and their flocks, their man-servants and their maid-servants.[19]

McGrigor's entourage was much removed from the expectations of medical officers in the Peninsula. Wellington, in a general order of October 1810, made it explicit that no officer in the medical department was allowed to have any soldier from the ranks as his servant or batman. This was a sore point as many doctors did feel that they needed, and deserved, someone to attend to them. The only course open was to hire from the local population. Soon after arriving in Coimbra in 1811, Walter Henry spotted 'a good looking Portuguese lad' lying in the shade taking a siesta. He hired him immediately as his servant, 'Although he could neither make splatterdashes nor play on the fiddle, like Sterne's La Fleur – he said he could cook, and brush my clothes, and polish my boots, and groom a horse.'[20] Antonio accompanied Henry up to the end of the war.

Language was an inevitable barrier to communication. Some British officers made a real effort, using books such as *Guthrie's Geographical, Historical and Commercial Grammar* as a guide to Portuguese, and Mordente's *Spanish Grammar*. The voyage to the Peninsula was a good opportunity for last-minute cramming. As educated men, the army's doctors expected to be able to master the necessary languages and converse easily. Most of them had received a basic education in Latin and Greek. A knowledge of French and other European languages was not rare. This classical education could prove unexpectedly helpful. When Walter Henry sought out a billet in Lisbon, he found that his landlord's grasp of English was little better than his Portuguese. The two men ended up having an animated conversation in Latin, which Henry says he had been taught to pronounce in the Continental rather than the English manner.

> We chatted away as classically as we might on the events of the day – the 'bellu internicum adversus Gallos' – the great 'Dux Wellington', the 'exercitus Britannicus' – the 'Rex Georgius' – the 'Spes Lusititaniae', and so forth, for half an hour, until we became cordial cronies.[21]

Proficiency in the language was the first step in getting to know the locals and beginning to understand another culture. Most of the views expressed by British officers, including the medical staff, were unashamedly nationalistic at best and xenophobic at worst. Samuel Broughton devotes a substantial part of his memoir to a description of the character of the people in the countries he visited. Of the Portuguese, '. . . an impoverished and miserable people, with the means of happiness in their possession, though with a total incapacity to make use of the blessings and natural advantages they possess.' The Spanish fared little better, 'The men are for the most part vulgar, vehement and noisy.'[22] He believed the Spaniards to have divided loyalties, with some being sincerely friendly to the British but others favouring the French. George Burroughs concurred with this view. When he entered Madrid, the citizens lauded the British army.

When this noble enthusiasm was at its height, I entered a book-seller's shop, and remarking to him, how very glad the people were to see us: 'Aye,' said he, 'they are so glad, that there is not a man among us, who would not give his wife to your embraces.'[23]

When the military situation was less favourable, the locals were more likely to keep their options open. On the retreat from Burgos, Burroughs met an innkeeper who had painted his sign 'Tria Naciones, junte in uno', the alliance of the British, Spanish and Portuguese. When asked what would happen when the enemy passed, he gave an 'arch look and a significant shrug' and pointed out that it could equally mean France, Germany and Spain.[24]

In his classic work *Life in Wellington's Army*, Anthony Brett-James summed up the British soldier's views of the people of the Iberian Peninsula. The Portuguese were dirty and indolent but good-natured and welcoming. The Spanish were better organised and cleaner but often arrogant and unfriendly.[25] This concords with the direct comparisons made by the doctors who experienced both countries. Samuel Broughton praises the Spanish for their greater industry and cleanliness, but the tone is grudging. The Portuguese were much more amiable and 'were they to live only a little more like civilised beings I should prefer their character to that of the Spaniards'. Assistant Surgeon Brookes of the 87th Foot lamented in 1809 that in Spain he had been greeted with little civility and the Portuguese were ten times as hospitable.[26] As the French were the enemy they were unlikely to be viewed in a favourable light. Broughton was predictably scathing, 'Two predominant foibles are conspicuously common to both sexes – excessive vanity, and a never-ceasing disposition to chatter, accompanied by a corresponding aversion from every species of thinking.'[27]

A subject which engendered particular outrage and bigotry was religion. Most British troops were Protestant and many were insular in their opinions. They were easily shocked by local religious customs and, in the Peninsula, were critical of the large numbers of priests who appeared extremely idle. Surgeon Boutflower was typically antagonistic to the Catholic church in Spain. He describes, 'every species of wickedness'. Allegedly, the Sabbath was disregarded, the dead were buried with 'disgusting levity', the convents were 'hotbeds of iniquity' and the clergy were responsible for 'nine tenths of seductions'.[28]

Spanish and Portuguese women received a variable press from British officers. One described the ladies at a ball as being a mixture of black eyes and black teeth. Charles Boutflower alternately praises and damns the Spanish womenfolk. Thus, on entering Badajoz,

What struck me was the vast superiority that the Spanish women have over the Portuguese in Person, Air, Appearance, and Dress. The latter are in general very slovenly, while the former are particularly neat in their mode of dress, and have an inexpressible elegance and dignity in their walk which I have never seen in other women.

When Boutflower became better acquainted with some of these ladies, he was less impressed. 'From habit and bad example the women here even of the first rank have contracted an indelicacy in their ideas and conversation which would shock the most abandoned in England.' Some were surprisingly ignorant, believing among other things that Englishmen were permitted to have several wives. The experience simply confirmed in Boutflower's mind the superiority of his 'own fair countrywomen'.[29]

Another medical officer who had difficulty making up his mind about the Spanish ladies was Samuel Broughton. In one letter they are 'deficient in delicacy and manners', but later 'with a little more polish from refined education that is at present within their reach, I cannot conceive a more agreeable, fascinating, and beautiful set of females'.[30] Much of the socialising was with the 'better classes', women from the upper echelons of Spanish society whom officers might meet at parties. As only the minority of British officers at an evening 'conversazione' or 'pertiglia' would be able to speak Spanish, Boutflower described these events as stupid. The Spanish women of the lower classes were, according to Adam Neale, 'irascible to a degree'. In Salamanca, he says that they fought a pitched battle eight or ten times a day, 'their tongues are the general weapon of attack'.[31]

Whatever their reservations about foreign women, some doctors' interest in them was more than intellectual. Samuel Broughton does not confess any indiscretions. Of Portuguese ladies he notes, 'They are not to be taken by storm, but require a long siege, which, if the lover has the patience to go through all the manoeuvres of it, is I believe rarely unattended with ultimate success.'[32] This has the flavour of second hand information. In contrast, Walter Henry, who seems to have had more fun than most, gives us plenty of detail of his amorous exploits. Opposite his billet in Lisbon lived two attractive and high-spirited Portuguese girls. In the evening they sat on a balcony which was only separated by a narrow street from his own. He chatted with them in his recently acquired Portuguese, and as it became dark, the conversation became more animated.

> Mutual compliments were then interchanged; I praised the brilliancy of the ladies eyes, and their fine persons; unusual in Lisbon, where dumpiness is a common characteristic of the women. I perceived that my lively neighbours were much at a loss to discern a laudable quality about me, and were obliged to content themselves by saying

'vos merced tem muito bonitas dentes' – you have good teeth. Except occasionally playing a modhina set to music, on the guitar, I firmly believe these girls never read, nor worked, nor drew, nor visited, nor went out, except to church; nor did anything but lounge through the house, look out of the windows, loll on the couches, make love when they could, and amuse themselves with the Gallegos.[33]

A few months later, Henry transferred to a village outside Lisbon. Here he was the only British officer and soon became embroiled in a full blown love affair with the daughter of his landlord, a beautiful girl called Theodora. The 'vigorous flirtation' included Henry writing amatory notes in Portuguese which his new love was unable to read. Unfortunately, the romance was doomed. Her family much disapproved of the match and when efforts by the local magistrate to turn the doctor out of his accommodation failed, the girl was spirited away. 'I saw her no more,' laments Henry.[34] No doubt there were other similar affairs, but there is no instance in the Peninsular War, that I can find, of a medical officer actually marrying a local woman.

The Waterloo campaign brought the army's doctors into contact with the womenfolk of the Low Countries. Again, there was some consternation at the lack of decorum. William Gibney, in his first campaign, was aggrieved that his landlady entered his room without knocking, 'bedroom or sitting room, it was all the same to her'. To make matters worse, she harangued him with all nature of complaints.[35] Assistant Surgeon John Haddy-James visited Bruges in the early days of the campaign. The streets were thronged with people including many women who, he says, were dressed similarly to the country people in England. However, there were differences.

... they do not, like our females, appear at all anxious to exhibit the contours of their figures, of which they allow little to be seen except what their short petticoats may discover – sometimes a pair of well-turned legs, but not infrequently the direct reverse.[36]

Soldiers' wives accompanied the army abroad despite the disapproval of many senior officers. Regulations dictated that up to six wives of the rank and file were randomly selected to travel on service with each company. In addition, a proportion of the officers were joined by their wives, and even by their children. Many wives resided in Lisbon, but some did travel with their husbands on campaign and, depending on their durability and the circumstances, were regarded by the regiment's other officers as either an asset or a hindrance. None of Wellington's doctors who have left accounts of the war mention their family being anywhere other than at home. It is likely that only a few were accompanied by their wives on campaign. We know that Francis Maguire, surgeon to the 4th Foot, took his wife with him as she is credited with saving the Colours of the King's Own from capture. The couple were on a transport returning from America in 1797 when it was captured by a French privateer. To prevent the regimental Colours from falling into French hands, Mrs Maguire wrapped them around her flat iron and dropped them into the sea. She was truly a woman of the wars, eventually receiving three pensions; one for her husband who died from yellow fever in India, one for her son Francis who was killed in the storming of San Sebastian, and one for her son Pete who was lost at sea.[37]

The intense interest taken by most soldiers in food and drink reflected the vagaries of life on campaign. Tales of gluttonous feasts and excessive consumption of alcohol are interspersed with stories of poor rations and near starvation. Rations were irregularly supplied throughout the Peninsular War and, to a lesser extent, in other campaigns. Foraging for additional food was often a necessity although pilfering was strongly discouraged. Army beef was usually like leather and the biscuit rock hard and even full of maggots. When Surgeon Joseph Burke of the 95th Rifles reprimanded a man with severe indigestion for his poor diet, his patient retorted that two years in Spain had turned his stomach into 'a scavenger's cart, obliged to take in every rubbage'.[38] British soldiers were not routinely taught to cook and did not necessarily make the best of the food available. William Fergusson condemned the widespread waste, asserting that Englishmen would starve in conditions where the French or Germans would survive with ease.[39] It would be wrong to imply that all the shortages were self-induced or avoidable. On the retreat from Burgos, George Burroughs says he was forced to eat wild turnips, hawthorn berries and acorns. This is confirmed by another regimental surgeon, 'roasted acorns were by many considered not unpalatable, and often served to appease the cravings of hunger'. He says that on occasions flour alone was supplied, 'which we made into cakes and baked as well as we could on a tin plate'. When even flour was unavailable, wheat was issued. This had to be prepared for eating by boiling or roasting.[40]

When officers were comfortably quartered in the larger towns and cities with a ready supply of money, there was an abundance of food. William Dent explained this to his mother in a letter from north-east Spain in 1814. 'If a man has plenty of money, he may live well, almost everywhere, but if he has not money, then he is obliged to bite the hob, and live on a soldier's rations.'[41] Fruit could be purchased cheaply from the local markets and familiar items such as tea, sugar, butter and hams were sold by the sutlers who accompanied the army at prices a little dearer than at home. Officers usually joined together in messes. Thus three or four men pooled their resources and cooked together. According to Dent, with a subscription of four to five pounds a month in addition to the rations, a small group such as this could live 'comfortably'. We can only guess what he meant by this, but there are a few anecdotes to suggest that in the good times medical officers could eat at least as well as at home. In January 1812 Surgeon Samuel Good dined with a brother officer off soup, boiled neck of mutton, pork cutlets, patties, roast goose, woodcocks and pudding washed down with champagne and Madeira.[42]

For the more adventurous, and sometimes from necessity, there was the opportunity to sample the local cuisine of Portugal and Spain. Predictably, the British were not overly impressed with food that was radically different from anything they had tasted previously. The Portuguese offerings were, moaned Samuel Broughton, ruined by the 'very liberal distribution of garlic, oil, and onions throughout all their dishes'.[43] Spanish food, according to Adam Neale, consisted almost entirely 'of an execrable mess, called gaspacho, which they eat thrice a day'.[44] Outside the Iberian Peninsula the troops experienced similar periods of hunger and satiety. In the weeks preceding Waterloo, officers were able to enjoy the local food. Assistant Surgeon Haddy James admits in his journal that 'an account of many dinners and much wine would be fatigueing'.[45] Well equipped officers carried canteens containing cutlery, bowls, cups and plates. Assistant Surgeon John Smith's portmanteau contained candlesticks and lamps. When the campaign got properly underway, the army's doctors' requirements became much simpler. William Gibney spent the day before Waterloo 'adding a little fighting to starving and marching'. In the evening he felt himself extremely fortunate to obtain some tongue of dubious origin and a thimbleful of brandy.[46]

Alcohol has been invoked as a significant cause of disease. It was an integral part of army life and was consumed in enormous quantities. This abuse was encouraged by prevailing views that it actually gave protection against the lethal diseases that bedevilled the army. In the West Indies, the local rum was supposed to have antiscorbutic properties and was also considered to be an effective prophylactic against yellow fever.[47] Similar views were held in India, and in the Peninsula the peasants were astonished that Wellington's troops drank so much wine and so little water.[48] The attitude of the regimental medical officers to alcohol often appears ambivalent. Some justified alcohol consumption as a way of restoring the men's morale. On the retreat from Burgos, a surgeon of the 71st Foot supported the use of both alcohol and tobacco.

> Notwithstanding the ideas entertained by total abstainers and temperance advocates, the exhilarating and beneficial effect of liquor in distressing circumstances is also well known, and was often exemplified on the retreat.[49]

In this tolerant climate the doctors did not deny themselves a fair share of the drink. Even the conservative James McGrigor – a man who in Ceylon commented, 'the army passed the time in much, too much, joviality for me' – carried his personal stock of wine whilst campaigning in India. When drinking the health of the 'Saint of the Day' with Colonel Beresford's champagne, he contributed six bottles of fine old hock.[50]

Wellington was concerned at the damage alcohol was undoubtedly causing to his army. Hence this general order of July 1812.

> As much of the sickness of the troops is attributed to the use of raw spirits by the soldiers in the hot season, the Commander of the Forces desires that the officers will see that the men of each mess in their companies mix their spirits with four times the quantity of water, as soon as the spirits are issued by the Commissary.[51]

This was followed by the threat to discontinue the supply of all spirits and wine to a regiment if its officers did not carry out the order. One of the reasons that alcohol was the main thirst-quenching drink was the shortage of accessible drinking water. Much of the diarrhoea suffered by the soldiers in the Peninsula, 'fits of the King Agrippa', as one officer termed it, was almost certainly caused by the drinking of impure water. Even apparently clear water could hold hidden hazards. Walter Henry recalls a bizarre incident in Spain. After drinking from a fountain in a town square, one hundred and fifty soldiers attended their regimental hospitals spitting blood. It transpired that this alarming symptom was caused by small leeches in the water which had attached themselves to the mouths, nostrils, throats, gullets and even the stomachs of the men. Henry and his colleagues set to work. 'We had a bloody day at the hospitals, although no lives were lost, except the leeches'.' They were removed with some difficulty with a combination of silk ligature nooses, strong solutions of salt, tobacco and powerful emetics.[52]

The British war strategy in the Peninsula depended on the mobility of the army. Medical staff officers could spend prolonged periods at headquarters or in general hospitals, but the regimental surgeons were frequently on the move and spent long hours on the road with their battalions. A typical day's march was fifteen miles, although this varied depending on the weather, the state of the roads, and the military necessity to cover longer distances. Forced marches over difficult terrain in extreme heat or cold were not uncommon and there was inevitable suffering. In addition to a mule for the regimental medical equipment, most regimental surgeons had a horse for their own transport and another mule for their personal baggage. Animals were bought from a local market such as the 'Rocino' held in an open area to the north of Lisbon. Campaigning took its toll on these beasts of burden. One Guards officer whose battalion had marched 1,700 miles lost six mules from fatigue. Their replacement, at around £20 each, was a considerable expense for the average medical officer. When William Dent had to buy two animals in 1813 he was forced to write to his mother to request the necessary money. Without them, he assured her, it would be impossible for him to be like the other officers and to do his duty.

The dangers of campaigning were not confined to the battlefield. With their regiments, doctors could feel relatively secure, but travelling alone in the Peninsula carried real risks. When Samuel Broughton rode alone along an isolated mountainous road near Pamplona in December 1813, the natives' graphic accounts of robbery and murder made him concerned for his safety. The bandits included deserters from the British Army. Hospital Mate James Byron Bradley had reason to fear for his life when he became lost in an isolated region of Portugal in 1812. He was ordered to accompany a convoy of sick and wounded troops from Castello Branco to Abrantes, but injudiciously delayed his journey to share a meal with a fellow doctor. When he set out on horseback to catch up with the convoy, he took a wrong turn and was soon wandering through the countryside completely lost and suffering from cold, hunger and fever. Eventually, he came across a sizeable barn.

By the light of a large fire on the ground, close to the building, I observed five or six Portuguese soldiers. I called aloud, and it appeared strange that I could not attract their attention. At length one of them left his party, and came slowly towards me. When within two or three yards he drew his sabre, and demanded what I wanted. I saw that he was a Portuguese dragoon, and his appearance and bearing were such to create some alarm. Being entirely alone, enveloped in total darkness, and having, in common with many British officers, a very unfavourable opinion of the Portuguese lower orders, I judged it prudent to ensure my own safety by letting him see at once how dangerous it would be to attempt anything hostile. I asked him the way to Sarnadas, and assumed a somewhat authoritative tone and manner, keeping him in front of me. He could not tell me, but I learned that he and his companions were in charge of stores for the army, which were deposited in the barn-like building. There was something extremely forbidding in the appearance of this man. He was a tall, brawny fellow, with a complexion so swarthy as to appear black, with enormous whiskers and mustachios. I said, 'I am the commander of a regiment of English, which are at the foot of the hill, and our route is to Sarnadas.' I thought it advisable to say a regiment of troops, as the number would deter him from meditating any attack on me; and that I was the commander of them, thinking, perhaps justly, that if he and his party might be disposed to attempt anything against a humbler individual, they would hesitate to do so against one whose presence they would know was so necessary to the regiment; and that whilst the commander of it was absent, it would remain at the foot of the hill until his return.

He had put several questions to me before I told him that I was accompanied, which were calculated to excite some suspicion – such as, if I were alone, if I had the means of paying a guide, &c. I thought it prudent to get away from him as soon as possible, and turned my horse round with that intention. In turning round, I fancied that his long sword was uplifted. It was a moment of great alarm; but, knowing that it was not a time to show any fear, I immediately turned my horse's head towards him again, spoke to him in a commanding tone respecting the stores which he had in charge, and during this time kept backing my horse, so as to have the dragoon in front, until I had gotten to the brink of the hill which I had just ridden up. When there, I suddenly turned round, called out 'Viva Senhor!' and sending the spurs into the animal's sides, galloped down the hill as fast as she could go.[53]

In reality the chances of perishing in an isolated incident of this sort were remote. The greatest danger to life, from both sickness and violence, was following a military reverse when the discipline and cohesion of the army deteriorated. The British lost no major battle in the Peninsula, but the army was forced into two ignominious retreats, that of Sir John Moore's force to Corunna in the winter of 1808–9, and Wellington's later withdrawal from Burgos in the winter of 1812. Both were periods of appalling hardship for all the troops and the army's followers. Although the Corunna retreat is better known, many veterans believed the withdrawal from Burgos to be even worse. Doctors accompanying the retreating armies have left some of the most evocative accounts of the miseries endured. Physician Adam Neale and Surgeon Henry Milburne were in Moore's force and Assistant Surgeon George Burroughs and an anonymous regimental medical officer of the 71st Foot, probably Surgeon Arthur Stewart, wrote of their experiences in 1812.

Neale witnessed the full extent of the suffering of the Corunna retreat on the climb of Monte Cebrero near Villafranca. His vivid account was widely circulated at home.

This country was now covered with deep snow. There was neither provision or shelter from the rain, nor dried fuel for our fires, nor place where the weary and footsore could rest for a single day in safety. All that had hitherto been suffered by our troops, was but as a prelude to this consummate scene of horrors. It was still attempted to carry forward our sick and wounded; the beasts which dragged them failed, and they were of necessity left in their wagons to perish amidst the snows. As we looked around on gaining the highest point of those slippery precipices, and observed the rear of the army winding along the narrow road, we could see the whole track marked out by our own wretched people who lay on all sides expiring from fatigue and the severity of the cold – while their uniforms reddened in spots the white surface of the ground . . . That no degree of horror might be wanting, this unfortunate army was accompanied by many women and children, of whom some were frozen to death on the baggage wagons, which were broken down or left upon the road for lack of cattle. Some died of fatigue and cold, while their infants were seen vainly sucking at their clay cold breasts.[54]

Henry Milburne became delayed at Astorga. Slightly wounded and with his servant ill, he marched nearly fifty miles without rest to join the rear of the army at Bembibre. Here he passed a great number of stragglers, sick women, and children. He was unable to continue on foot, and as the enemy were very close, had to abandon his luggage including his valuable surgical instruments. He did eventually reach Corunna.[55]

The scenes between Burgos and the Portuguese border in November 1812 are reminiscent of the eyewitness accounts of Napoleon's retreat from Moscow. The weather was bitterly cold, the rivers flooded, and the roads blocked with dead animals, wagons and abandoned equipment. At a bivouac near Ciudad Rodrigo, the surgeon of the 71st was shocked at the state of his comrades.

It is melancholy to see the wretched plight of most of our poor fellows, their frames emaciated, and worn with fatigue, their countenances shrunk with privation, suffering and care, the state of their clothes ragged in the extreme, many of them being almost without a cover to their nakedness, or protection from the severity of the weather, their shoes worn to pieces, nay, many obliged to trudge on their bare feet, with foot sores, wounds, and blisters. The suffering of the officers, in comparison, certainly was not less; numbers were knocked up, and obliged to be transported in hospital wagons, or on gun carriages. How altered in their appearance may be judged from the fact that I with difficulty recognised some of my acquaintances belonging to other corps whom I casually encountered on the march under such circumstances.[56]

As was the case four years earlier, the women with the army were most vulnerable. George Burroughs paints a pathetic picture. Those in poor health sat on the bullock carts, 'sobbing to the disagreeable squeaking of the greaseless wheels'. Many were wearing gaudy dresses and attempted to shield themselves from the sun and rain with parasols. Some were local women, 'If you asked them where they were going they said they did not know, they were going with the English.'[57]

When morale was low soldiers took solace in plundering. On the road to Corunna the men broke into wine cellars and indulged in frenzied drinking, some even drowning in wine. Bad though such events were, the apotheosis of alcohol abuse and disorder in the Peninsula followed the successful reduction of a siege. When British soldiers entered Badajoz in 1812, the wine and spirit stores were promptly ransacked and the army dissolved into an intoxicated mob. The doctors on the scene were shocked by what they saw. James McGrigor entered the town to determine the number of wounded.

> In a little time the whole of the soldiers appeared to be in a state of mad drunkenness. In every street and in every corner we met them forcing themselves like furies into houses, firing through the keyholes of the doors so as to force locks, or at any person they saw at a window imploring mercy. In passing some houses which they had entered we heard the shrieks of females, and sometimes the groans of those whom they were no doubt butchering.[58]

There is no evidence that the army's medical officers were any part of these depravities, but they were not above reproach. In a review of courts-martial of the Peninsular War, Charles Oman notes that the medical department was subject to relatively few trials, but that drunkenness was the most serious failing.[59] This sometimes resulted in brawling and 'other discreditable incidents in public'. Many of the charges against doctors appear to have been trivial, petty insubordinations and minor breaches of rules. A few cases attracted more attention. In December 1810 a regimental surgeon appeared before a court-martial charged with confining in the guard-room a Portuguese whom he accused of stealing a horse. He had no authority to make such an arrest. He was found guilty and sentenced to be reprimanded, but was acquitted on a charge of conduct prejudicial to discipline and good order. Wellington was irritated by this leniency and issued a general order condemning the surgeon and insisting that a reprimand should be read to the doctor at the head of the troops stationed at Torres Vedras.[60] The most outrageous disciplinary offence by a doctor was almost certainly that of Hospital Mate George Welch. He commenced his misdemeanours by disobeying the order of a superior. He then abandoned nine sick men on the road between Abrantes and Lisbon and left other sick in his care unassisted for several days. When he returned to his hospital, he ran through the wards with a sword threatening convalescents who had left their beds without his permission. At his court-martial in December 1809 he was dismissed from the service.[61]

Oman concludes that duelling was rare. Only four duels in the Peninsula led to courts-martial. All were associated with deaths. Wellington, although he was later foolish enough to duel with Lord

Winchester, was much opposed to duels on active service as he could not afford to lose good officers. A few medical officers became involved in 'affairs of honour'. There were no real winners in these encounters. Patrick Egan, assistant surgeon to the 23rd Dragoons, was tried by court-martial for challenging a superior officer to a duel and was sentenced to be cashiered. In consideration of his previous good character, the Prince Regent over-ruled the judgement but ordered his removal to another regiment. William McChristie, assistant surgeon to the 69th Foot, was forced to resign by his colonel after fighting a duel with a fellow officer in 1814. He re-entered the medical service the following year as a lowly hospital assistant. At least these officers were given a second chance. Thomas Montgomery, assistant surgeon in the ordnance medical department, was killed in a duel in Guadeloupe in 1812.

Behaviour like that at Badajoz provided the justification for the army's draconian disciplinary measures. Wellington was a traditionalist with respect to punishments. Malefactors could expect hanging or flogging. In fairness to the commander in chief, he had little choice of other punishments. He was limited by the provisions of the Mutiny Act and the Articles of War, and there were no army prisons in Portugal or Spain. Flogging was with a cat-of-nine-tails on the back of the perpetrator who was tied to a triangle or spontoon. The number of lashes varied from around 300 to 1,200. Regimental surgeons had the unenviable responsibility of judging at what point the punishment was life-threatening and to step in and postpone the remainder until the man had recovered. A contemporary critic of flogging describes the surgeon 'with dubious look, pressing the agonised victim's pulse, and calmly calculating to an odd blow, how far suffering may be extended, until in its extremity it encroach upon life'.[62] William Fergusson, then a surgeon in the 5th Foot, had to supervise the horrific and potentially fatal punishment of 1,000 lashes. A soldier of the light company had broken into a Sussex farm and had severely wounded the woman of the house with a bayonet.

> When brought up for punishment, he stripped off as in scorn, and presented as fine a model of compact form, hard muscle, and dark thick skin, as I ever beheld. The drummers were well grown sturdy lads, who had always performed their duty well, and to them, after the punishment began he particularly directed his abuse, daring them to do their worst, for they never would extract a single groan from him. Seven hundred and seventy-five lashes were most severely inflicted, when perceiving from his countenance alone that nature was giving way, I had him taken down and carried to the hospital.
>
> In a few weeks he was reported cured, and the commanding officer declared that the sentence should be inflicted to the utmost lash. He

was accordingly brought out again. It was winter, and the snow was on the ground. He was tied up with his back to the wind. At the first lash the newly organised skin gave way, the blood streamed down his back, and he who on the first infliction was all defiance, now writhed and cried out. As the flogging proceeded, the lash became clogged with blood, which at every wave of the drummers arm was driven in showers by the wind over the snow-covered ground; his cries became actual yells, and the integuments of his newly-cicatrised back were literally cut to pieces. I stopped the punishment when he had received sixty lashes: but his second cure was now a very different affair. Healthy suppuration could not be established after such reiterated injury, and sloughing and deep-seated abscesses were formed amongst the great muscles of the back. When I left the regiment, on promotion, some months afterwards, he was still in the hospital, a poor hectic wretch, utterly broken down from the terrible effect of the second flogging. I never learned when he ultimately recovered.[63]

Astonishingly, some soldiers did survive the effects of repeated floggings. George Guthrie records the case of a man in his regiment who had received a total of 15,000 lashes in the course of his service. Robbery with armed force without extenuating circumstances could lead to a death sentence. Other crimes punishable by execution were murder and desertion. Murder most commonly led to the gallows, whilst desertion was the one offence which regularly resulted in a firing squad. Assistant Surgeon James Dickson witnessed an execution by the latter method in Flanders in 1794. Unlike for flogging, the regimental surgeon played no active role in executions but stood with the rest of the army in order of battle in complete silence.

The prisoner marched on foot with his hands tied and his helmet off his head, surrounded by a part of his own regiment at slow time along the whole line. He was then brought into the centre of the picquets, and after some time spent in prayer with a priest, he was desired to kneel down. Six soldiers of his own regiment were then drawn up before him and ordered to load their carbines. He spoke a few words to his captain, and they put the cage over his eyes, upon which the executioners were ordered to advance within six yards of him. He was to give the signal by dropping a handkerchief; this he did after a few minutes; and the soldiers immediately presented but were ordered by the provost-marshal to recover their arms, and go through the motions for firing. He received four balls in his head and one in his neck; one must have missed him. His grave was immediately dug, and he was buried on the spot.[64]

Doctors were at limited risk of a violent death in action. Their professional role in battle and their surprisingly low chance of receiving a fatal wound have been discussed in Chapter II. However, the battles that punctuated the long periods of relative inactivity were inevitably periods of heightened awareness and anxiety for all the army's officers. The memoirs of a number of medical officers recount in graphic detail the hours leading up to a major battle. The emotions expressed are mostly an eager anticipation mixed with excitement and some nervousness. Men tried to calm themselves with light-hearted banter. William Gibney before Waterloo,

> It was wonderful with what indifference we spoke or rather joked with each other on coming events. To one, tall and big, the information was vouchsafed that his chances of being hit were good, so huge an individual forming a target not to be missed. To another, with an unusually prominent nasal organ, its liability to attract the enemy's attention to him was pointed out; and so on everlastingly.[65]

Few admitted to real fear. Once the battle was underway, Gibney says he had a feeling of 'je ne sais quoi'. Waterloo was his first experience of fighting and this was not unusual in 1815. It is difficult to be precise about how many medical officers at Waterloo had been in battle before, but only approximately half of the regimental doctors had previously been on campaign. The relevant information is contained in Dalton's Waterloo Roll Call and Drew's List of Medical Officers in the British Army. There were 104 regimental medical officers at Waterloo; 70 in infantry regiments and 34 in the cavalry; 36 were surgeons and 68 were assistant surgeons; 24 of the 36 surgeons and 33 of the 68 assistant surgeons had previous experience of campaigning – just over half the total number. Twenty had participated in more than one earlier campaign. The figures for individual campaigns are as follows: Peninsula (52), Walcheren (12), Holland (7), Egypt (3), North America (3), South Africa (2), and West Indies, India and Germany (1). Drew is not always comprehensive with respect to campaign experience and these figures are probably a slight under-estimate.

With so many rookie doctors at Waterloo, it is not surprising that at least one or two became visibly alarmed as the fighting intensified. In his famous memoir of the campaign, Captain Cavalrie Mercer included a cameo featuring an assistant surgeon in the ordnance medical department, Richard Hitchins.

> We breathed a new atmosphere – the air was suffocatingly hot, resembling that issuing from an oven, we were enveloped in thick smoke, and malgre the incessant roar of cannon and musketry, could

distinctly hear around us a mysterious humming noise, like that which one hears of a summer's evening proceeding from myriads of black beetles; cannon-shot, too, ploughed the ground in all directions, and so thick, was the hail of balls and bullets that it seemed dangerous to extend the arm lest it should be torn off.

In spite of this serious situation in which we were, I could not help being somewhat amused at the astonishment expressed by our kind-hearted surgeon, who heard for the first time this sort of music. He was close to me as we ascended the slope, and, hearing this infernal carillon about his ears, began staring round in the wildest and most comic manner imaginable, twisting himself from side to side, exclaiming, 'My God. Mercer, what is that? What is all this noise? How curious! – how very curious!' And then, when a cannon-shot rushed hissing past, 'There! – there! What is it all?' It was with great difficulty that I persuaded him to retire: for a time he insisted on remaining near me, and it was only by pointing out how important it was to us, in case of being wounded, that he should keep himself safe to be able to assist us, that I prevailed on him to withdraw.[66]

A number of medical officers showed great courage in action. At the Battle of Laswaree in India in 1803, Surgeon George Fryer charged with the 8th Light Dragoons until in the midst of the fight he was ordered out of the way. He was short-sighted, proceeded in the wrong direction and was almost captured.[67] Another notable example of bravery is that of Assistant Surgeon Edward Johnson of the 28th Foot who volunteered to carry a vital dispatch from Tarifa ordering his regiment to withdraw from its abortive attempt to relieve Cadiz in June 1810. He soon came under fire from the French, and then was nearly accidentally attacked by British troops. He survived all this unscathed, but his luck ran out when local guerrillas mistook him for a French officer and he was knocked from his horse with a lance, breaking his arm. Once on the ground he received around thirty further wounds, including a fractured skull, before it was discovered that he was a British officer. Johnson claimed that he opened his coat to display his red uniform to the guerrillas before the cowardly attack. Fortunately, he was rescued by a party of his own regiment and the dispatch was recovered. Following his ordeal the doctor was transferred to Tarifa for medical treatment. His gallant action was not honoured by the British government but he did receive the decoration of the Order of Charles the Third from the Spanish King.[68]

When the army was in action, medical officers ran the risk of becoming prisoners of war. Most civilised countries saw little point in detaining doctors for long periods but a few were imprisoned. Listings of British army prisoners in France include six surgeons and seventeen assistant surgeons.[69] Several of these officers were captured after the Battle of

Talavera when they were left in the town to tend the wounded. Although Wellington had suggested that captured medical officers should be promptly returned by either side, the doctors at Talavera were sent to the prison depot at Verdun and only released a year later. Sadly, we have no further details of Surgeon John Johnson of the 9th Foot who escaped by feigning insanity. However, Assistant Surgeon James Elkington has left a detailed account of the whole episode in his journal. Initially the doctors were taken to the Retiro Palace in Madrid from where Elkington and a few comrades made a desperate bid for freedom.

> November 7th [1809] – George and A.Beamish, Herriot, Curby, Rule, and myself, having procured a rope, attempted to escape, and descended from the window into the garden, but one of the sentries was alarmed, and after two hours spent endeavouring to get out of the gardens, we fell into a picquet and were conveyed to the Guard room, from whence we were removed to the common dungeon (George Beamish and Rule had fortunately got clear and returned to their rooms). We remained a fortnight in this place, very cold, there being six windows, iron grated, without glass, and were supplied with black bread and water only; but having money and a canteen cooking machine, we procured many comforts and passed our miserable confinement in tolerable good humour.[70]

Later in the month, Elkington left Madrid in the company of twelve other British officers and a hundred British soldiers. There were also 2,000 Spanish prisoners. The convoy passed through Valladolid, Burgos, Tolosa, and reached Bayonne just before Christmas. The marches were exhausting and at night officers and men were confined in immense barns. Verdun was reached by coach in January 1810. The castle in the town was one of the better POW depots and Elkington was treated as well as any prisoner of war could expect. Officers were allowed to walk the ramparts and even to visit local villages. Much of the time was passed in the 'club-room' where there were newspapers and games such as chess, backgammon, billiards and cards. In the evenings, comic plays were enacted.

> The living was cheap and good. Thus had I conceived I was to have been only a short period here, I could not have wished to have passed my time in a better quarter; but being uncertain as to the duration of our confinement, it became every day more tiresome and irksome.[71]

The surgeons left with the wounded at Talavera decided to appeal directly to Napoleon for their release. The following plea reached the French Emperor in May 1810.

The undersigned medical officers of His Britannic Majesty's Service, having been for the sake of humanity left in charge of the English and French wounded on the retreat of the British army from Talavera became prisoners of war. Whilst performing their duties at Talavera they received the commendations of Marshals Mortier, Victor and Sebastiani. They humbly request to be allowed to return to their country, throwing themselves on the known clemency of the Emperor.

Elkington says that the last sentence was not universally approved of by the officers but he believed that some flattery was required to achieve their objective. Perhaps because the Emperor had just married the Archduchess of Austria he was generous, and the medical officers received their passports and left Verdun after a stay of four months. For Elkington, the threat of imprisonment by the French had not ended. During the British retreat through northern Spain in 1812, he was left to tend the sick in Burgos – a duty for which he was promised promotion. When the enemy entered the town, the French commandant ordered him to report in the evening to sign his parole as a prisoner of war. This was delayed until carts had collected the final British wounded from the hospital at the nearby village of Villa Toro where Elkington was in charge. It was likely that he would again be deported to France.

This was a death blow to me, and I immediately went to Captain Menzies, a wounded officer in Burgos, to ask his advice about attempting to escape. He advised me not to try as my health was so delicate; he thought I could not go through the fatigue. Some officers of the German Legion, however, were of a different opinion. Seeing the cars ready to start, I had no time to lose. I bought a bottle of brandy and two pounds of meat, and rode to the gate. The sergeant of the guard wished to detain me, but I showed him my pass of the 24th, which he did not examine minutely, and talking of Verdun, where his regiment had been quartered, he allowed me to pass.

On arrival at Villa Toro, I got my horse and mule ready, with my Portuguese boy mounted on the latter, and, seeing the cars approaching, I took a dose of brandy and started off at a gallop. After a good ride over flat but partly ploughed land, I came to a village at the foot of the mountains. The inhabitants told me they were sure the French would not follow me up the mountain; so I ascended, and at the top halted, and with my glass distinctly saw some French cavalry in the village I had just left. I immediately struck off the high road, and, judging as well as possible my proper direction, I continued on till dark, when I fell in with a peasant, whom I compelled to show me the way to the priest's house on my way to Aquillo-de-Campo, my

217

intention being to reach the coast at Santander, as I knew Sir Home Popham and some English vessels were there.[72]

Elkington rode his horse to exhaustion and finally found a billet with some Spanish troops. He shared some coffee with the Spanish General Renovales who informed him of the latest military situation – General Hill had reluctantly conceded Madrid to the French, Wellington had already abandoned the siege of Burgos, and Hill and Wellington were planning to unite around Salamanca. On his arrival in Santander, the doctor found Sir Home Popham and acquainted him with this intelligence. The rear admiral, in command of a squadron harassing the coast of Spain, thought it of enough import to immediately send a frigate to England carrying the news. Elkington sold his horse to Popham ('at a bargain price') and took the opportunity of a safe passage home.

Elkington's adventures are the stuff of Napoleonic novels. It must be acknowledged, however, that most soldiers spent considerable periods of the wars in relative inactivity with boredom the main enemy. For officers billeted in small towns or villages, perhaps for several winter months, life could be extremely monotonous. William 'Tiger' Dunlop, assistant surgeon in the 89th Foot, describes his existence in Canada in 1813.

> We passed the remainder of the winter as officers are obliged to do in country quarters. We shot, we lounged, we walked and did all the flirtation that the neighbourhood of a mill, a shop, a tavern, with two farmhouses, within a reasonable forenoon's walk, could afford. We were deprived, however, of the luxury of spitting over a bridge, which Dr Johnston says is the principal amusement of officers in country quarters, for though we had a bridge close at hand, the stream beneath it was frozen.[73]

Compared with the dangers of battle and real disease, homesickness seems a trivial malady. But it was real enough to those afflicted. For Wellington's soldiers, Spain and Portugal were lands alien in culture, economy, language and religion. At least some of the Peninsular army's doctors pined for the familiar pleasures of home. These feelings were understandably most intense at times of traditional celebration such as Christmas. Assistant Surgeon John Murray writes to his mother in Scotland from Spain on 13 December 1812:

> This being a wet Sunday's forenoon I dedicate my time to write you a letter, and who knows, but some of you at Slap may be similarly employed in writing to me. Our pleasures are mainly of the negative kind, that is, we rejoice that we are not much exposed to the cold and wet, that we have a dry bed to sleep in, and that we have plenty to eat.

218

But we have little to look forward to, wherewith to amuse and enjoy ourselves at Christmas which, were I at home amongst you, I should anticipate as a time of much merriment and social conviviality. We have no formal society to lose and play forfeits with – no hand through a dance – or to make us cracked and crazy for stealing our hearts.[74]

Such thoughts were not designed to improve morale, and both men and officers sought distraction in the form of varied amusements and recreations. These were in part highly organised, but many medical officers fell back on their own resources to pass the time. Reading was popular although in the Peninsula there was normally a shortage of suitable books. Those who could read French, Portuguese and Spanish had more choice. By contemporary standards, the doctors had eclectic and intellectual tastes which reflected their classical education. Charles Boutflower's comment that he had passed a couple of hours, 'in the perusal of a French poem I procured at Coimbra, called Pitie from the Pen of De Lille', is typical. A constant frustration was the lack of news from home and even a dearth of information about the military affairs in which they were participants. In a letter home to his father from Flanders in 1794, James Dickson complains, 'With regard to news you cannot expect to hear any from me. For a month past I have been perfectly ignorant of what is going on both at home and abroad. You know much more than I do about the operations of the campaign.' He was unable to find an English newspaper and asked his father to send him one, preferably the *General Evening Post*.[75] In the Peninsula, officers also relied on friends and relatives to send them copies of the *Morning Post*, *The Globe* and the *London Chronicle*. The arrival of the English newspapers was a great occasion. Most who wanted a newspaper could get hold of one although news of vital events was still more quickly available at home. Samuel Broughton, writing to friends in England from Toulouse in the spring of 1814, notes that he had just received news of affairs in Paris, 'with which you must long ago have been apprized'.[76]

Many enjoyed writing and a few aspired to more than the normal letters and journals. This was despite the practical difficulties of writing on campaign. John Murray prematurely concludes a letter to his father from Almarez in 1812 because he was 'writing in a most awkward position with the worst pen and ink in the universe'.[77] Of course some wrote medical tracts but others attempted accounts of particular localities, military history and even novels. For instance, Assistant Inspector of Hospitals Andrew Halliday, who served in the Peninsula and at Waterloo, wrote extensively on both medical and military matters. His works include accounts of Portugal and the Portuguese army which were published in 1811 and 1812 and also a narrative of the 1815 campaign. He considered writing a detailed history of the war in Portugal, presumably a more wide-ranging work than his account of the Portuguese army. For this project he sought the support of Wellington but in his reply the Duke was characteristically downbeat at the prospect of an author attempting to describe his campaigns.

> The events in this country of the last three years are fit subjects for the historian, and if well and truly related, may be deemed deserving the consideration of political and military men. But I am apprehensive that the time is not yet arrived in which either the facts themselves can be stated with accuracy or truth, or the motives for the different occurrences be stated.[78]

Halliday was recommended to postpone his history 'to some future period'. Wellington was probably dubious that a doctor, who was neither a historian, politician or soldier, could possibly do justice to the subject. Others dabbled in more romantic material. In addition to his well respected medical works, Surgeon John Gideon Van Millingen wrote a collection of highly imaginative military anecdotes entitled *Stories of Torres Vedras*. This is now a very rare book and perhaps just as well as the stories are almost unreadable.[79]

One of the favourite leisure pursuits of the British medical officers was sightseeing. In Portugal and Spain, they often spent spare time as serious tourists keen to recount their experiences to friends at home. Indeed, some of their campaign journals are little more than travelogues. Samuel Broughton subtitles his collection of letters as a description of 'the leading features of the provinces passed through, and the state of society, manners, habits &c. of the people'. Bull fights are often described and rarely in complimentary terms. Charles Boutflower, who visited the Madrid bullring in 1812, thought the spectacle, 'the most delightful there can be to the people of this Nation, but which to a mind tinctured with the smallest degree of humanity cannot be witnessed without horror'.[80] He comments that few British officers returned to witness a second bullfight. Less contentious, and more popular, was a visit to the local theatre. In the main theatre in Lisbon, Broughton says that the entertainments included operas, ballets, farces, dancing and comedies.[81] When Walter Henry visited the theatre in Toulouse in 1814 to see Henry the Fourth, there was still great local elation at the recent British victory. On Wellington's entry into the royal box the performance stopped and actors and spectators joined in shouts of exclamation. 'It was all like magic,' enthused the young surgeon.[82]

Horseplay and practical jokes provided free entertainment. The most elaborate hoax of the Peninsular War was a report spread around Lisbon that an officer intended to walk across the Tagus on cork boots. A large crowd gathered but nothing happened. The most notorious regimental surgeon in the British Army was Maurice Quill of the Connaught Rangers. Stories of his comic and eccentric behaviour appear in several memoirs, notably those of George Bell and William Grattan. Typical is Bell's account of Quill's behaviour at the Battle of Vitoria. As the fighting began in earnest, Quill ran back from the front to collect and bring up his mule and surgical equipment. He was mistaken by a general officer and his aide-de-camp as a fellow officer running away and attempts were made to stop him. Instead of complying Quill ran more quickly.

'No, no,' he said. 'I'm off; seen enough fighting for one day.'

The general became angry and demanded his name.

'Oh, never mind my ugly name, everybody knows me. Your life's not worth a dollar this blessed day. Go to the front and be killed if you like – everybody's being killed but myself – oh, such slaughter!'

Finally Quill arrived back at the mule and panniers, and the general and his aide-de-camp realised that they had been the butt of a joke and took it in good heart.[83] In an even more bizarre, and possibly apocryphal, anecdote, Quill won a bet that he would both dine with Wellington and also borrow some money off him. By the end of the war he was so well known that he was written into the romantic novels of Charles Lever and James Grant. Both authors are little remembered now but were very popular in Victorian England. In his review of the literature of the Peninsular War, Lieutenant Colonel Kempthorne was quick to point out that Quill was not typical of the army surgeon of that date 'who was more usually a sober-minded Scotsman'.[84]

More serious and structured recreations included country sports and team games. Hunting, shooting and fishing were all popular. When Surgeon William Bowen Miller of the 79th Foot went shooting with dogs near Busaco, no sooner had the game been raised than a distant bugle sounded 'Assembly' and the doctor and his companion had to call off the dogs and rush back to their billets.[85] Organised sports played by both officers and men were athletics, cricket, football, rackets and 'throwing the stone'. The serious intent of all this recreation was to prevent men resorting to less savoury activities such as gambling on cards and dice. None of the medical officers admits to these pursuits in his memoirs, but that a few participated is clear. Lieutenant George Woodberry noted of his companions playing cards in southern France in 1813, 'P. and H. seem to be among the losers, and poor P. swears every day he won't play again, but next day it is he who starts.' P. was Lucas Pulsford, the regiment's assistant surgeon.[86]

The financial rewards of an army medical career were not great. Doctors could potentially earn much more in civilian practice although this was not guaranteed. Rates of pay in the army varied through the period. In 1804 it was 11s.4d. a day for regimental surgeons and 7s.6d. for assistant surgeons. Staff surgeons received 15s. a day and hospital mates 7s.6d. These salaries need to be seen in the context of average living expenses and the wages paid in civilian life. It was calculated by a non-medical officer that the annual living expenses for him and his wife were a minimum of around £80. By the end of the war, a textile worker could earn a guinea a week. There was little scope for extra earnings on campaign. Occasionally, medical officers were able to share in prize money. This was usually after a victory, although William Dent expected to receive a share of £12 from the Walcheren prize fund, 'no trifle in these hard times'.[87] After Waterloo, only those doctors actually serving in the action of 15–18 June, fewer than half of the officers in the campaign, were eligible for part of the prize. To determine the amount, a comparison with officers of combatant rank was worked out. For example, an inspector general of hospitals could expect the same share as a colonel and a staff surgeon the same as a major or captain.[88] The medical officers at Waterloo received the Waterloo Medal, as did all ranks, but those only serving in the Peninsula had to wait until 1848 to be awarded the Military General Service Medal. Some officers were personally honoured. John Gunning, the senior surgeon on the field at Waterloo, received the Order of the Belgian Lion. James McGrigor, Wellington's favourite doctor, became a Knight Bachelor and a Knight of Hanover.

When a regiment was reduced, the officers were generally put on half-pay with the understanding that they could be recalled if required. However, to qualify for half-pay a medical officer had to have served for five years at home or three years abroad. Pensions were allocated according to rank and additional money might be allowed if a soldier had a significant disability resulting from the wars. Any wound had to be inspected by an army medical board within a year and a day of the original injury. Even the basic pension was not automatic. A regimental surgeon could only retire with the certainty of a pension after thirty years' service. An average amount was around ten shillings a day.

In peace-time, many army doctors entered civilian medicine. A common arrangement was for them to form a partnership with the local druggist. Any earnings from this private practice supplemented their half-pay and most could achieve a comfortable existence. This state of affairs suddenly changed in 1815 when the Apothecaries Act created consternation among half-pay medical officers. The Act was a vital step in the early regulation of the medical profession but it had a number of unfortunate implications.[89] Essentially, it meant that all those who kept an apothecary's shop were required to pass an examination before examiners appointed by the Society of Apothecaries, and all candidates were required to give proof of having served five years as apprentices. Penalties were imposed on unlicensed practitioners. The Society of Apothecaries had complete control of the education of three quarters of those who contemplated entering the medical profession, and the future livelihood of most old army doctors was now dependent upon passing this new examination. Their response was one of outrage and indignation. A retired army surgeon expressed the general opinion in a thundering letter to *The Lancet*.

> I was one of a number who had been interested, many years, with the medical charge of 600 to 800 men, who had seen much disease in various parts of the world; had been painfully conversant with gunshot wounds; and had performed of the capital and minor operations of surgery, not a few – I, submit to examination by the drug-pounders of Blackfriars!!![90]

Another popular term of abuse describing the Society of Apothecaries was 'The Hags of Rhubarb Hall'. In the face of sustained hostility in the decade after Waterloo, a clause was inserted into the Act allowing army and navy surgeons to practise as apothecaries without any further examination.

Reading the memoirs, journals and letters of Wellington's doctors it is apparent that for many the greatest rewards of army life were not material. Campaigning could be almost indescribably hard with the constant threat of disease and death. But despite this a 'joi de vivre' exudes from much of their writing. They were actors in enormous events, within touching distance of the greatest men of the age. As doctors they had a unique view of the war with privileged access to the extremes of misery and exultation. It is appropriate that Wellington's own physician, John Hume, should have the last word.

> I came back from the field of Waterloo with Sir Alexander Gordon, whose leg I was obliged to amputate on the field late in the evening. He died unexpectedly in my arms about half-past three in the morning of the nineteenth. I was hesitating about disturbing the Duke, when Sir Charles Broke-Vere came. He wished to take his orders about the movement of the troops. I went upstairs and tapped gently at the door, when he [Wellington] told me to come in. He had as usual taken off his clothes, but had not washed himself. As I entered, he sat up in bed, his face covered with the dust and sweat of the previous day, and extended his hand to me, which I took and held in mine, whilst I told him of Gordon's death, and of such of the casualties as had come to my knowledge. He was much affected. I felt the tears dropping fast upon my hand, and looking towards him, saw them chasing one another in furrows over his dusty cheeks. He brushed them suddenly away with his left hand, and said to me in a voice tremulous with emotion, 'Well, Thank God, I don't know what it is to lose a battle; but certainly nothing can be more painful than to gain one with the loss of so many of one's friends.'[91]

NOTES

1. Neale, A, *Letters from Portugal and Spain*, pp.327–8.
2. Gordon, A, *A Cavalry Officer in the Corunna Campaign*, p.9.
3. Kempthorne, G A, *The American War 1812–1814*, p.140.
4. Maurice, F, *The History of the Scots Guards*, pp.294–5.
5. Blanco, R L, *Wellington's Surgeon General*, p.57.
6. Henry, W, *Surgeon Henry's Trifles*, p.22.
7. Boutflower, C, *The Journal of an Army Surgeon during the Peninsular War*, p.7.
8. Broughton, S D, *Letters from Portugal, Spain, and France*, p.22.
9. Boutflower, pp.13, 108.
10. Burroughs, G F, *A Narrative of the Retreat of the British Army from Burgos*, p.13.
11. *Selections from the dispatches and general orders*, pp.522–3.
12. Gronow, R H, *The Reminiscences and Recollections of Captain Gronow*, Vol.II, p.195.
13. Oman, C, *Wellington's Army*, p.264.
14. Smith, J G, *The English Army in France*, Vol.I, p.122.
15. Burroughs, p.14.
16. ibid., pp.32–3.
17. Dickson, J, *James Dickson M.A. 1769–1795, Army Surgeon*, p.60.
18. ibid., p.54.
19. McGrigor, J, *Autobiography and Services of Sir James McGrigor*, pp.114–15.
20. Henry, p.26.
21. ibid., p.23.
22. Broughton, p.186.
23. Burroughs, p.39.
24. ibid., p.52.
25. Brett-James, A, *Life in Wellington's Army*, pp.58–60.
26. Broughton, p.134: Glover, M, *Wellington's Army in the Peninsula*, p.157.
27. Broughton, p.284.
28. Boutflower, p.39.
29. ibid., pp.14, 18, 28.
30. Broughton, pp.186, 255.
31. Neale, p.226.
32. Broughton, p.59.
33. Henry, p.32.
34. ibid., pp.33–5.
35. Gibney, W, *Eighty Years Ago, or the Recollections of an Old Army Doctor*, p.165.
36. Haddy James, J, *Surgeon James's Journal*, p.7.
37. Haythornthwaite, P, *The Armies of Wellington*, p.130.
38. Costello, E, *Edward Costello. The Peninsular and Waterloo Campaigns*, p.71.
39. Fergusson, W, *Notes and Recollections of a Professional Life*, p.71.
40. Anon, *Reminiscences of a Regimental Medical Officer*, p.116.
41. Dent, W, *A Young Surgeon in Wellington's Army*, p.45.
42. Maurice, p.358.
43. Broughton, p.24.
44. Neale, p.254.
45. Haddy James, p.11.
46. Gibney, p.183.
47. Buckley, R N, *The Destruction of the British Army in the West Indies*, p.84.
48. Howard, M R, *Red Jackets and Red Noses*.
49. Anon, *Reminiscences of a Regimental Medical Officer*, p.115.
50. McGrigor, p.101.

51. *Selections from the dispatches and general orders*, p.618.
52. Henry, pp.53–4.
53. Maxwell, W H, *Peninsular Sketches*, Vol.II, pp.190–2.
54. Neale, A, *The Spanish Campaign of 1808*, pp.190–1.
55. Milburne, H, *A narrative of circumstances attending the retreat*, pp.27–9.
56. Anon. *Reminiscences of a Regimental Medical Officer*, pp.114–15.
57. Burroughs, p.43.
58. McGrigor, p.275.
59. Oman, C, *Courts Martial of the Peninsular War 1809–14.*
60. *Selections from the dispatches and general orders*, p.417.
61. Oman, *Courts Martial of the Peninsular War 1809–14.*
62. Haythornthwaite, p.68.
63. Fergusson, pp.22–3.
64. Dickson, p.75.
65. Gibney, p.174.
66. Mercer, C, *Journal kept through the Campaign of 1815*, pp.169–70.
67. Haythornthwaite, p.136.
68. Blakeney, R, *A Boy in the Peninsular War*, pp161–3.
69. Lewis, M, *Napoleon and his British Captives*, pp.291–2.
70. Elkington, J G, *Some episodes in the life of James Goodall Elkington*, p.83.
71. ibid., p.85.
72. ibid., p.95.
73. Dunlop, W, *Tiger Dunlop's Upper Canada*, pp.20–1.
74. Murray, J, Letter to his mother, 13 December 1812.
75. Dickson, p.89.
76. Broughton, p.292.
77. Murray, J, Letter to his father, 9 September 1812.
78. Brett-James, A, *Wellington at War 1794–1815*, p.209.
79. Kempthorne, G A, *The Medical Department of Wellington's Army*, p.220.
80. Boutflower, pp.159–60.
81. Broughton, p.46.
82. Henry, p.97.
83. Bell, G, *Soldier's Glory*, p.76.
84. Kempthorne, *The Medical Department of Wellington's Army*, p.220.
85. Brett-James, A, *Life in Wellington's Army*, p.210.
86. ibid., p.156.
87. Dent, p.31.
88. Cantlie, N, *A History of the Army Medical Department*, Vol.I, p.394.
89. Chaplin, A, *Medicine during the Reign of George III*, pp.13–14.
90. Cantlie, p.436.
91. Brett-James, A, *The Hundred Days from Eyewitness Accounts*, p.182.

Appendix I

Contents of a regimental medical chest[1]

Medicines[2]

Ammonia	Chalk	Caustic Alkali	Scilla
Antimony	Cantharis	Spanish Soap	Ginger
Silver Nitrate	Colocynth	Wine	Mercury Ointment
Capaiva Balsam	Iron Sulphate	Spirits	Vitriolated Zinc
Calomel	Camomile	Magnesium	Dr James's Powder
Camphor	Senna	Peppermint Oil	Sulphuric Acid
Calomine	Gum Ammoniac	Castor Oil	Verdigris
Soapwort	Gum Arabic	Mercury Pills	Alum
Lead Acetate	Guaicam Resin	Digitalis	
Opium	Mercurous Chloride	Ipecacuanha	
Rose Petals	Mercury Nitrate	Jalap	
Cinchona	Saltwort	Rhubarb	

Materials

Horn Cups	Common Splints	Grain Scales and Weights
Surgeon's Tow	Ounce Scales and Weights	Urethra Syringe
Linen	Vials in Sorts	Glyster Syringe and Pipes
Skins of Leather	Gallipots in Sorts	Pewter Bleeding Porringer
Linen Rollers	Graduated Glass Measure	Bolus Knives
Flannel Rollers	Writing Paper	Spreading Spatula
Eighteen-tailed Bandages	Wrapping Paper	Pot Spatula
Bag Trusses	Pens	Tin Panakin
Bougies in a Case	Ink Powder	Tin Funnel
Tape	Wafers	Packthread
Thread for Ligatures	A Bolus Tile	Surgeon's Sponges
Pins	Mortar and Pestle	Vial Corks
Fine Lint	Pill Boxes	

1. From *Instructions to Regimental Surgeons*, 1803.
2. It is often difficult to translate the names of early nineteenth-century drugs into recognisable forms. This is a representative but not comprehensive list of drugs routinely available to a regimental surgeon.

Appendix II

Set of surgical instruments for a regiment[1]

An Amputating Saw with spare Blade
1 Metacarpal Saw with spare Blade
24 Curved Needles
2 Amputating Knives
1 Catlin
2 Tenaculums
1 Bullet Forceps
1 Pair of Bone Nippers
2 Screw Tourniquets
4 Field Tourniquets with Handle
2 Callico Compresses
2 Trephines with sliding Keys
1 Trephine Forceps
1 Elevator
1 Lenticular
A Brush
Key Instruments for Teeth, to fit Trephine Handle
8 Scalpels
3 Silver Catheters
2 Elastic Catheters
1 Trocar with Spring and introductory Canula
Canula for Hydrocoele
1 Probang
1 Long Silver Probe

1. From *Instructions to Regimental Surgeons*, 1803.

Appendix III

List of stores for a general hospital of 500 men[1]

2 Hospital Tents and Marquees, Poles, &c.
500 Palliases
500 Blankets
500 Sheets
500 Coverlids
500 Bolster-cases
2 cwt. Rice
1 cwt. Oatmeal
56 lb. Sago
1 45 gal. Copper and Trevet
50 Camp-kettles
200 Pint-pots
100 Quart-pots
200 Trenchers
500 Spoons
1 cwt. Portable Soup
2 Round Tents, complete
200 Linen Shirts
200 Nightcaps
1 Jar of Oil with Wick
1 Large Tea-kettle
1 Flesh-fork and Soup-ladle
1 Scales and Weights
1 Steelyard
2 Brass Cocks
2 Spades
2 Shovels
2 Saws
2 Hatchets
500 Nails

2 Hammers
2 dozen Knives and Forks with Carvers
10 gal. Vinegar
2 cwt. Salt
60 Biers for wounded men
200 yards Flannel
10lb. Tea
1 cwt. Sugar
Quarter Cask Port Wine
100 Bowls
Birch Brooms, Sweeping Brushes
Mops, Scrubbing Brushes
6 Water Buckets
6 Bedpans
6 Stool-pans
200 Chamberpots
10 Basins
3 Urinals
12 Saucepans
10 Lamps
3 gal. British Spirit and Cask
2 cwt. Hard soap
1 cwt. Soft soap
10 Baggage water-decks
1 Box of Stationery and Books
Candles
Flour
Raisins
1 Bathing Tub

1. From S G ? Ward, *Wellington's Headquarters*, 1957.

Appendix IV

Return of surgical cases treated and capital operations performed in the general hospital at Toulouse from 10 April to 28 June 1814[1]

Wounds	Number	Died	Discharged to duty	Transferred to Bordeaux	Mortality (%)
Head	95	17	25	53	18
Chest	96	35	14	47	36
Abdomen	104	24	21	59	23
Wounds to arms	304	3	96	205	1
Wounds to legs	498	21	150	327	4
Compound fractures	78	29	-	49	37
Wounds of spine	3	3	-	-	100
Wounds of joints	16	4	-	12	25
Primary Amputations	48	10	-	38	21
Secondary Amputations	52	21	-	31	40

1. From Guthrie, G J, *Commentaries on the Surgery of the War*, p.154.

Appendix V

Return of capital operations, primary and secondary, performed
in the British general hospitals, Brussels, or brought in from
the field between 16 June and 31 July 1815[1]

Primary Operations	Number	Died	Mortality (%)
Shoulder Joint	6	1	16
Thigh	54	19	35
Leg	43	7	16
Arm	21	4	19
Fore-arm	22	1	5
Total	146	32	22

Secondary Operations	Number	Died	Mortality (%)
Shoulder Joint	12	6	50
Hip Joint	1	0	0
Thigh	94	43	46
Leg	50	16	32
Arm	51	13	25
Fore-arm	17	5	29
Carotid Artery Tied	1	0	0
Trephine	2	1	50
Total	228	84	37

1. From Guthrie, G J, *Commentaries on the Surgery of the War*, p.158.
   Return does not include those who died on the battlefield or were sent
   to Antwerp.

Appendix VI

Patients treated and causes of death in the regimental and general
hospitals of the Peninsular War, 1812–14[1]

Year	1812	1813	1814	Total for 1812–14
Total Treated	176,180	123,019	53,073	352,272
Discharged Cured	119,798	79,010	34,591	233,399
Transferred	39,757	29,090	12,825	81,672
Died	7,193	6,866	2,909	16,968
Cause of Death				
Dysentery	2,340	1,629	748	4,717
Continued Fever	2,020	1,598	387	4,005
Vulnera (Wounds)	905	1,095	699	2,699
Typhus	999	971	307	2,277
Gangrene	35	446	122	603
Unknown	182	59	124	365
Intermittent Fever	148	139	4	291
Pneumonia	58	133	96	287
Phthisis (Tuberculosis)	49	158	72	279
Diarrhoea	79	106	34	219
Varii	97	71	35	203
Morbi Chronici	102	58	15	175
Remittent Fever	67	65	18	150
Hydrops	26	72	21	119
Fractures	0	6	64	70
Apoplexia	19	21	16	56
Tetanus	4	23	24	51
Enterus	4	32	7	43
Mortificatio	0	32	7	39
Febris Hectica	0	15	23	38
Hepatitis	5	23	8	36
Syphilis	19	11	5	35
Hydrothorax	5	13	15	33
Ulcera	5	20	6	31
Rheumatism	2	11	2	15
Carditis	6	4	1	11
Epileptic	3	6	2	11
Variola	3	1	2	6
Cholera	4	0	0	4
Other	7	48	45	100

1. From McGrigor, J, *Sketch of the Medical History of the British Armies.*

Appendix VII

Mortality and sickness in the Peninsular Army 1811–13

The greatest number of deaths (shown by solid line) coincided not with a major battle but with the retreat from Burgos when the army was severely affected by dysentery and typhus and the sick rate (broken line) was 40%.

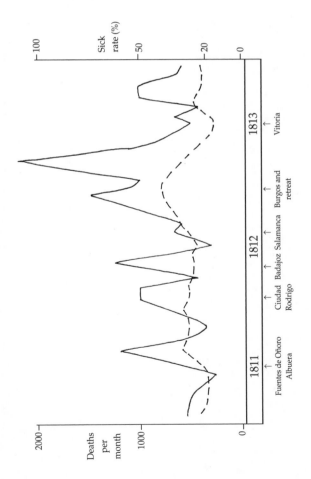

Bibliography

Manuscripts
RAMC Muniments Collection, Wellcome Library for the History and
    Understanding of Medicine, London:

The Diaries of James Goodall Elkington (336;484).
The Papers of William Fergusson (202–212; 1023–1024)
The Papers of Sir James McGrigor at the Medico-Chirurgical Society,
    Aberdeen (microfilm 799).
Letters from John Murray, Assistant Surgeon to the 39th Foot and
    Surgeon to the 66th Foot during the Peninsular War (830).
William Dent's Letters 1810–1814 (536).

Primary Sources (Medical)
Anon., *Reminiscences of a Regimental Medical Officer*, United Service
    Journal (1851), pp. 110–16.
Bacot, J, *A Sketch of the Medical History of the First Battalion of the First
    Regiment of Foot Guards during the Winter of 1812–13*, Medico-
    Chirurgical Transactions (1816), Vol. 7, pp. 373–86.
Bell, C, *Letters of Sir Charles Bell selected from Correspondence with his
    Brother George Joseph Bell*, London, 1870.
Borland, J; Lempriere, W and Blane G, *Report of the prevailing malady
    among His Majesty's forces serving in the Island of Walcheren*, Medical and
    Physical Journal (1810), Vol. 23, pp. 183–7.
Boutflower, C, *The Journal of an Army Surgeon during the Peninsular War*,
    Manchester, 1912.
Broughton, S D, *Letters from Portugal, Spain and France, written during the
    campaigns of 1812, 1813 and 1814, addressed to a friend in England*,
    London, 1815.
Burroughs, G F, *A Narrative of the Retreat of the British Army from Burgos*,
    London, 1814.
Cooper, S, *A Dictionary of Practical Surgery*, New York, 1834
Dent, W (ed. L W Woodford), *A Young Surgeon in Wellington's Army*, Old
    Woking, 1976.

241

Dickson, J (ed. A A Cormack), *James Dickson M.A. 1769–1795 Army Surgeon*, Aberdeen, 1968.

Dunlop, W, *Tiger Dunlop's Upper Canada*, Toronto, 1967.

Elkington, J G (ed. H P Elkington), *Some episodes in the life of James Goodall Elkington, an Army Surgeon in the Peninsular Days with extracts from his journal*, Journal of the Royal Army Medical Corps (1911), Vol. 16, pp. 79–104.

Fergusson, W, *Notes and Reflections of a Professional Life*, London, 1846.

Fifth Report of the Commissioners for Military Enquiry, London, 1808.

Gibney, W (ed. R D Gibney), *Eighty Years Ago, or the Recollections of an Old Army Doctor*, London, 1896.

Gilpin, D A, *Remarks on the Fever which Occurred at Gibraltar in 1814*, Edinburgh Medical and Surgical Journal (1809), pp. 311–17.

Good, S, *The Journal of Samuel Good*, in F Maurice, *The History of the Scots Guards 1642–1914*, London, 1934.

Guthrie, G J, *Commentaries on the surgery of the War in Portugal, Spain, France and the Netherlands from the Battle of Roliça in 1808 to that of Waterloo in 1815 with Additions Relating to those in the Crimea in 1854–1855*, London, 1855.

Guthrie, G J, *A Treatise on Gunshot Wounds of the Extremities*, London, 1827.

Haddy James, J (ed. J Vansittart), *Surgeon James's Journal*, London, 1964.

Hamilton, R, *The Duties of a Regimental Surgeon Considered*, London, 1787.

Hargrove, G, *An Account of the Islands of Walcheren and South Beveland against which the British expedition proceeded in 1809*, Dublin, 1812.

Hennen, J, *Principles of Military Surgery*, Philadelphia, 1830, 3rd edn.

Henry, W (ed. P Hayward), *Surgeon Henry's Trifles. Events of a Military Life*, London, 1970.

Hooper, R, *Account of Diseases of the Sick landed at Plymouth from Corunna*, Edinburgh Medical and Surgical Journal (1809), Vol. 5, pp. 398–420.

Horner, W E, *A military hospital at Buffalo New York in the year 1814*, Medical Examiner and Record of Medical Service (1852–3), Vol. 8, pp. 753–774; Vol. 9, pp. 1–25.

Instructions to Regimental Surgeons for regulating the concerns of the sick and of the hospital, London, 1803.

Jackson, R, *A Sketch of the History and Cure of Febrile Diseases*, Stockton, 1817.

Jenks, G S, *The Journal of George Samuel Jenks*, in C R Liddell, *Memoirs of the Tenth Royal Hussars*, London, 1891.

MacLean, C, *An analytical view of the medical department of the British Army*, London, 1808.

McGrigor, J, *Autobiography and Services of Sir James McGrigor*, London, 1861.

—— *Medical Sketches of the Military Expedition to Egypt from India*, London, 1804.

—— *Observations on the Fever which appeared in the Army from Spain on their return to this country in January 1809*, Edinburgh Medical and Surgical Journal (1810) Vol. 6, pp. 19–32.

—— *Sketch of the Medical History of the British Armies in the Peninsula of Spain and Portugal during the late campaigns*, Transactions of the Medico-Chirurgical Society (1815), Vol. 6, pp. 381–489.

—— (ed. M McGrigor), *The Scalpel and the Sword. The Autobiography of the Father of Army Medicine, Sir James McGrigor*, Dalkeith, 2000.

McLean, H, *An enquiry into the nature and causes of the great mortality among the troops at Saint Domingo*, London, 1797.

Milburne, H, *A Narrative of Circumstances attending the retreat of the British Army under the Command of the late Lieutenant General Sir John Moore*, London, 1809.

Millingen, J G Van, *The Army Medical Officer's Manual Upon Active Service*, London, 1819.

Moises, H, *An Inquiry into the Abuses of the Medical Department in the Militia of Great Britain with some necessary Amendment proposed*, London, 1794.

Monro, D, *Observations on the Means of Preserving the Health of Soldiers and of Constituting Military Hospitals and on the Diseases Incident to Soldiers*, London, 1780.

Neale, A, *Letters from Portugal and Spain*, London, 1809.

—— *The Spanish Campaign of 1808*, Edinburgh, 1828.

Pinchard, G, *Notes on the West Indies including observations relating to the Creoles of Spain, of the West Colonies and the Indians of South America, interspersed with remarks upon the Seasoning or Yellow Fever of the Climate*, London, 1816.

Pringle, J, *Observations on Diseases of the Army in Camp and Garrison*, London, 1752.

Ranby, J, *The method of treating gunshot wounds*, London, 1744.

Regulations for the management of the general hospitals in Great Britain, London, 1813.

Smith, J G, *The English Army in France: Being the Personal Narrative of an Officer*, London, 1831.

Thomson, J, *Lectures on Inflammation*, London, 1813.

—— *Report of Observations in the British Military Hospitals in Belgium after the Battle of Waterloo with remarks concerning amputation*, Edinburgh, 1816.

Tresal, J B, *Essai sur la fièvre adynamique qui a regné dans l'île de Walcheren dans l'année 1809, précédé d'un aperçu topographique de la même île*, Paris, 1815.

Turnbull, W, *The Naval Surgeon*, London, 1806.

Wright, T, *A History of the Walcheren Remittent Fever*, London, 1811.

Primary Sources (Military)

Aitchison, J (ed. W F K Thompson), *An Ensign in the Peninsular War*, London, 1981.

Anglesey, Marquess of, *One Leg. The Life and Letters of Henry William Paget, First Marquess of Anglesey KG, 1768–1854*, London, 1961.

Anon., *An accurate and impartial narrative of the war by an officer of the Guards, comprising the campaigns of 1793, 1794 and the retreat through Holland to Westphalia in 1795*, London, 1796.

Anon., *Operations of the British Army in Spain by an Officer of the Staff*, London, 1809.

Anon. (ed. C Hibbert), *A Soldier of the Seventy-First*, London, 1975.

Anon., Reminiscences of a Light Dragoon, United Service Journal (1840; 1841), pp. 53–61; 86–93; 223–7; 357–70; 455–65, 509–18; 517–27.

Anon., *The British Cavalry on the Peninsula*, Sunderland, 1996.

Austin, T (ed. H H Austin), *Old Stick Leg. Extracts from the Diary of Major Thomas Austin*, London, 1926.

Bayly, Col. (ed. W R Galway), *The Diary of Colonel Bayly, 12th Suffolk Regiment 1796–1830*, Journal of the Royal Army Medical Corps (1923), pp. 220–31.

Barallier, Capt., *Adventure at the Battle of Salamanca*, United Service Journal (1851), pp. 274–7.

Bell, G (ed. B Stuart), *Soldier's Glory*, London, 1956.

Blakeney, R, *A Boy in the Peninsular War*, London, 1899.

Boothby, C, *A Prisoner of France – the memoirs, diary and correspondence of Charles Boothby, Captain Royal Engineers during his last campaign*, London, 1898.

Bragge, W (ed. S A C Cassels), *Peninsular Portrait 1811–1814. The letters of Captain William Bragge, Third (King's Own) Dragoons*, Oxford, 1963.

Browne, T N (ed. R N Buckley), *The Napoleonic War Journal of Thomas Henry Browne 1807–1816*, London, 1987.

Burgoyne, J F, *Life and Correspondence*, London, 1873.

Campbell, N, *Napoleon at Fontainebleau and Elba, being a Journal of Occurrences in 1814–1815*, London, 1869.

Codrington, E, *Memoirs of Admiral Sir Edward Codrington*, London, 1873.

Cooke, J (ed. E Hathaway), *A True Soldier Gentleman. The Memoirs of Lt John Cooke 1791–1813*, Swanage, 2000.

Cooper, J, *Rough Notes of Seven Campaigns in Portugal, Spain, France and America during the years 1809–15*, Carlisle, 1914.

Costello, E (ed. A Brett James), *Edward Costello. The Peninsular and Waterloo Campaigns*, London, 1967.

Cotton, E, *A Voice from Waterloo*, London, 1889.

Dallas, R W (ed. C T Atkinson), *A Subaltern of the 9th in the Peninsula and Walcheren*, Journal of the Society for Army Historical Research (1950), Vol. 28, pp. 59–67.

De Jonnes, A M, *Adventures in Wars of the Republic and Consulate*, London, 1920.

De Lancey, Lady (ed. B R Ward), *A Week at Waterloo in 1815*, London, 1906.

Dobbs, J (ed. I Fletcher), *Recollections of an old 52nd Man*, Staplehurst, 2000.

Donaldson, J, *Recollections of the Eventful Life of a Soldier*, London, 1856.

Douglas, J (ed. S Monick), *Douglas's Tale of the Peninsula and Waterloo 1808–1815*, London, 1997.

Dyneley, T, *Letters written by Lieutenant-General Thomas Dyneley while on active service between the years 1806 and 1815*, London, 1984.

Green, J, *The Vicissitudes of a Soldier's Life*, Louth, 1827.

Green, W (eds J and D Teague), *Where My Duty Calls Me*, West Wickham, 1975.

Gordon, A, *A Cavalry Officer in the Corunna Campaign 1808–9. The journal of Captain Gordon of the 15th Hussars*, Felling, 1990.

Grattan, W (ed. C Oman), *Adventures in the Connaught Rangers*, London, 1902.

Gronow, R H, *The Reminiscences and Recollections of Captain Gronow*, London, 1900.

Gunn, J (ed. R H Roy), *The Memoirs of Private James Gunn*, Journal of the Society for Army Historical Research (1971), Vol. 49, pp. 90–120.

Hale, J (ed. P Catley), *The Journal of James Hale Late Serjeant in the Ninth Regiment of Foot*, Windsor, 1998.

Hall, F, *Peninsular Recollections 1811–12*, Journal of the Royal United Service Institution (1912), Vol. 56, pp. 1389–1408, 1535–46, 1735–9.

Harness, W (ed. C M Duncan-Jones), *Trusty and Well-Beloved. The Letters Home of William Harness, an Officer of George III*, London, 1957.

Harris, Rifleman (ed. H Curling), *Recollections of Rifleman Harris*, London, 1928.

Hay, W, *Reminiscences 1809–1815 under Wellington*, London, 1901.

Howard, T P (ed. R N Buckley), *The Haitian Journal of Lieutenant Howard, York Hussars 1796–1798*, Knoxville, 1985.

Jackson, T, *Narrative of the Eventful Life of Thomas Jackson, late Sergeant of the Coldstream Guards*, Birmingham, 1847.

Jordan, A, *Biographical Memoirs of Andrew Jordan formerly a Waterloo Soldier and now city missionary*, Londonderry, 1855.

Keep, W T, (ed. I Fletcher), *In the Service of the King. The Letters of William Thornton Keep at Home, Walcheren and in the Peninsula 1808–1814*, Staplehurst, 1997.

Kincaid, J, *Adventures in the Rifle Brigade* and *Random Shots from a Rifleman*, Glasgow, 1981.

Larpent, F S (ed. G Larpent), *The Private Journal of F Seymour Larpent Judge-Advocate General*, London, 1854.

Larrey, D J, *Memoires de Chirurgie Militaire et Campagnes de Baron Larrey*, Paris, 1983.

Lawrence, W (ed. E Hathaway), *A Dorset Soldier. The Autobiography of Sergeant William Lawrence 1790–1869*, Tunbridge Wells, 1993.

Leach, J, *Rough Sketches of the Life of an Old Soldier*, London, 1831.

Le Marchant, J G (ed. D Le Marchant), *The Memoirs of the Late Major-General Le Marchant*, London, 1841.

Mercer, C, *Journal of the Waterloo Campaign*, London, 1969.

Morris, T (ed. J Selby), *Thomas Morris: The Napoleonic Wars*, London, 1967.

Napier, G T (ed. W C E Napier), *The Early Military Life of General Sir George T Napier*, London, 1886.

Ney, Marshal, *Memoirs of Marshal Ney*, London, 1833.

Nicol, D, *The Gordon Highlanders in Spain. A Forgotten Page in their History; from the unpublished diary of Serjeant Nicol*, in E B Low, *With Napoleon at Waterloo*, London, 1911.

O'Neil, C, *The Military Adventures of Charles O'Neil*, Worcester,1851.

Pearson, A (ed. A H Haley), *The Soldier Who Walked Away*, Liverpool, 1988.

Percival, R, *An Account of the Island of Ceylon*, London, 1805.

Roberts, D, *The Military Adventures of Johny Newcome*, London, 1904.

Schaumann, A, *On the Road with Wellington*, London, 1924.

Sherer, Moyle, *Recollections of the Peninsula*, London, 1824.

Shipp, J (ed. C J Stranks), *The Path of Glory. Being the Memoirs of the Extraordinary Military Career of John Shipp*, London, 1969.

Simmons, G, *A British Rifleman*, London, 1899.

Simpson, J, *Paris after Waterloo*, London, 1853.

Smith, H (ed. G C Moore), *The Autobiography of Sir Harry Smith 1787–1819*, London, 1910.

Surtees, W, *Twenty-Five Years in the Rifle Brigade by the late Quartermaster William Surtees*, London, 1973.

Swabey, W (ed. F A Whinyates), *Diary of Campaigns in the Peninsula for the years 1811, 1812 and 1813*, London, 1984.

Tomkinson, W (ed. J Tomkinson), *The Diary of a Cavalry Officer in the Peninsular and Waterloo Campaigns 1809–1815*, London, 1894.

Verner, W, *Reminiscences of William Verner (1782–1871) 7th Hussars*, Society for Army Historical Research Special Publication, London, 1965.

Wellington, Duke of, *Dispatches during his various campaigns in India, Denmark, Portugal, Spain, the Low Countries and France from 1799 to 1818 compiled from official and authentic documents by Lieutenant Colonel Gurwood*, London, 1837–9.

Wheatley, E (ed. C Hibbert), *The Wheatley Diary*, London, 1964.

Wheeler, W (ed. B H Liddell Hart), *The Letters of Private Wheeler 1809–1828*, London, 1951.

Wood, G, *The Subaltern Officer: A Narrative*, London, 1825.

Secondary Sources (Medical)

Adams, G W, *Doctors in Blue*, New York, 1952.

Anon., *Biographical Sketch of G J Guthrie*, The Lancet (1850), Vol. 1, pp. 727–36.

Billroth, T, *Historical Studies on the Nature and Treatment of Gunshot Wounds from the Fifteenth Century to the Present Time*, Connecticut, 1933.

Blanco, R L, *Wellington's Surgeon General: Sir James McGrigor*, Durham, NC, 1974.

Buckley, R N, *The destruction of the British Army in the West Indies 1793–1815*, Journal of the Society for Army Historical Research (1978), Vol. 56, pp. 79–92.

Cantlie, N, *A History of the Army Medical Department*, Edinburgh, 1974.

Chaplin, A, *Medicine in England during the Reign of George III*, London, 1919.

——— *Mortality Rates in the British Army 100 Years Ago*, Proceedings of the Royal Society of Medicine (1915), Vol. 9, pp. 89–99.

Creighton, C, *A History of Epidemics in Britain*, London, 1965.

Crowe, K E, *The Walcheren Expedition and the new Army Medical Board; a reconsideration*, The English Historical Review (1973), Vol. 88, pp. 770–85.

Crumplin, M K H, *Surgery at Waterloo*, Journal of the Royal Society of Medicine (1988), Vol. 81, pp. 38–41.

Dible, H, *Napoleon's Surgeon*, London, 1970.

Drew, R, *Commissioned Officers in the Medical Services of the British Army 1660–1960*, Vol. I (A Peterkin; W Johnston), London, 1968.

Edmonds, T R, *On the Mortality and Sickness of Soldiers engaged in War*, The Lancet (1838), Vol. 2, pp. 143–8.

Ellis, H, *John Hunter's teachings on gunshot wounds*, Journal of the Royal Society of Medicine (2001), Vol. 94, pp. 43–5.

Feibel, R M, *What happened at Walcheren: the primary medical sources*, Bulletin of the History of Medicine (1968), Vol. 42, pp. 62–72.

Gabbay, J, *Clinical Medicine in Revolution*, British Medical Journal (1989), Vol. 299, pp. 106–9, 166–9.

Giao, M R F, *British surgeons in the Portuguese Army during the Peninsular War*, Journal of the Royal Army Medical Corps (1934), Vol. 62, pp. 299–303.

Gillet, M C, *The Army Medical Department 1775–1818*, Washington, 1981.

Gore, A, *The Story of Our Services Under the Crown*, London, 1870.

Hodge, W B, *On the mortality arising from military operations*, Quarterly Journal of the Statistical Society (1856), Vol. 19, pp. 219–71.

Howard, M R, *British Medical Services at the Battle of Waterloo*, British Medical Journal (1988), Vol. 297, pp. 1653–6.

—— *In Larrey's Shadow.Transport of British Sick and Wounded in the Napoleonic Wars*, Scottish Medical Journal (1994), Vol. 39, pp. 27–9.

—— *Medical Aspects of Sir John Moore's Corunna Campaign 1808–1809*, Journal of the Royal Society of Medicine (1991), Vol. 84, pp. 299–302.

—— *Red Jackets and Red Noses. Alcohol and the British Napoleonic Soldier*, Journal of the Royal Society of Medicine (2000), Vol. 93, pp. 38–41.

—— *Walcheren 1809: A Medical Catastrophe*, British Medical Journal (1999), Vol. 319, pp. 1642–5.

Howell, H A L, *Robert Jackson MD Inspector of Hospitals*, Journal of the Royal Army Medical Corps (1911), Vol. 16, pp. 121–39.

—— *The British Medical Arrangements during the Waterloo Campaign*, Proceedings of the Royal Society of Medicine (1924), Vol. 17, pp. 39–50.

Kempthorne, G A, *The American War 1812–1814*, Journal of the Royal Army Medical Corps (1934), Vol. 62, pp. 139–40.

—— *The Army Medical Services at Home and Abroad 1803–1808*, Journal of the Royal Army Medical Corps (1933), Vol. 61, pp. 144–6, 223–32.

—— *The Egyptian Campaign of 1801*, Journal of the Royal Army Medical Corps (1930), Vol. 55, pp. 217–30.

—— *The Medical Department of Wellington's Army*, Journal of the Royal Army Medical Corps (1930), Vol. 54, pp. 65–72, 131–46, 212–20.

—— *The Walcheren Expedition and the Reform of the Medical Board*, Journal of the Royal Army Medical Corps (1934), Vol. 62, pp. 133–40.

—— *The Waterloo Campaign*, Journal of the Royal Army Medical Corps (1933), Vol. 60, pp. 204–7.

Kiple, K F, *Plague, Pox and Pestilence*, London, 1997.

Laws, M E, *Medicine at Montivideo 1807*, The Lancet (1955), Vol. 1, pp. 610–11.

McGuffie, T H, *The Walcheren expedition and the Walcheren fever*, English Historical Review (1947), Vol. 62, pp. 191–202.

Porter, R, *The Greatest Benefit to mankind. A Medical History of Humanity from Antiquity to the Present*, London, 1997.

Richardson, R, *Larrey. Surgeon to Napoleon's Imperial Guard*, London, 2000.

Trohler, U, *To Improve the Evidence of Medicine. The 18th Century origins of a critical approach*, Edinburgh, 2000.

Watts, J C, *George James Guthrie. Peninsular Surgeon*, Proceedings of the Royal Society of Medicine (1961), pp. 764–8.

Woodford, J, *To Do The Sick No Harm. A study of the British Voluntary Hospital System to 1875*, London, 1974.

Zinsser, H, *Rats, Lice and History*, London, 1935.

Secondary Sources (Military)
Blond, G, *La Grande Armée*, London, 1995.
Bond, G C, *The Grand Expedition*, Athens, GA, 1979.
Brereton, J M, *The British Soldier. A social history from 1661 to the present day*, London, 1986.
Brett-James, A, *Life in Wellington's Army*, London, 1994.
—— *The Hundred Days from Eyewitness Accounts*, London, 1964.
—— *The Walcheren Failure*, History Today (1963; 1964), Vol. 13, pp. 811–20; Vol. 14, pp. 60–8.
—— *Wellington at War 1794–1815*, London, 1961.
Cambridge Modern History, Vol. 9, 'Napoleon', Cambridge, 1934.
Chandler, D, *The Campaigns of Napoleon*, New York, 1974.
—— *Dictionary of the Napoleonic Wars*, London, 1979.
Dalton, C, *The Waterloo Roll Call*, London, 1978.
Davies, G, *Wellington and his Army*, Oxford, 1954.
Elting, J R, *Swords Around a Throne. Napoleon's Grande Armée*, London, 1988.
Fletcher, I (ed.), *The Peninsular War*, Staplehurst, 1998.
Fortescue, J W, *A History of the British Army*, London, 1935.
Glover, M, *Wellington's Army in the Peninsula 1808–1814*, Newton Abbott, 1977.
Graves, D E, *Where Right and Glory Lead. The Battle of Lundy's Lane 1814*, Toronto, 1997.
Guy, A J, *The Road to Waterloo*, London, 1990.
Hall, C D, *British Strategy in the Napoleonic War*, Manchester, 1999.
Hall, J, *A History of the Peninsular War*, Vol. VIII, *The biographical dictionary of British Officers killed and wounded 1808–1814*, London, 1998.
Haythornthwaite, P, *The Armies of Wellington*, London, 1994.
—— and Fosten, B, *Wellington's Specialist Troops*, London, 1988.
Horward, D D, *Napoleonic Military History. A Bibliography*, London, 1986.
—— *Napoleon and Iberia. The Twin Sieges of Ciudad Rodrigo and Almeida 1810*, Tallahassee, 1984.
Hoskins, W G, *Exeter Militia List 1803*, London, 1972.
Keegan, J, *The Face of Battle*, London, 1988.
Lawford, J P and Young, P, *Wellington's Masterpiece. The battle and campaign of Salamanca*, London, 1973.
Lewis, M, *Napoleon and his British Captives*, London, 1962.
Longford, E, *Wellington. The Years of the Sword*, London, 1994.
Maxwell, W H, *Peninsular Sketches*, London, 1858.
Muir, R, *Tactics and the Experience of Battle in the Age of Napoleon*, New Haven, CT, 1998.

Napier, W F P, *History of the War in the Peninsula and in the South of France from the year 1807 to the year 1814*, London, 1828–40.

Oman,Carola, *Sir John Moore*, London, 1953.

Oman, Charles, *A History of the Peninsular War*, Oxford, 1902–30.

——— *Courts Martial of the Peninsular War 1809–14*, Journal of the Royal United Service Institution (1912), Vol. 56, pp. 1699–1716.

——— *Wellington's Army 1809–1814*, London, 1913.

Paget, J, *Wellington's Peninsular War*, London, 1990.

Pope, D, *Life in Nelson's Navy*, London, 1997.

Robertson, I C, *Wellington at War in the Peninsula*, Barnsley, 2000.

Rogers, H C B, *Wellington's Army*, London, 1979.

Rothenberg, G E, *The Art of Warfare in the Age of Napoleon*, London, 1977.

Siborne, H T, *The Waterloo Letters*, London, 1983.

Sutherland, J, *Men of Waterloo*, London, 1966.

Ward, S G P, *Wellington's Headquarters*, Oxford, 1957.

Weller, J, *Wellington in India*, London, 1972.

——— *Wellington in the Peninsula 1808–1814*, London, 1962.

Wellesley, M, *The Man Wellington through the eyes of those who knew him*, London, 1937.

Index

Hunter, John, 7, 143.
Huskisson, William, 74.
Hussey, Sir Vivian, 136.
Hythe, 111.

immunity to disease, 175.
India, 50, 82, 177–178, 182, 190.
insanity, 179.
Inspector-General, 4–5.
ipecacuanha, 165.
Isle of Wight, 112.

Jackson, Robert, 9–10, 12, 14, 16, 24, 118, 163.
Jackson, Sergeant Thomas, 131.
Jamaica, 161.
James's powder, 162, 165.
Jenner, Edward, 189.
Johnson, Assistant Surgeon Edward, 215.
Jordan, Andrew, 99.
jungle fever, 82.

Keate, Thomas, 3, 5–6, 21, 118.
Keegan, John, 62.
Keep, William, 37, 173–174.
Kempthorne, Lieutenant-Colonel, 221.
Ker, Charles, 6.
King's German Legion, 188.
Knight, Francis, 3, 10, 118.

Lancet, The, 190, 223.
lancets, 164.
Lancey, Sir William Howe De, 151.
Lane, Lieutenant Henry, 55.
Larpent, Judge-Advocate, 42, 103–104.
Larrey, Dominique Jean, 44, 59, 67–68, 77, 129–130, 132–136, 138, 140, 142, 148–149, 152, 188.
Laswaree, battle of, 215.
Lawrence, Sergeant William, 73, 103.

Leach, Rifleman Jonathan, 166.
lead poisoning, 162.
leeches, 164.
Lesassiery, Alexander, 46.
Lever, Charles, 221.
Lidderdale, Surgeon William, 195.
Lind, James, 184.
Lisbon, 69, 112, 196–198, 203.
Liverpool, Earl of, 29, 69.
lockjaw, 148.
London, 155.
louse, body, 167.
Lundy's Lane, battle of, 59, 109–110, 126, 145.

Madras, 177.
Madrid, 106, 201, 220.
Maguire, Surgeon Francis, 205.
Mahratta War, 50.
Maida, battle of, 127.
Maling, Surgeon John, 131.
malingering, 18, 112, 176–177, 180–181.
Mann, James, 110.
Marshall, Henry, 157, 190.
Martinique, 51, 159, 166.
Masséna, Marshal, 69.
McChristie, Assistant Surgeon William, 212.
McGill, Surgeon William, 45.
McGrigor, James: relationship with Wellington, 1–2, 6, 85–87; opinions on army doctors, 8, 13, 18, 22–24, 28–29; education, 15; qualifications, 15; joins army, 18–19; writings, 29, 169; on importance of medical department, 30; on doctors in action, 58; arrives in Peninsula, 84–85; on transport of sick, 85–86; on general hospitals, 101–102, 104; at Walcheren, 109; after Corunna, 111, 167–168; on regimental hospitals, 113–114,

and wounded, 81; general hospitals, 95–107; regimental hospitals, 115–117; hospital admissions, 118; surgery of, 135–136; local population, 201–202.

pensions, 222.

Pepys, Sir Lucas, 3–4, 7–10, 118.

Percy, Pierre-Françoise, 67, 88–89, 99.

peritonitis, 142.

Physician-General, 4.

Pinchard, Physician George, 159, 179.

Plymouth, 112–113, 167.

Ponsonby, Lieutenant-Colonel Frederick, 150.

Popham, Sir Home, 218.

Portsmouth, 111, 167.

post-mortems, 174.

poultices, 139.

Pringle, John, 92, 113, 173.

prize money, 222.

prostitution, 172.

Pulsford, Assistant Surgeon Lucas, 221.

purgatives, 162.

Purveyor-in-Chief, 4.

purveyors, 11–12.

Pyrenees, battle of, 30, 47, 75.

quarantine, 188.

Quartermaster-General, 95.

Quatre Bras, battle of, 42, 58.

Quill, Maurice, 221.

Ranby, John, 36.

rations, 205.

rickettsia, 167.

Robb, Deputy Inspector of Hospitals John, 51.

Roberts, Lieutenant-Colonel David, 26.

Roliça, battle of, 35.

Rosetta, 176, 200.

Ross-Lewin, Lieutenant, 47, 49.

roundshot, 126.

Royal Hospital Corps, 119.

Rush, John, 3.

Salamanca, battle of, 33, 40, 43, 46–47, 63.

salaries, 222.

San Sebastian, siege of, 39, 41.

Santander, 105–107, 218.

scarificator, 164.

Schaumann, Commissary August, 76, 81, 98.

Scheldt estuary, 178.

senna, 165.

septicaemia, 135.

sergeant of hospital, 114.

Sheffield, 155.

shellshock, 179.

Sherer, Captain Moyle, 181–182.

Shipp, Lieutenant John, 178.

shock, 149.

Siborne, William, 55.

sick states, 68.

sightseeing, 220.

Simmons, Major George, 36–37, 44–45, 74–75, 81, 150–151.

Simpson, James, 108.

Smith, Assistant Surgeon John Gordon, 198–199, 206.

Smith, Major Harry, 51, 73, 77, 137.

Society of Apothecaries, 222–223.

soldiers: morale 40; previous occupations, 156, 184–185; age, 156; height, 156–157; medical examination of, 157, 184–185; and women, 172; arrival on campaign, 185; clothing, 186–187; diet, 187; discipline, 187–188; wives, 204–205.

South Africa, 178.

splenomegaly, 174.

splints, 140.

sports activities, 221.
St Domingo, 158, 162.
St Jean de Luz, 105.
Standing Instructions for
    Hospitals, 95.
Stewart, Surgeon Arthur, 209–210.
stretchers, 39, 77.
Subijana de Alava, 52–54.
suicide, 179.
Surgeon-General, 4.
Surgeon's Hall, 12.
surgery, army, 5, 25–52;
    amputation, 25–26, 129–136;
    workload, 126; equipment, 126,
    139, 287; mortality after,
    135–136, 233, 235; probing,
    136–137; foreign bodies,
    137–138; dressings, 138–139;
    fractures, 140; head and neck,
    140–141; chest, 141–142;
    abdomen, 142–143; competency,
    143; pain of, 144–145; soldiers
    attitudes to, 145; infection,
    145–146; hospital gangrene,
    146–148; tetanus, 148;
    antiphlogistic treatment,
    148–151; change in status of,
    152.
surgery in civil life, 125.
Surtees, William, 61–62, 75, 180.
Swabey, Lieutenant William, 76,
    83, 179.
sword injuries, 127.
syphilis, 172.

Tagus river, 77.
Talavera, battle of, 41, 43, 47–48,
    98, 141, 215–216.
Tarifa, 215.
tents, 186, 199.
tetanus, 148.
theatre, 220.
Thomson, Professor John, 107–108,
    129, 142.

tobacco, 206.
Tomkinson, William, 77, 139.
Torres Vedras, lines of, 100, 211.
Toulouse, battle of, 28, 63, 107,
    134–135, 148.
tourniquets, 130, 133, 164.
transport of sick and wounded,
    67–89; French ambulance, 67–68;
    sick convoys, 69–71; bullock
    carts, 72–73; Royal Wagon
    Train, 73–74; spring wagons,
    74–75; mules, 75–76; sedan chair
    77; by water, 77–79; transport
    ships, 78–79; officers retinue, 80;
    accidents, 81; sick abandoned,
    81; help from comrades, 81–82;
    criticism of, 83–84; nineteenth
    century, 89.
trephining, 140.
Tresal, Jean-Baptiste, 174–175.
Trotter, Thomas, 184.
Tulloch, Lieutenant Alexander
    Murray, 190.

uniform, 20.
Uxbridge, Lord, 144.

vaccination, 189.
Valladolid, 87.
Van Millingen, Staff Surgeon John
    Gideon, 42, 64, 220.
Veere, 109.
Vera, 103.
Verdun, 216–217.
Verner, William, 141.
Villafranca, 209.
Vimeiro, battle of, 42, 49, 62.
Vitoria, battle of, 30, 35, 42, 52–55,
    104, 221.
Vizeu, 169.

Walcheren expedition, 5, 82,
    173–175.
wardmasters, 93, 96, 102.

Wasdell, Staff Surgeon, 52.

Waterloo campaign: casualties, 33–34, 58; evacuation of wounded, 40, 44, 88; dressing stations, 41; shortages, 42–43; doctor's account, 55–58; aftermath of battle, 61–63; general hospitals, 107–108; surgery of, 136, 135, 137–138, 144, 150–151, 233, 235; local population, 204; medical officer numbers, 214.

weaponry, 126–127.

Webbe, Inspector of Hospitals John, 173.

Weir, John, 6.

Welch, Hospital Mate George, 211.

Wellington, Duke of: relationship with McGrigor, 1–2, 6, 85–87; promotion, 21; opinions on army doctors, 22, 29–30, 87, 200–201, 220; on evacuation of wounded, 40, 69, 86–87; kindness to wounded, 87–88; Flanders campaign, 95; opinions on hospitals, 104, 106–107, 115; wounded, 142; views on soldiers, 156; illness, 177; views on accommodation, 197–198; on alcohol, 207; on punishment, 212; after Waterloo, 223.

West India Regiments, 157, 186.

West Indies: deaths from disease, 28, 157–158; field hospitals, 51; general hospitals, 109, 186; hospital corps, 119; diseases of, 158–162, 166, 190.

Westminster Hospital, 91.

Wheatley, Edmund, 38.

wheelbarrows, 77.

Wheeler, Private William, 77, 105–106, 147–148.

Wildman, Captain Thomas, 144.

Wood, Captain George, 62, 120–121.

Woodberry, Lieutenant George, 221.

Woolcombe, Dr, 156.

Woolwich, 113.

wounds: experience of wounding, 36–38; re-wounding 41; types of, 126–127; amputation for, 129–136; dressings, 138–139; fractures, 140, 143; head injuries, 140–141; of chest, 141–142; of abdomen, 142–143.

Wright, John, 9.

Wright, Thomas, 110–111.

writing on campaign, 219–220.

wurst, 67.

York, Duke of, 6.

Young, Thomas, 118.